LITIGANTS IN PERSON AND THE FAMILY JUSTICE SYSTEM

This book is about those who represent themselves as Litigants in Person in the family justice system. It calls for a refocusing of the debate about the historical challenges associated with Litigants in Person as well as the role they should play within the family justice system in England and Wales.

Drawing together interviews with Litigants in Person and decades of research into self-representation from across multiple jurisdictions, this book provides an account of the family justice system through the eyes of its users. It employs an innovative socio-legal framework comprising feminist theory, a Bourdieusian theory of class, vulnerability theory, and actor-network theory to explore the journey that Litigants in Person take through the legal, cultural and social context of the family court.

It provides fresh insight into the diverse challenges that people face within this process and how these relate to wider pressures within the family justice system. It argues that there are important lessons to be learned from Litigants in Person. By understanding how and why people come to the point of self-representing, and the kinds of experiences they have when they do, the book advocates the importance of forging a more positive and effective relationship between Litigants in Person and the family justice system.

Litigants in Person and the Family Justice System

Jessica Mant

•HART•
OXFORD • LONDON • NEW YORK • NEW DELHI • SYDNEY

HART PUBLISHING

Bloomsbury Publishing Plc

Kemp House, Chawley Park, Cumnor Hill, Oxford, OX2 9PH, UK

1385 Broadway, New York, NY 10018, USA

29 Earlsfort Terrace, Dublin 2, Ireland

HART PUBLISHING, the Hart/Stag logo, BLOOMSBURY and the Diana logo are trademarks of Bloomsbury Publishing Plc

First published in Great Britain 2022

A catalogue record for this book is available from the British Library.

A catalogue record for this book is available from the Library of Congress.

ISBN: HB: 978-1-50994-735-5
ePDF: 978-1-50994-737-9
ePub: 978-1-50994-736-2

Typeset by Compuscript Ltd, Shannon

To find out more about our authors and books visit www.hartpublishing.co.uk. Here you will find extracts, author information, details of forthcoming events and the option to sign up for our newsletters.

ACKNOWLEDGEMENTS

This book marks the conclusion of a research project that has shaped me as an academic. During its various stages, I have drawn inspiration and support from countless colleagues, mentors, and friends. I am indebted to all of you for the impact you have had on me, both professionally and personally.

I would like to thank the Economic and Social Research Council for funding my PhD project, as well as the Centre for Law and Social Justice at the University of Leeds for providing a vibrant socio-legal community for the formative years of my career. I am also grateful to the School of Law and Politics at Cardiff University, for exposing me to new ideas and providing the space and support for me to finish this book.

This book would not have been possible without the accounts of the 23 parents who generously welcomed me into their lives and I am extremely grateful to those that trusted me with their stories of the court process.

Finally, thank you to my husband, for always making coffee and being ready for new adventures. Here's to more 'sploring for the Dr BGs.

CONTENTS

LIST OF ABBREVIATIONS

ANT	Actor Network Theory
CAFCASS	Child and Family Court Advisory and Support Service
DRA	Dispute Resolution Appointment
FFH	Fact-Finding Hearing
FHDRA	First Hearing Dispute Resolution Appointment
FPR3A	Part 3A, Family Procedure Rules 2010
LASPO	Legal Aid, Sentencing and Punishment of Offenders Act 2012
LIP	Litigant in Person
LIPSS	Litigant in Person Support Strategy
MIAM	Mediation Information and Assessment Meeting
NHS	National Health Service
PD3AA	Practice Direction 3AA
PD12B	Practice Direction 12B (The Child Arrangements Programme)
PD12J	Practice Direction 12J

TABLE OF CASES

1

Introduction

When a family breaks down, there are several things that need to be decided. Generally, this might include things like where children should live, how often they spend time with each parent, and how any property or assets should be divided. Although these decisions are often difficult and emotional, most parents work these issues out by themselves and do not need to rely on the legal system. Some families will use mediation, where a mediator will help them to work through the issues and come to agreements. Others might instruct solicitors to negotiate arrangements on their behalf. However, this is not possible for all families, especially in situations where former partners are struggling to communicate effectively, contending with complex circumstances, high levels of conflict, power imbalances, or even safety concerns and domestic abuse. Traditionally, these would be the families most likely to find themselves in the family court. Although used only by a tiny proportion of families in England and Wales, the family court has always operated as a safety net by providing a formal environment where court orders can secure safe and appropriate arrangements in otherwise chaotic and difficult family circumstances. However, this safety net has been placed under significant strain by swathes of legal aid reforms, including the almost complete removal of eligibility for funded advice and representation for private family law problems under the Legal Aid, Sentencing and Punishment of Offenders (LASPO) 2012. Now, approximately 80 per cent of cases that reach the family court involve people who are representing themselves as 'Litigants in Person' (LIPs), and many of those arrive for their hearings without prior legal advice or an advocate to help them navigate the legal, procedural, and cultural norms of the family court process.

The family court process is not designed with LIPs in mind. It remains predicated on a full-representation model, which presumes that every party has a lawyer with legal and procedural knowledge, as well a general understanding of how hearings work and how different people within the family court are supposed to interact with each other. When a lay individual is expected to navigate an unfamiliar legal process, it is likely that they will make mistakes, and judges and other professionals involved will need to take time to assist them and explain things. As a result, cases are more difficult or take longer when they involve LIPs. This has ramifications not only for the families at the centre of those cases, but also the resilience of the wider family justice system to cope with other cases. The number of LIPs in the family justice system therefore raises concerns for the future of this system, as well as the accessibility of family justice for all those who rely upon it.

This book is about those people who are representing themselves as LIPs within the family justice system. For the first time, it draws interviews with LIPs who have been through the family court after LASPO together with decades worth of research on LIPs and their role within the family justice system. It follows the various journeys that LIPs may take through this system and traces the ways that their experiences are shaped by the turbulent context of post-LASPO family justice. In doing so, it advocates for a fresh conceptualisation of the relationship between LIPs and the family justice system – one that explicitly places the experiences, concerns, and perspectives of LIPs at the centre of debates about the future of family justice.

I. Litigants in Person and the Family Justice System

Although there are many more people appearing as LIPs now than ever before, self-representation is by no means a new phenomenon. Rather, LIPs have always been a common feature of the family justice system in England and Wales, with as many as 43 per cent of family court cases involving at least one self-representing party in 2011 (Ministry of Justice 2021a). This begs two important questions. First, who are LIPs, and why do they choose to represent themselves in the family court when many of them might have chosen other (less adversarial, and arguably in some cases, more appropriate) options for resolving their family law problems? Second, why are LIPs and their experiences so important for understanding the wider context of family justice?

Turning first to the matter of who comes to court as a LIP, there are several large-scale studies from which we can draw a tentative view of the typical characteristics and circumstances of LIPs, as well as an indication of how this profile has changed over the past few decades. For instance, studies from across England and Wales, Australia, and Northern Ireland all indicate that LIPs continually tend to be those from more deprived socio-economic backgrounds and with lower levels of formal education (Dewar et al. 2000; Moorhead and Sefton 2005; Trinder et al. 2014; McKeever et al. 2018; Cusworth 2020; 2021). LIPs tend to be those who fall into the gap of being unable to afford their own lawyer but cannot access legal aid because their incomes or assets take them over the financial threshold that has traditionally governed eligibility. Aside from socio-economic status, studies also suggest that LIPs tend to have characteristics which give rise to experiences of vulnerability. In 2005, it was found that 15 per cent of LIPs in child disputes had what was termed a 'vulnerable characteristic', which included being a victim of domestic abuse,[1] or having physical or mental health problems (Moorhead and Sefton 2005: 70). Expanding the scope of vulnerability to include things like

[1] A variety of terms may be used to denote experiences of domestic abuse, but the term 'victim' is used purposely throughout this book to acknowledge the ways that the court process is frequently used as a mechanism of re-victimisation or continuing abuse. See further, ch 2.

learning difficulties, extreme nerves and anxiety and language barriers, subsequent research found that as many as half of LIPs could be described as having vulnerable characteristics (Trinder et al. 2014: 27). This suggests a typical profile of a LIP as someone who is likely to have low levels of economic, cultural, and social resources to draw upon for support during their time in court. It also suggests that LIPs are disproportionately likely to already be marginalised by broader power structures which frame intersectional experiences of social class, race, gender, disability, or ill health within society.

Since the widespread withdrawal of state funded legal representation that came with the implementation of LASPO, LIPs have been the rule rather than the exception. This means that the family court is now seeing many more LIPs who come with the various characteristics and backgrounds discussed here. However, LASPO did not only result in more LIPs. Rather, the blanket withdrawal of legal aid has added a whole new category of LIPs: those on the lowest incomes and with the fewest resources because their family disputes are now categorically excluded from scope.[2] In fact, emerging data suggests that, since LASPO, significant proportions of LIPs are arriving at court include people who have accessed no prior advice, people with low levels of literacy, people without access to a phone or the internet, as well as many who do not speak English as a first language (House of Commons Justice Committee 2015; Lee and Tkacukova 2018). In the post-LASPO context, the question of who comes to court as a LIP is far more complicated, and the best response is to recognise that LIPs are now an even more diverse population of individuals who are potentially contending with an even more amplified range of marginalised circumstances, backgrounds, and characteristics.

Why might someone in these circumstances choose to represent themselves? To answer this question, it is important to note that people take different routes into the family justice system. Some are forced to engage with the family court process because the other party has initiated court proceedings and they must represent themselves as respondents because they cannot secure representation.[3] Others initiate proceedings as a last resort when communication has broken down or their ex-partner is behaving unreasonably. Sometimes, LIPs represent themselves because of an internal sense of justice, or a desire to assert their own rights as far as possible. More commonly, they do not trust others to represent them effectively. These sentiments often stem from a broader mistrust of lawyers, previous negative experiences with legal professionals, or a belief that a lawyer would not be well-placed to properly convey the personal issues concerned in their

[2] See especially, Cusworth (2021) where researchers classified just under a third of LIPs in England as living in the most deprived quintile of England.

[3] This is particularly common in cases involving domestic abuse. Evidence from across multiple jurisdictions indicates that perpetrators commonly use family court applications as a strategy to continue abusive behaviours, especially after relationships have ended. See especially: Birchall and Choudhry 2018: 42.

family cases (MacFarlane et al. 2013: 48–50; McKeever et al. 2018: 84). The extent to which marginalised communities place trust in the legal system can therefore be an important factor in some LIPs' decisions to go it alone in the family court. However, mistrust of lawyers does not necessarily correlate with self-confidence in one's own ability. It is relatively rare for LIPs in the family court to report that they can manage the process without help. Even those that do state that they feel confident in their ability to represent themselves often find later that they have underestimated the procedural complexity of the family court process (MacFarlane et al. 2013: 8).

The issue of trust (or mistrust) is important and will be revisited throughout this book, as it significantly underpins the relationships that LIPs have with others in the family justice system. It is not, however, the primary reason that people represent themselves in the family court. Rather, the overwhelming reason is because most people cannot afford legal representation. Some LIPs are concerned about only being able to afford an inexperienced lawyer who would not represent their interests effectively and perceive self-representation as their best option (Trinder et al. 2014: 16–17; McKeever et al. 2018: 84–88). For others, instructing any lawyer at all is entirely beyond their financial means (Dewar et al. 2000: 33; Hunter et al. 2003). Most LIPs, therefore, do not actively reject legal representation and choose to represent themselves in court – rather, they self-represent because legal aid is inaccessible, and lawyers are unaffordable.

Why then, do so many people use the family court at all? After all, court proceedings are just one possible way to try to resolve a family dispute and for many families, mediating or negotiating an agreement is often far less stressful and potentially cheaper for all involved. To understand how individuals get to the point of needing to rely on the safety net of the family court, it is important to appreciate that for many families, these options may not be appropriate means of resolving disputes. Mediation, for instance, can only be effective if both parties are willing to engage meaningfully with the process, and if there are no significant power imbalances between the parties that would render negotiations unfair. However, even in situations where mediation or alternative dispute resolution might be viable routes for resolving disputes, the realistic accessibility of these options has historically hinged upon the availability of legal aid to support legal advice. To understand how people end up as LIPs in the family court, we must first unravel the ways that restrictions on legal aid have shaped the landscape of family justice.

II. The Family Justice Landscape

The family justice system in England and Wales consists of a panoply of different options and processes that individuals might use to try to reach fair arrangements, such as litigation, solicitor-led negotiations, mediation, and other models of alternative dispute resolution.[4] In theory, individuals can choose the most appropriate process for their circumstances, but realistically, this choice has ultimately been constrained by a range of neoliberal policies which have, first, limited the availability of state funding and, second, aimed to divert families away from lawyers and the court, and towards mediation.

The legal aid scheme was introduced with lofty ambitions of securing access to justice for all by subsidising the costs of legal services for those who could not afford to privately instruct a lawyer. From enaction, family law practice was one of the main areas that drew upon legal aid to support advice and representation. Part of this is because since the scheme was implemented, family life has become increasingly more complex, with major shifts in societal attitudes towards divorce, same-sex relationships, and co-parenting arrangements. As such, family law itself has become correspondingly more intricate, as legislators work to keep up (Maclean and Eekelaar 2019: 9–11). This means that there has always been enormous demand for free or affordable family law advice, legal support to negotiate solutions, and representation in court to determine what should be done at the point of family breakdown. With increased demand, however, comes increased cost to the state. Efforts to limit the expense of the legal aid budget have been multifaceted but consistent across administrations on both the left and the right of the political spectrum. Policies ranged from those attempting to constrain the amount of legal aid work that lawyers could take on, limit the fees that could be claimed for legal aid work, and narrow citizens' eligibility for legal aid through increasingly strict means testing (Hynes and Robins 2009).

Concerns about the cost of legal aid have also been underpinned by another debate, where questions have been raised about whether the involvement of lawyers and the court in family disputes is in fact an appropriate way to reach resolutions. Under this logic, lawyers are not conceptualised as a means of understanding one's rights and entitlements, nor as facilitators of agreements. Rather, the involvement of lawyers is instead something that exacerbates and entrenches conflict, increasing the chances that families will end up in the family court, which should be avoided at all costs (House of Commons Public Accounts Committee 2007; Legal Services Commission 2007). This narrative aligns neatly with concerns about the spiralling costs of lawyers who provide publicly funded legal services through legal aid. Therefore, although other forms of dispute resolution exist, mediation has consistently been promoted as a one size fits all, cheaper, quicker alternative to going to court which minimises conflict between parents (Barlow et al. 2017: 10–14). However, the appropriateness and efficacy of mediation varies, and it has never been able to offer a universal remedy for all disputes. Moreover, the success of out-of-court resolution options like mediation can often depend on whether people are able to access legal advice in the first place. This is because

[4] See generally: Barlow et al. 2017.

many families who seek advice about their disputes have often not considered the potential benefits of mediation until a lawyer is able to offer them a bespoke understanding of their options, as well as the benefits and disadvantages of each of these options (Ingleby 1992; Eekelaar et al. 2000). Without this early intervention, many may pursue their cases to court unnecessarily without recognising the potential value of alternative options.

As a result, despite the intentions of policymakers, self-representation in the family court has always been a common phenomenon. Although there are some LIPs who pursue court proceedings because they are determined to have their day in court, LIPs are not typically a population of litigious troublemakers. Rather, they are most often families caught in the gaps formed by the way these policies have disrupted the delicate ecosystem of family law. In 2010, this became even more amplified. In that year, a fresh set of reforms to the legal aid scheme were proposed under a new statute now known as LASPO.

Coming into force in April 2013, LASPO introduced sweeping cuts to several areas of law, the extent of which was incomparable to the incremental restrictions and constraints of previous reforms. While earlier reforms had sought to place gradual limits on eligibility or expenses, LASPO entirely reversed the position by creating a default of ineligibility. Now, only those legal problems specified as eligible within the statutory framework are entitled to claim legal aid for the purposes of obtaining advice or representation. As one of the areas that relied most heavily on the legal aid budget, private family law was one of the key targets for these changes. After LASPO, private family law is excluded almost entirely from scope. Only limited exceptions are available for those who can provide evidence of domestic abuse or can prove that their case warrants exceptional funding on the basis that denying them legal aid would contravene the state's obligations under the European Convention on Human Rights.[5]

At the same time, LASPO included yet another attempt to incentivise disputing families to turn to mediation instead of the family court. While legal aid funding was withdrawn for advice and representation, it was retained for the purposes of covering the costs of attending mediation. In practice, this means that disputing families on very low incomes are only able to access public funding to support their participation in mediation, and if they want to consult a solicitor or use the family court, they will need to do so at their own expense. Predictably, given the trajectory of earlier reforms, this did not play out in the manner that the then-government had hoped. Although mediation is the only route for which public funding is available for most families, rates of attendance at mediation fell significantly after LASPO. At the same time, rates of self-representation in the family court increased exponentially (Ministry of Justice 2021a; 2021b).

Although it would be near impossible to try and establish a causal link between the withdrawal of legal advice and the increase in self-representation, it is likely to

[5] LASPO 2012, sch 1 and s 10, respectively.

be a key factor.[6] This is because the removal of legal aid has not only affected the individuals who would previously have relied upon it but has also closed off entire income streams for those firms and advice organisations who have traditionally supported them. While most people became ineligible for legal aid, many lawyers and advisors were forced to close their doors or move into other areas of provision (Maclean and Eekelaar 2019: 18–19). This means that the context of family justice has shifted from one that has struggled on under increasing pressure, to one in which demand for free support is soaring yet capacity to provide that support has been eroded to a minimum. It is perhaps unsurprising, then, that after LASPO, even more people in even more diverse and difficult circumstances are finding themselves forced to rely on the safety net of the family court.

The implementation of LASPO can be understood as a significant turning point for family justice for two key reasons. The first is that the post-LASPO context is fundamentally different from that which existed before 2013. Although LASPO contained nothing new in the way of policy rationale, it fundamentally altered the ways that people have traditionally engaged with family law. As with previous reforms, LASPO was underpinned by the objective of reducing expenditure on legal aid and sought to further entrench the idea that family disputes are personal matters that should be resolved without state-funded support. However, never have individuals been wholesale excluded from legal aid based on their type of legal problem. Similarly, LASPO merely intensified existing cynicism about the legitimacy of lawyers' involvement with family law issues. Yet, never has a policy intervened to close off legal advice as a gateway to resolution pathways, leaving a varied market of non-legal support which LIPs must navigate with limited prior experience or knowledge.

The post-LASPO context is therefore one in which people are more frequently falling to the safety net of the family court not only as their last resort, but sometimes as their only option. At the same time, there has been limited change within this court process. Consequently, judges, legal professionals, and academics have accused the LASPO reforms of creating a false economy in which money saved from the legal aid budget has simply been displaced to the family court, which is now unsustainably strained under the additional costs and burdens that come with increased numbers of LIPs (Cookson 2013; National Audit Office 2014; Richardson and Speed 2019). In short, LASPO brought an already-pressurised family court process to breaking point and, operationalising the enduring neoliberal narrative of personal responsibility, positioned LIPs themselves as the root of these problems.

The second reason that LASPO can be understood as a turning point is that it has forced many to finally consider the future of family justice. By exacerbating these problems to such a degree, LASPO has amplified the importance of finding

[6] In 2019, the government acknowledged that the removal of legal aid funding for advice is likely to have had the unintended consequences of a reduced number of referrals to mediation by lawyers and an increased number of LIPs in the family court (Ministry of Justice 2019a: 142–45).

solutions and instigating change, rather than simply papering over the cracks of a family justice system that has always struggled to support its users. For example, writing at the point of LASPO's implementation, Trinder et al advocated the importance of considering ways in which the court process might need to be reformed to become more accessible to the newly diverse range of LIPs who were likely to be using it post-LASPO (2014: 11–20). LASPO is by no means the end of the story of legal aid reform. Instead, it marks a key milestone at which many are finally recognising the extent of the damage that has been done and starting to ask questions about what might come next (Kaganas 2017: 181).

III. Where Next for Family Justice?

In this book, I argue that LASPO offers an opportunity for access to justice and family law scholars, practitioners, and policymakers to begin anew and to start addressing some of the systemic problems that have always characterised the family justice system. Instead of requiring the family justice system to struggle on with yet another set of incremental changes, the severity of LASPO has, in effect, torn up the rulebook on how the various institutions of family justice are supposed to respond. As such, it provides an imperative to draw together rigorous, empirical evidence with theoretically-informed academic scholarship, in order to reflect upon the needs, challenges, and long-term possibilities for family justice. At the same time, there are immediate practical questions about what comes next and what might be done. Both of these long- and short-term deliberations must be considered carefully. Care is needed because, first, the LASPO changes were not an isolated reform stemming from one single government administration. Rather, they were implemented as part of an ever-delicate political context which is underpinned by specific ideas about who family law is for, the appropriate role of the court process, as well as conflicting ideas about the extent to which various government administrations are willing to extend state-funded support to citizens. Any potential future for family justice that is geared towards supporting LIPs will need to be carefully negotiated so that it is capable of both addressing longstanding problems as well as garnering political support from policymakers.

Second, these questions must be considered contextually. This is because there are other issues and events that have intersected the landscape of family justice. For instance, in tandem with protracted concerns about the accessibility of advice and representation, the family court has also been at the centre of repeated criticism for systemic problems relating to the recognition of domestic abuse. The debates and campaigns for improvements in this area have provided impetus for several major reviews and reforms within the family justice system, to varying degrees of success.[7] Given the challenges that stem from a lack of legal representation on

[7] See generally: Barnett 2020.

either side of a case involving domestic abuse, the ramifications of LASPO have been heavily implicated in the continued failures of the family court in respect of adequately responding to domestic abuse. Moreover, the family justice system is also still finding its way through the enormous impact and ongoing ramifications of the COVID-19 pandemic. The sudden closure of face-to-face services and suspension of in-person court hearings had a multifaceted impact on the ways that the family court has been able to function, as well as its capacity to support LIPs that are even further impaired in their ability to seek support and frequently lack appropriate technology.[8]

Given this complexity, it is difficult to disentangle the different voices that govern our understandings of these problems and how they affect LIPs' relationship with the family justice system. For instance, the implementation of LASPO has inspired responses ranging from barrister walk-outs to media campaigns in favour of reversing legal aid cuts (Bowcott 2015; Bach Commission 2017; Legal Aid Practitioners Group 2017). Although these responses are rooted in concerns about access to justice, it is very easy to fall into the trap of conflating a crisis of access to justice with a crisis of legal professionalism. In the present context, lawyers have been excluded from work and are facing challenges to the assumption that they are needed within family law. Clearly, increased investment in legal aid would be an ideal solution for addressing both of these concerns and improving the accessibility of family justice. However, this is likely to be an unrealistic possibility, given the lack of appeal among economically-conscious policymakers. Moreover, reinstating legal aid to pre-LASPO levels would not necessarily address the pre-existing problems that characterised the legal aid scheme and framed differential experiences for those attempting to use family law.[9] Many people have always been practically excluded from the benefits of legal aid, and the different working conditions of publicly and privately funded lawyers meant that even when there was broad eligibility, there was never quite equal access to good quality legal help when comparing the experiences of those relying on legal aid and those who could afford to pay privately for legal services. To this end, it is important to remember that it is not only the absence of legal advice and representation which causes barriers for access to justice. Rather, it is the system that exists without this support (McKeever et al. 2018: 153–56). By cutting off access to advice and representation, LASPO has not *created* barriers to the family justice system: it has exacerbated existing obstacles, and plainly exposed the disadvantages that people experience within it *due to the way that the system works.*

To appropriately investigate the relationship between LIPs and the family justice system, it is therefore imperative that we consciously expose and elevate the experiences and perspectives of LIPs themselves. After all, it is only by viewing the

[8] See generally: Ryan et al. (2021).

[9] There is an important difference between increasing theoretical eligibility for legal aid and facilitating meaningful access to legal advice. See: Minnoch (2021).

processes of family justice through the eyes of its users that we may begin to reflect on the problems that characterise that system. Fortunately, there is no shortage of research that incorporates LIPs' voices, which can be explicitly drawn out for this purpose. Internationally, several major studies have used variety of research methods to investigate the phenomenon of self-representation in civil and family law, including examination of case files and legal aid records, focus groups, and interviews with legal professionals, judges, court staff, and support services. Importantly, these methods have frequently been combined with researcher observations of hearings involving LIPs and interviews with LIPs (Dewar et al. 2000; De Simone and Hunter 2009; MacFarlane et al. 2013; Toy-Cronin 2015; McKeever et al. 2018). As a result, there is already an indicative picture of what self-representation is like for people in jurisdictionally akin countries like Canada, Australia, New Zealand, and Northern Ireland. In England and Wales, there is also an impressive body of data that draws together the experiences of legal professionals, judges, and court staff with those of LIPs themselves (Moorhead and Sefton 2005; Trinder et al. 2014). Although these studies pre-date the implementation of LASPO, they provide a vital insight into how LIPs have experienced the family justice system throughout the turbulent context of policy reforms that have been exacerbated to the extreme.[10] These large-scale studies can also be reinforced by some more recent, albeit smaller-scale, studies in England and Wales which employ interviews and surveys to amplify the experiences that LIPs are having of the post-LASPO context of civil and family justice (Leader 2017; Lee and Tkacukova 2018; Barry 2020). Although this literature has often focused on drawing a comprehensive view of self-representation by drawing together perspectives of all participants involved in such hearings, it is nevertheless possible to hone in on the wealth of LIP experiences denoted in these studies, and to purposefully use these perspectives as a lens through which to consider the future of their relationship with the family justice system.

The purpose of this book is to address this need to give voice to LIPs who rely on this system. In the chapters that follow, I draw together 23 first-hand accounts from LIPs who have experienced family court proceedings in England and Wales after LASPO and situate these against decades of research concerning the experiences of self-representation from around the globe. In doing so, I consider how the family justice system may begin to learn from LIPs' experiences, perceptions, and understandings, and argue that these should not only inform the future relationship between LIPs and the family justice system, but also be central to the debate about what comes next for family justice. Exposing and centring LIP voices may, in practice, mean that LASPO need not be understood as the end of family justice – rather, it may provide a turning point from which we can finally begin this learning process.

[10] Due to its timing and scale, the study conducted by Trinder et al. (2014) is particularly useful for understanding what the family court process was like for LIPs at the point that LASPO was just about to come into force.

IV. Learning from LIPs

The empirical interviews that inform this book were conducted with 23 LIPs who volunteered to share their time and stories with me. These LIPs were all individual parents who were representing themselves in a range of different private law children proceedings during 2017, when the implications of the LASPO changes were beginning to become apparent within the family justice system.

In total, the sample included 16 mothers and 7 fathers, with ages ranging between 18 and 45 years old. The sample was disproportionately represented by those who identified as White British, with just one man who identified as black African, one woman who identified as white European, and two women who identified as South Asian. English was a second language for the latter three interviewees. Most (10) interviewees had completed secondary education, with a minority (three) possessing an undergraduate degree or above, and six interviewees having no formal qualifications. In terms of employment, there was a roughly even split, with 10 interviewees in full-time employment, a further four in part-time employment, and nine who were unemployed at the time of their interview.[11]

Recruiting LIPs to participate in interviews is challenging. Unless a researcher stations themselves in court waiting rooms,[12] it is difficult to identify and locate people who are representing themselves in these proceedings. Even then, the research would be limited to LIPs who had attended the same court building, encountered the same judges, lawyers, and practices. There are also specific ethical implications associated with cold-approaching people in court waiting rooms, as waiting for family court hearings is likely to be a time when they are feeling anxious and distressed about their impending hearing and its potential outcome. For both reasons, the decision was taken to recruit LIPs opportunistically, by promoting the project away from the pressure of the court environment and allowing LIPs to volunteer to participate of their own accord. To this end, the project was promoted through prominent face-to-face advice services across England and Wales, including the Citizens Advice Bureaux and Support Through Court, as well as through relevant social media groups and online forums about family law and the family court. By taking an opt-in recruitment strategy, it was possible to speak to LIPs who had a diverse range of experiences and ensure as far as possible that

[11] It is important to acknowledge that, as a consequence of the opportunistic recruitment strategy used, this sample is disproportionately White British, and all LIPs had used the family court after a breakdown of a heterosexual relationship. Although this was never intended to be a representative sample, this unfortunately limits the extent to which interviews can provide insight into the experiences of non-heteronormative families and people of other races and cultures who may rely on the family court in England and Wales. This is an enduring issue across family law scholarship, however there are some notable exceptions which should be regarded as best practice. See, eg: Bendall 2014; Dunne 2016; Parveen 2018; Alrouh et al. 2022.

[12] This strategy has been taken in many large-scale studies. See, eg: Dewar et al. 2000; Hunter et al. 2003; Moorhead and Sefton 2005; Trinder et al. 2014; Lee and Tkacukova 2018.

they were emotionally ready to discuss their thoughts, feelings, and perceptions of the court process.

At the beginning of each interview, LIPs were asked to talk generally about their circumstances, such as whether they had other children, where they were living, whether they had any other legal problems, and any other information about themselves that they felt were important for me to know in order to understand what court was like for them. During these conversations, it transpired that a significant number (12) had experienced domestic abuse in their relationship with the other parent. Mental health issues were also common, with 10 LIPs citing diagnoses including anxiety, depression, and post-traumatic stress. Six LIPs were contending with life-long learning difficulties, and one had a long-term physical health condition. While it is not possible or desirable to essentialise these experiences according to broad categories of age, gender, or disability, the breadth of circumstances across the sample means that it can speak to at least some of the ways that these characteristics may intersect and manifest within the institutional context of the legal system.

LIPs had a range of different experiences of seeking advice alongside their court hearings, as well as of the court process itself. Fourteen were based near or within large cities across England and Wales and nine were from small towns and rural areas, which are often more difficult to reach through conventional recruitment strategies. Although two LIPs had paid for some legal advice, the majority (21) explained that they could not afford legal representation and had either been unable to obtain legal aid or had not applied due to anticipating it would not be available. Although several LIPs were mistrustful of lawyers, none said that this was their sole reason for self-representing. LIPs also had a range of different experiences within the court process itself. For instance, three LIPs went through the court process more than once due to ex-partners making counterapplications for variations to existing orders. As a result, these LIPs had experiences of acting as both applicant and respondent in relation to the same case. In terms of who they faced in court, 17 LIPs had experiences of both semi-represented hearings (in which they represented themselves against legal representatives) and unrepresented hearings (in which they represented themselves against other LIPs) during their time in the process. The remaining six LIPs stated that they had only self-represented against another LIP throughout their entire proceedings, and this meant that they were able to provide a useful contradictory insight into the ways in which hearings were managed without any lawyers at all.

The sample broadly aligns with those of existing studies which have also found a high prevalence of factors like unemployment, low levels of education, domestic abuse, and mental health issues among LIPs. There are, nevertheless, a few anomalies that should be noted. First, there was a relatively high proportion of mothers who volunteered to be interviewed compared to earlier studies, where LIPs are either evenly split by gender or include a higher number of fathers (Dewar et al. 2000: 38; Moorhead and Sefton 2005: 67; MacFarlane et al. 2013: 23; Trinder et al. 2014: 12). Indeed, within the public Facebook groups I used to advertise the project, there appeared to be no shortage of male LIPs – indeed, their voices tended to overwhelm these groups, due to the high numbers of posts which related to father's rights groups.[13] To an extent, the larger proportion of mothers may be attributable to how I was perceived by LIPs. For example, several mothers who had negative experiences of the family court were cautious of men who were also involved in the court process. Almost all female LIPs expressed their concerns for my safety because of my decision to include a photograph of myself online when promoting the project, and to interview male LIPs by myself in unfamiliar locations. These conversations left me with the impression that women would not have been so well represented in this sample had the project been conducted by a male-presenting researcher. Similarly, it may be possible that some fathers were less likely to perceive a female-presenting researcher as open to their perspectives and motivations. Nevertheless, the gender distribution of the sample did align with earlier studies in relation to their status as applicants or respondents, in that all fathers were applicants, whereas only five mothers had made applications (Moorhead and Sefton 2005: 67; Trinder *et al.* 2014: 12).

Second, several LIPs had spent a great deal of time in the court process. In Trinder et al.'s research, the median number of substantive hearings attended by LIPs was three for semi-represented cases and two for unrepresented cases (2014: 58). For comparison, the median number of substantive hearings attended by the LIPs I interviewed was four. Moreover, four LIPs attended eight or more hearings, which is unlikely to be a typical experience.[14] However, this means that their experiences are nevertheless extremely useful for gaining an insight into the problems that may be occurring for a minority of LIPs who find themselves unable to progress smoothly through the court process.

Third, an unusually high number of LIPs had attended hearings involving cross-examination, including fact-finding hearings in which the court determines the truth of allegations of domestic abuse (13) and final hearings at which the court imposes final court orders (7). Given that several LIPs had experienced protracted disputes, the high number of final hearings is unsurprising, as it is likely that they were unable to reach agreements earlier in the process as many family litigants are encouraged to do. More atypical, however, was the number of fact-finding hearings, given the extensive literature which indicates that it is relatively rare for such hearings to be ordered.[15] Nevertheless, the high number of LIPs who were able to discuss cross-examination was extremely useful for gaining an insight into how LIPs may experience this process. This is especially important considering the

[13] On this, see generally: Melville 2017.

[14] A possible explanation for this is that 14 LIPs were recruited through social media groups, which Tkacukova (2020) has suggested is an environment that can foster problematic attitudes and misunderstandings about the family court, and potentially hinder the progress of cases. While it is not possible to determine the role that social media played in this, all four of these LIPs were dealing with chaotic circumstances and protracted disputes.

[15] See generally: Hunter and Barnett 2013; Barnett 2014; Hunter et al. 2018.

many examples of research that have questioned the efficacy of judicial guidance and the extent to which domestic abuse is effectively recognised and responded to in family court practice.[16]

Lastly, because interviews were conducted prior to the outbreak of COVID-19 in England and Wales in 2020, it is not possible to garner any first-hand insight into the potential impact of the pandemic and associated restrictions on LIPs' experiences of the family court. Nevertheless, LIPs' perceptions and understandings that are explored throughout this book are likely to be valuable for thinking through at least some of the ways that LIPs may have experienced the family justice system during this time. Additionally, it is possible to draw these experiences together with emerging research and data that has been produced more recently to reflect more precisely on the implications of the pandemic for both how LIPs relate to others in the family court process, as well as the potential efficacy of the way that this system has been able to support them.

This book will use the accounts of these 23 parents to trace the different ways in which LIPs may experience and relate to the family justice system. By playing close attention to how their perceptions and encounters aligned with and differed from each other, it will provide an insight into the rich diversity of issues that LIPs face within this system. Their accounts will be drawn together with a broad range of LIP experiences derived from the rich array of large- and small-scale studies discussed here. These studies provide a wealth of data concerning self-representation across different legal systems and political contexts but have not yet been drawn together for the specific purposes of examining the family justice system from the perspective of its unrepresented users. In doing so, this book will provide an important theoretical and empirical contribution to this literature, with the hope of reframing how the relationship between LIPs and the family justice system is conceptualised within academic scholarship and policy, and to better situate LIPs within debates that will shape the future of the process that exists to serve them.

V. Chapter Outline

The structure of this book will be as follows. Chapter two begins by setting out the shifting landscape of family justice that frames LIPs' experiences. By tracing these key changes, events, and issues, this chapter provides a vital starting point for thinking about the different factors that shape the relationship that LIPs have with the family justice system, and the frequent absence of LIPs' perspectives from debates about the future of family justice. Chapter three builds upon this understanding by reflecting on how LIPs are currently conceptualised within the

[16] See further discussion of this in ch two.

family justice system. It considers what theoretical and empirical tools might be used to rethink the relationship between them. In doing so, it underscores that any exploration of this relationship must not only be empirical, as it has been to date, but also theoretical. This combination is important for such an exploration to adequately capture both the diversity of LIPs' experiences as well as how those experiences relate to broader power structures that frame society. To this end, chapter three outlines an analytical framework that draws together multiple theoretical tools for these purposes and sets out how these tools can be used as a pragmatic lens through which to gain a deeper, richer, and broader understanding of LIPs' experiences of the court process.

Chapters four, five, and six use this analytical lens to explore in detail the journeys that LIPs may take through the family court process. Chapter four focuses upon how LIPs navigate the family justice system. Here, I discuss the ways that LIPs may engage with procedural requirements within the court process, operationalise the legal principles and concepts that govern their cases, and negotiate a complex web of unspoken social hierarchies and cultural expectations as they move through the family court. Chapter five explores the extent to which LIPs can contribute to the proceedings that concern their family disputes. It draws together the different ways that LIPs may communicate with others in the process, by speaking in their hearings, conveying information through paperwork, and finding alternative ways to feel heard within the confines of oral and written court procedures. Chapter six examines the extent to which LIPs are able to play a meaningful role in the court process. It considers the different kinds of relationships that LIPs may have with other participants, including judges, legal professionals, and other LIPs, and the crucial importance of all these relationships for meaningful participation.

Chapter seven steps back from the detail of the interactions and experiences that LIPs have within the court process and reflects upon how these different journeys may shape perceptions of family justice. It explores the extent to which the court process aligns with LIPs' expectations of the family court and the different ways that LIPs may understand the decisions reached through this process. It also considers how negative perceptions may perpetuate cyclical exclusion of LIPs and emphasises that LIPs' perceptions are crucially important for ensuring public faith in the family justice system.

The book will conclude with chapter eight, which revisits the tensions that characterise the relationship between LIPs and the family justice system. It reflects upon the value of centring LIPs within ongoing academic and policy debates, arguing that this activity further complicates current understandings about the challenges that LIPs face, and focuses critical attention on the capacity of the family justice system to respond to their needs. It argues that while LASPO is frequently cited as the demise of family justice, it can also be conceptualised as an opportunity to begin to think creatively about the future relationship between LIPs and the family justice system.

2

The Changing Landscape of Family Justice

The landscape of family justice is anything but static. The journeys that LIPs take through the family justice system have always been framed by a complex and tumultuous political context. Various neoliberal policy initiatives and reforms have shaped this context, informed by the idea that citizens should take full responsibility for resolving their own legal problems and that the state should be minimally involved in this process. The post-LASPO era has exacerbated this context to an extreme degree. Now, LIPs are caught within a context of diminished legal support, overwhelmed lawyers and advice services, and a strained court system attempting to maintain its important role as a safety net for those who rely upon it.

To further complicate matters, this context has also been intersected by two distinct and important issues which closely interrelate with the challenges facing family justice. The first of these issues is the family court's enduring failure to appropriately respond to domestic abuse. For decades, the family justice system has been subject to longstanding criticism concerning its ability to adequately support litigants who raise allegations of abuse. Reforms and initiatives are frequent but often ineffective, due to deep-rooted cultural misunderstandings of how abuse manifests as well as its relevance to future family arrangements. These problems have been further aggravated by the increasingly limited availability of legal support for victims, which has in turn created additional pressure for the already-strained court process as it strives to do better.

The second of these issues is more recent but nevertheless has enormous significance for the landscape of family justice. In early 2020, the COVID-19 pandemic transformed the ways that people in England and Wales were able to interact with each other as well as engage with legal support and the court process. Closures of face-to-face support services, suspension of court hearings, and a rapid shift to online processes have all fundamentally altered the practices of the family justice system. As an institution already reeling from the impact of LASPO, the family court has been faced with the additional challenge of trying to support LIPs who are even less likely to have been able to access prior advice and frequently lack appropriate technology.

This chapter will set out the changes and events that have framed this shifting landscape of family justice. The task of unravelling these different issues is a vital starting point for beginning to think about how LIPs fit into the future of family justice. This is because, first, it is only by tracing the ways that the family justice system has developed and adapted that we can gain an appreciation for how this system may be capable of changing in the future. Second, it is only by considering how all these influences have operated together that we can adequately map the current state of family justice. In practice, looking at any of these issues in isolation obfuscates the reality that they can each be understood as reiterations of the same overarching problem: that the family justice system in England and Wales is not designed with LIPs in mind, and debates about the future of family justice are not adequately rooted in the experiences and perspectives of these users.

I. Neoliberalism and the Family Justice System

At its core, neoliberalism is a theory of governance which assumes that economic, political, and social life can be governed by reference to market principles. Although it has manifested differently across jurisdictions, it has significantly influenced government policies across the world since the 1970s, with states reducing their commitments to social provision and instead focusing on promoting private property rights and free trade (Harvey 2005). In short, neoliberalism has the effect of reconfiguring all aspects of social life in economic terms, with the result that policies are valued in terms of their cost-effectiveness or capacity to promote economic growth. This economisation of social policy obfuscates the value of any non-economic policy goals, such as social inclusion, equality of participation within society, or access to justice (Larner 2000; Fraser 2013; Brown 2015). Consequently, any remnants of existing policies that were introduced in pursuit of such aims, are – at best – conceptualised as inefficient and wasteful due to their economic cost, and – at worst – harmful to society because they supposedly impair incentives for individuals to embark on journeys of self-determination.

This approach to governance is pervasive because it is posited as a sensible and pragmatic response to economic challenges, such as the need to address national deficits. This was a major driver of the austerity policies introduced by the Cameron-Clegg coalition Government in England and Wales, although neoliberal governance was already evident in privatisation policies introduced under the Thatcher and New Labour Governments of the 1980s and 1990s (Page 2015). However, this philosophy is not merely pragmatic – it is also rooted in a particular vision about the nature of inequality and the appropriate role that the state should play in terms of implementing policies that recognise or address inequality within society.

For the purposes of this book, there are two key assumptions of neoliberalism which are relevant to understanding the way that policies have shaped the family justice system. The first is the assumption of a level playing field in society, and the implicit (and explicit) expectations of self-sufficiency and responsibility in legal aid policies. Although the philosophy of neoliberalism advocates a retreat from state control or intervention, neoliberal policies nevertheless employ governance techniques which encourage or incentivise behaviours amongst its citizens (Barlow et al. 2017: 2–3). The second is the corresponding assumption that the appropriate role for the state is that of minimal involvement and diminishing commitments to the provision of subsidies like state welfare. In the context of family justice, these assumptions are most obvious in moralistic policy initiatives which encourage or incentivise people to 'take responsibility' for their family disputes, thus conceptualising them as personal problems in which wider society has no interest, and the state is unaccountable for outcomes (Boyd and Treloar 2013).

The family justice system has developed to provide several different processes that families might pursue to reach resolutions to their family disputes. While litigation is perhaps the most serious route, there are also options including solicitor-led negotiations and alternative dispute resolution, including mediation. In theory, individuals can choose the most appropriate process for their circumstances, but realistically, this choice has ultimately been constrained by a range of neoliberal policies which have, first, limited the availability of state funding and, second, aimed to divert families away from lawyers and the court, and towards mediation. For example, before individuals are permitted to make a court application, they must first attend a Mediation Information and Assessment Meeting (MIAM), at which a mediator will encourage them to consider using mediation instead, if there are no identified issues of domestic abuse. MIAMs have been compulsory for those reliant on legal aid since 1996, and for all potential court users since 2011.[1] This policy gave a clear steer for how families should resolve their family law problems: by negotiating future arrangements away from expensive sources of state funded support such as legal aid lawyers and the court system.

Despite its many potential benefits for families, mediation has never been a popular option among those dealing with a family dispute, and political efforts to encourage mediation have never been truly successful. One reason for this is that mediation requires both parties to meaningfully participate. This can be impossible if parties are not yet emotionally ready to discuss the relevant issues or to reach compromises (Hitchings et al. 2013). Another explanation is that mediation-focused policies have consistently failed to recognise the important relationship between out-of-court dispute resolution and legal advice. Although it is often thought that the very act of involving lawyers in family disputes is something which can exacerbate conflict, decades of evidence suggests that the practice of family lawyers is strongly underpinned by a conciliatory approach, and a commitment to reducing conflict wherever possible (Ingleby 1992; Davis et al. 1994; Eekelaar et al. 2000). In particular, solicitors have historically been key facilitators in referring clients to mediation, providing an important framework of legal advice to inform negotiations, and wherever possible, supporting clients to negotiate private settlements without the need to go to court.

[1] See: Family Law Act 1996, s 26 as well as Practice Direction 3A which was subsequently enshrined under the Children and Families Act 2014, s 10.

The success of out-of-court resolution options like mediation can therefore often depend on whether people are able to access legal advice. Such advice might involve clarifying misconceptions that people may have about their legal rights and entitlements, managing expectations as to what might realistically be achieved through family law processes, or bespoke suggestions for how to manage interim arrangements in a way that does not exacerbate tensions (Eekelaar et al. 2000; Wright 2006). For most separating couples, the main objective on both sides is usually to maintain a reasonable relationship with their ex-partner, especially if there are children involved. As such, feelings of guilt or vindication relating to the relationship breakdown can often play a significant role in private negotiations. Solicitors perform an important role by ensuring that any agreements reached incorporate an understanding of their future needs and the future needs of their children, rather than the immediate trauma of the relationship breakdown (Wright 2007). As Ingleby (1992: 2) explains, family lawyers do not simply pick up the pieces by meeting the day-to-day needs of their clients, but they also put the pieces back together again by helping them to negotiate a final resolution which is forward-looking.

The accessibility of legal advice, however, has historically hinged on the availability of legal aid. Introduced under the Legal Aid and Advice Act 1949, legal aid has historically been available through a judicare model, which involves providing state funding to private law firms for the purposes of providing legal services to those who could not otherwise afford to instruct lawyers. Although the legal aid scheme was characterised by ambitious post-war aspirations of equitable access to law, it has never quite achieved these aspirations. Rather, the expense of the judicare model meant that the legal aid scheme was a common target for cost-saving measures, particularly as neoliberal ideas about the appropriateness and affordability of state-funded welfare provision began to take hold within public policy. Several successive government administrations introduced reforms to limit eligibility for the scheme through increasingly strict means testing.[2] This meant that even those who are eligible for legal aid have often been excluded from its benefits because they were expected to take financial responsibility for their problems by paying expensive and sometimes unaffordable contributions towards the cost of legal services (Hynes 2012; Hirsch 2018).

Beyond limiting eligibility of individuals, however, these cost-saving initiatives were also targeted at the providers of legal services themselves. This was because the cost of the scheme was inextricably linked with the growing demand for legal advice and representation. This is especially true in family law, where the law has necessarily become more complicated to keep up with the reality of modern family life. Greater acceptability of different family forms and relationships, as well as increasing numbers of families co-parenting across different households, all came with a greater demand for family dispute resolution and orders under the Children

[2] See, eg: Legal Aid Act 1988 and Access to Justice Act 1999.

Act 1989. The corresponding increase in demand for legal aid raised government concerns about 'supplier-induced inflation' and a suspicion that firms reliant on income from legal aid were not incentivised to provide services efficiently, especially compared to those motivated by private profits (Moorhead 2004). These concerns indicated a shift in the relationship between lawyers and the state, in which government policy became geared towards promoting efficiency, greater scrutinisation of firms offering legal aid funded services, and limiting remuneration for lawyers undertaking legal aid work. In short, the insufficient support for the legal aid sector meant that this work quickly became unprofitable and arduous. While some firms were able to offset the impact of this by taking on private clients alongside their legal aid clients, many organisations began to move away from legal aid work entirely.

This restrictive climate of legal aid provision significantly impaired the effectiveness with which lawyers were able to support people to make the most of out-of-court dispute resolutions. For one thing, it created a stark distinction between the experiences of people relying on legal aid funded legal services as compared with people who could afford to instruct lawyers privately. Privately instructed lawyers were typically under pressure from clients to be proactive, and to provide effective and efficient resolutions to their family disputes. This meant taking early action, attentively following up on their cases, facilitating greater access to a range of dispute resolution options, and usually avoiding court altogether (Davis et al. 1994; Eekelaar et al. 2000). In contrast, research suggests that the service legal aid clients received was often reactive and tended to 'drift' towards adjudication, because their lawyers were frequently inexperienced and overwhelmed by so many cases and such limited support (Davis et al. 1994: 138).

As eligibility for legal aid was gradually eroded, many solicitors began to offer 'unbundled' legal services for ineligible clients who were able to pay fixed fees for help with specific tasks. This was an innovative way of attempting to sustain their businesses and make legal services more accessible despite restrictions to legal aid (National Audit Office 2014; Webley 2015: 316–17; Maclean 2015a). However, this format of providing sporadic support was not always enough to help people avoid ending up adjudicating as LIPs and remained incomparable to the comprehensive service received by clients who could afford to privately instruct lawyers.

This climate also sometimes meant that LIPs began to draw more heavily on the help of McKenzie Friends once they ended up in the court process. Traditionally, McKenzie Friends have been friends, family members or support workers, who might come with LIPs to provide practical and emotional support in the courtroom.[3] As legal assistance became more limited, however, a market developed for 'professional' McKenzie Friends who would offer this support in exchange for

[3] See: *McKenzie v McKenzie* [1970] 3 WLR 472. McKenzie Friends are not permitted to undertake restricted activities under the Legal Services Act 2007, s 12 such as advocacy or conducting litigation. See further: *Practice Guidance (McKenzie Friends: Civil and Family Courts)* [2010] 1 WLR 1881.

variable fees (Legal Services Consumer Panel 2014; Smith et al. 2017). By helping to ensure paperwork is correct and helping LIPs to engage with hearings, McKenzie Friends can be extremely helpful for everyone in the court process, and their support might even help LIPs to continue with cases that would have otherwise collapsed. There is some indication that some professional McKenzie Friends may even be ex-legal aid lawyers or social workers who have been forced out of work but are still able to offer a wealth of experience and knowledge that LIPs have been unable to access within the fragmented climate of legal advice (Smith et al. 2017: 18).

However, there is also evidence to suggest that a minority of McKenzie Friends would sometimes breach boundaries of acceptability within court by seeking to act for LIPs, such as by negotiating or calling the court on their behalf (Moorhead and Sefton 2005: 57–58; Legal Services Consumer Panel 2014: 26). Additionally, given their lack of legal expertise, there is also the risk that McKenzie Friends will offer misguided advice on how to proceed with a case, or even attempt to 'egg LIPs on' or 'stir things up' within proceedings to pursue their own agendas through the cases of others (Moorhead and Sefton 2005: 172–73; MacFarlane et al. 2013: 78; Legal Services Consumer Panel 2014: 19–21). These McKenzie Friends have been regarded with scepticism and even resentment by lawyers, court staff, and the judiciary.[4] While some of this may have stemmed from the further threats that McKenzie Friends posed to the legal profession, it is also rooted in concern for the many LIPs who are ill-placed to judge the quality and reliability of their McKenzie Friends. The gradual erosion of legal aid and state support has therefore demarcated the experiences of those eligible for legal aid, those who can afford to pay privately for legal services, and the majority who are caught in the middle and expected to navigate a fragmented and unpredictable landscape of support services. As Cornford (2016: 33) poignantly summarises, within the history of legal aid policy and family law reform, there is 'interestingly little discussion about the fact that people's ability to … use law is allowed to differ in accordance with their income'.

The history of the family justice system has been significantly shaped by neoliberal policies which have sought to not only reduce state expenditure, but also reframe family disputes as personal affairs for which lawyers and the court system are not necessary. Underpinning these policies is an assumption that most individuals have the resources and capacity to manage these disputes, which has meant that certain population groups have disproportionately struggled to access legal services. For many, these fraught political efforts to limit reliance on lawyers has had the unintended consequence of undermining the potential utility of out-of-court dispute resolution options. By tracing the ways that such policies have

[4] This is evident, for instance, in calls for greater professional regulation or policies that would prevent McKenzie Friends from claiming remuneration for their services (Legal Services Consumer Panel 2014: 13–4; Hunter 2017: 17).

influenced the landscape of family justice over the past few decades, it is possible to see that LIPs are not typically litigious troublemakers who pursue cases to the family court unnecessarily. Instead, they are most often families who find themselves caught in the gaps formed by the way these policies have disrupted the delicate ecosystem of family law. These increasing pressures on the family justice system all culminated at the point that LASPO was implemented.

II. Family Justice at Breaking Point?

By withdrawing legal aid almost entirely from private family law, the LASPO reforms marked the most significant disruption to the family justice system yet – effectively closing off legal advice to most families engaging with family law and facilitating a mass increase in how many of these families end up as LIPs in the court process. In addition to increasing the number of LIPs, the LASPO changes also facilitated an entire new category of LIPs. These 'new' LIPs now include those on the lowest incomes and with the fewest resources who have now been categorically excluded from legal aid eligibility based on their legal problem. This much larger and newly diverse population of LIPs is now faced with the challenge of navigating a debilitated family justice system with limited capacity to support them. The full implications of this are still unfolding, but it is no exaggeration to suggest that LASPO was a defining moment for the relationship between LIPs and the family justice system.

The four aims of LASPO stipulated in the initial policy consultation were to discourage unnecessary litigation, target legal aid at those who need it most, make significant savings to the cost of the legal aid scheme, and deliver better overall value for money for the taxpayer (Ministry of Justice 2010). These were to be achieved by withdrawing legal aid eligibility for several legal problems including social welfare law, employment law, and several issues relating to immigration, clinical negligence, debt, and housing law. Although public family law was to remain within scope, private family law disputes were to be entirely removed, with a narrow exception for those who can corroborate that they have experienced domestic abuse through prescribed forms of evidence. This meant that, in practice, disputing families on very low incomes would only be able to access public funding to support their participation in mediation, and if they wanted to consult a solicitor or use the family court, they would need to do this at their own expense.

Almost all responses to the LASPO consultation argued that these reforms were unnecessary and would impede access to justice for the most vulnerable in society. Nevertheless, the then-government proceeded on the basis that large scale withdrawal of legal aid was not only necessary from a financial perspective, but would be beneficial for the justice system and those who rely upon it:

> Legal aid has expanded far beyond its original intentions, available for a wide range of issues, many of which need not be resolved through the courts. This has encouraged

> people to bring their problems to court when the courts are not well placed to provide the best solutions … (Ministry of Justice 2011: 8).

In many ways, the further removal of funding for private family law under LASPO was merely an extension of previous neoliberal reforms. After all, prior limitations on eligibility, remuneration for providers, and encouragements to try mediation and avoid court were all inherently linked to making savings and delivering value for money. However, the vast scale of the LASPO reforms distinguishes them from earlier policy initiatives. The default position is now one of non-eligibility, where individuals may not expect state-funded legal support in relation to their family disputes, and use of the family court is generally stigmatised.

In establishing this position, the government stated that legal aid should instead be reserved only for the 'most vulnerable' (Ministry of Justice 2010: 3–6). The assessment of who would fall into this category involved a consideration of several factors, including: the importance of the legal issue, the litigant's ability to present their own case, the availability of alternative sources of funding, and the availability of other routes to resolution (Ministry of Justice 2011: 11–12). Under this assessment, individuals are understood to be most vulnerable if they can provide specific forms of evidence to prove that they have experienced domestic abuse, although in practice this is far from straightforward.[5] An exception is also made if people can demonstrate that their case warrants exceptional funding on the basis that denying them legal aid would contravene the state's obligations under the European Convention on Human Rights.[6] This extremely narrow conception of vulnerability implicitly constructs most people contending with family breakdown as self-sufficient individuals who should know better than to invoke court proceedings to resolve their personal problems.

There are also clear barriers to family law even among those who are theoretically still eligible for legal aid. For instance, there has been limited success for those who might have benefited from the exceptional funding scheme. The intention was that this would cover cases where individuals would be unable

[5] After LASPO, the task of establishing domestic abuse for the purposes of a legal aid application was characterised by several barriers, including a narrow range of accepted forms of evidence which were originally subject to a time-bar. The rules have gradually been expanded to include a broader range of evidence, to remove the requirement that evidence be subject to a time-bar, and to introduce discretion to means test evaluations in cases where victims have 'trapped capital' that they could not realistically access or use towards the costs of their legal services. These expansions have been incremental, emerging from notable judicial reviews launched by the Rights of Women and Public Law Project and following years of sustained campaigning from countless access to justice organisations and domestic abuse support services. See further: Civil Legal Aid (Procedure) (Amendment) Regulations 2016, Reg 33; Civil Legal Aid (Procedure) (Amendment) Regulations (No 2) 2017, Reg 33; *R (on app of Rights of Women) v The Lord Chancellor and Secretary of State for Justice* [2015] EWHC 35 (Admin); *R (on app of GR) v Director of Legal Aid Casework* [2020] EWHC 3140 (Admin).

[6] See: LASPO 2012, s 10.

to represent themselves effectively, for instance due to a disability or learning difficulty. However, an onerous application process and low success rates have deterred family lawyers from attempting to access this funding to support clients through legal aid (Marshall et al. 2018). Additionally, research has continually established that survivors of domestic abuse are unlikely to take action without legal support and are unlikely to apply for legal aid if they assume or perceive that it is not available (Hunter et al. 2003; De Simone and Hunter 2009). The introduction of additional evidential and procedural hurdles for legal aid applicants combined with already-strict means testing means that the post-LASPO population of LIPs is likely to include some individuals who were explicitly categorised as deserving of state-funded advice and representation, and for whom the option of self-representation is likely to be seriously unsuitable.

The LASPO scope changes have also dealt another blow to already-struggling legal aid providers and further impaired the capacity of lawyers and advisers to meet the now soaring levels of demand for free advice. Across civil legal aid, legal aid providers have decreased by a third since LASPO (Ministry of Justice 2021b). The Ministry of Justice does not collect data on what proportion of these are family law providers, but there is evidence to suggest that these providers have been disproportionately affected. For example, post-LASPO observations of family firms suggest that smaller firms and those relying mostly on legal aid clients are facing significant challenges sustaining their businesses now that they cannot derive an income from legal aid (Maclean and Eekelaar 2016). Although some firms are continuing to offer pro bono advice to clients who find themselves ineligible for legal aid, the majority have been overwhelmed since LASPO, and simply cannot meet the current level of demand (Maclean and Eekelaar 2019: 46–59). Due to the shortfall caused by LASPO, swathes of firms have had to diversify their income streams by either moving away from legal aid work entirely, or by offering other services like mediation (Russell 2019; Wong and Cain 2019). As a result, 'advice deserts' are now common, with some geographical areas having no organisations at all willing to take on a legal aid contract. Moreover, these areas are disproportionately likely to be post-industrialist or deprived areas where people are heavily reliant on welfare payments and public service employment and have been hit hardest by concurrent austerity measures (Marshall et al. 2018). Instead, individuals are turning to rely on non-legal services such as student-led advice clinics and Support Through Court, which can each provide practical help with paperwork and court forms. Support with private family law paperwork now forms almost half of the work undertaken by Support Through Court volunteers, but these services are now struggling to refer clients elsewhere for legal advice because there are so few options available (Marsh 2014: 48–49).

All of this means that legal advice has become practically inaccessible for those on the lowest incomes after LASPO. Despite the government's expectations that the reform would incentivise more people to use mediation, it was not surprising that without referrals from lawyers, mediation take-up significantly decreased after LASPO (Ministry of Justice 2021b).[7] Instead, the number of people representing themselves in court as LIPs has increased exponentially. The number of cases involving LIPs increased from 43 per cent to 74 per cent over the year following the reforms, and since then has remained steady at around 81 per cent (Ministry of Justice 2021a).[8] For most LIPs, therefore, MIAMs are simply a gateway to the court process, and people may be even more inclined to use adjudication to resolve their disputes without the benefit of advice and support to reach their own resolutions. Others may simply have no other option but to self-represent, due to the unsuitability of mediation for many couples and the unavailability of legal aid for representation.

The increased number of people representing themselves in the court process, combined with the challenges that many of them face before arriving at court, means that LASPO has also made a significant difference to the system in which their cases are heard. To elaborate on these implications, it is useful to briefly outline the court process itself.[9] The first hearing in child arrangement proceedings is always a First Hearing Dispute Resolution Appointment (FHDRA). The purpose of this initial hearing is to determine whether cases can first be resolved by agreement. If this is not possible, the case will progress to a substantive hearing known as a Dispute Resolution Appointment (DRA), where relevant issues are discussed further. Over the course of a case, there may be multiple DRAs, all of which require LIPs to prepare different kinds of information each time in advance of going to court. Usually, this can involve composing arguments which are supported by relevant law, writing statements that give accounts of past incidents which are relevant to the court's consideration, or give crucial information about the needs of both parents and children when the court is making these considerations. At each DRA, judges will continue to ascertain if there are any aspects of a potential arrangement on which the parties can agree. If a judge decides that resolutions cannot be achieved through these hearings, the case will culminate in a Final Hearing, where an order will be made for the parties. Additionally, if allegations of harm are made against one parent during proceedings – usually during the FHDRA – parties are directed to attend a Fact-Finding Hearing (FFH) before they continue to subsequent DRAs. The purpose of this hearing is to establish the truth of such allegations, for the purpose of them being considered in the future deliberations of judges.[10] Both Final Hearings and FFHs involve cross-examination and a definitive judgment at the end of proceedings.

[7] At the time of writing, MIAM take-up continues to be approximately a third of pre-LASPO levels, and mediation starts are approximately half of pre-LASPO levels. Both rates temporarily decreased even further during the initial outbreak of the COVID-19 pandemic.

[8] It is important to clarify that although the proportion of LIPs in family cases has significantly increased, overall use of the family court remains relatively low in relation to the number of families with dependent children in England and Wales. See generally: Cusworth 2020; 2021.

[9] See: Child Arrangements Programme, Practice Direction 12B.

[10] Although, as discussed later in this chapter, the use of FFHs in practice is significantly criticised, with research from both before and after LASPO indicating that findings of abuse are often not adequately considered, and FFHs inconsistently directed in the first place.

Each of these stages perform a distinct function within the court process in terms of progressing cases to a conclusion. However, there is a significant amount of research to indicate the ways in which increased numbers of LIPs are putting the family justice system under strain and impairing these functions. First, the presence of LIPs has for decades been linked to increased work for others within the court process, due to the problems that LIPs have in completing and submitting paperwork, the additional time that is required to explain things to LIPs, and the frequency with which hearings had to be adjourned (Dewar et al. 2000; Moorhead and Sefton 2005; Trinder et al. 2014; McKeever et al. 2018). Second, when facing a LIP, lawyers and judges encounter difficulties in performing their traditional roles within the court process. For example, lawyers are frequently required to take on the extra work of preparing trial bundles and extending help to LIPs whilst also maintaining their ethical obligations and confidence of their own clients (Williams 2011; Bevan 2013; Trinder et al. 2014; McKeever et al. 2018). Judges also sometimes need to change their approach, ranging from basic signposting, giving procedural leeway to LIPs, to acting on behalf of LIPs during key tasks like cross-examination, and even sometimes managing hearings in an entirely inquisitorial way (Dewar et al. 2000; Moorhead and Sefton 2005; Trinder et al. 2014; Corbett and Summerfield 2017). The inconsistency between these approaches stems from judicial anxiety about maintaining their traditional position of impartiality, as well as time and resource constraints (Moorhead and Sefton 2005; Moorhead 2007). Third, there is evidence to suggest that many cases reaching the family court are more challenging and contentious than they were before LASPO, with more people needing to return to court to enforce contact arrangements which might otherwise have been addressed by solicitors (Cusworth 2021). In terms of the court process, therefore, evidence tends to emphasise that the presence of LIPs within court hearings places significant demands on other parties, and that this increase in LIPs is unsustainable.

Further, given that support is now so limited, there is some evidence to suggest that the use of McKenzie Friends has increased since LASPO, and that professional McKenzie Friends may be expanding further into offering services which are geared more towards giving advice and doing out-of-court work, or even being granted rights of audience and conducting cross-examination when judges have few other options (Caplen 2016; Corbett and Summerfield 2017: 22–23; Hunter 2017: 17). In many ways, McKenzie Friends may be playing an even larger role in helping LIPs who cannot access legal advice or representation, especially as many altruistically pitch their services at those on very low incomes (Barry 2019: 85; Smith et al. 2017: 35). Additionally, fee-charging McKenzie Friends may no longer be the only ones at risk of providing misguided advice and information. Rather, negative experiences of the court process can mean that agenda-driven advice or conspiracy myths may be circulated among LIPs themselves through social media and other informal networks, which LIPs are also increasingly relying upon as sources of support in the post-LASPO context (Leader 2017: 208–11; Melville 2017).

The post-LASPO context is therefore one in which people are more frequently falling to the safety net of the family court as LIPs. At the same time, there has been limited change within this process to move beyond the full-representation model.[11] This lack of change limits the capacity of those working within it to respond to the significant shift in court users. Instead, LIPs, lawyers, and judges must try to find ways to adapt and adjust the traditional routines of the court process, which is all-the-more difficult now that there are not only more LIPs in court, but these LIPs are coming to court with a much greater variety of support needs.

The various policy reforms and narratives that led to LASPO, as well as the impact of the 2013 reforms themselves, mean that LIPs' relationship with the family justice system is far from straightforward. This complex political context has shaped this relationship in multiple ways – by limiting eligibility for LIPs at the same time as constraining resources available to those who might provide LIPs with support, this relationship is one in which the interests and objectives of LIPs and the system exist in tension with one another. However, this is even further complicated by two other key issues that closely intersect with this relationship: first, the ongoing problems related to the family court's response to cases involving allegations of domestic abuse, and secondly, the effects of the COVID-19 pandemic for family justice processes, many of which are still unfolding at the time of writing.

III. Domestic Abuse and Family Justice

Allegations of domestic abuse are disproportionately common in private family disputes.[12] It is also not uncommon for applications to the family court to be used as a mechanism of furthering abusive behaviour after the victim has left the perpetrator (Birchall and Choudhry 2018: 42). Even when this is not the case, abusive relationship dynamics render mediation an inappropriate route to resolution, due to the inherent power imbalances involved. For these reasons, abusive relationships frequently end up in the family court – after all, the family court is intended to be a safety net for those families who would benefit from the security that a court order provides.

The family justice system has, however, frequently fallen short of these expectations. A wide body of literature spanning decades before LASPO was even proposed indicates the difficulties that victims have in establishing the truth and relevance of their abuse within disputes over children. For example, lawyers, mediators, and judges have struggled to consistently identify or respond appropriately to historical abuse, non-physical abuse, or abuse which has 'only' been perpetrated against the other parent, rather than the child (Hunter and Barnett 2013; Barnett

[11] This notion and articulation of the 'full-representation' default in family court hearings is drawn from Trinder et al. 2014: 53.

[12] Studies suggest that allegations of abuse are raised in somewhere between 42% and 69% of children disputes that reach the family court (Barnett 2020: 20).

2015: 51; 2016: 228–9). In many of these cases, even where abuse has been identified, research has found that victims have often nevertheless been pressured into participating in mediation and even agreeing to unsafe contact arrangements which facilitate further harassment and intimidation from perpetrators (Hester and Radford 1996; Hester et al. 1997: 15–8; Coy et al. 2012: 35; Women's Aid 2016: 27–8; Thiara and Humphreys 2017).

When cases involving abuse allegations reach the family court, judges are required to respond in particular ways. Practice Direction 12J (PD12J), for instance, provides specific judicial guidance on how to identify these situations and to manage allegations of domestic abuse within hearings.[13] However, research demonstrates that victims nevertheless experience difficulties trying to establish their abuse within the court process. For example, the 2014 revision of PD12J set out clear expectations that judges 'should' direct parties to participate in FFHs in which parties are cross-examined in order to establish the factual basis of any abuse allegations and their relevance to any decisions made in relation to the child. The guidance also stipulated that if judges direct that a FFH is not necessary, they are required to justify why this direction was made. This was reiterated in the 2017 revision of PD12J, which clarified these requirements by replacing the instruction 'should' with 'must'. However, despite this clarification and improved guidance, FFHs have always been relatively rare, due to a lack of understanding about abuse combined with mounting pressure on judges to promote contact with both parents (Hunter and Barnett 2013; Barnett 2014: 443–54; 2015: 52–53; Hunter et al. 2018). For many women, this is linked with limited awareness of gender equality issues, in which judges often have underlying preconceptions of abused mothers as 'being difficult' or standing in the way of contact,[14] and men with a history of aggressive behaviour being treated with leniency because they want to play a role in their child's life (Birchall and Choudhry 2018: 30–32). As part of this, even when FFHs are held, judges have been observed to disaggregate violent incidents from broader patterns of abuse (Barnett 2017). However, without these hearings, evidence suggests that allegations tend to disappear altogether, as the focus of court hearings turns to ensuring contact and potentially unsafe arrangements are made without all the facts (Barnett 2015: 67; Birchall and Choudhry 2018: 23–26).

The implementation of LASPO has only served to exacerbate these problems. For instance, the restriction of legal aid to those who can both provide evidence of domestic abuse and satisfy the means test means that many victims are at risk

[13] Guidelines were first introduced following *Re L, V, M, H (Contact: Domestic Violence)* [2001] Fam 260, and subsequently incorporated into PD12J, which underwent notable revisions in both 2014 and 2017, and is currently under review again in light of further evidence of non-compliance. See further: Hunter et al. 2020: 84–86; Ministry of Justice 2020: 17.

[14] Commentators have criticised the family court's 'pro contact culture', whereby judges are pressured to order contact between children and their parents wherever possible. See: Hunter et al. 2020: 42–43. This approach often conflicts with the expectations set in other legal contexts, where mothers are expected to protect their children from perpetrators rather than ensure contact with them. See generally: Hester 2011.

of being financially pressured into mediation or having to self-represent in court, especially if their abuse is not identified at an early stage (Hunter 2011: 356–57; Birchall and Choudhry 2018: 28). Further, despite the emphasis that has been placed on discouraging unnecessary litigation, there was little attention paid within the LASPO proposals to the ways that serial or vexatious applications provide an opportunity to further harass victims, who in turn are often LIPs themselves as any funds become exhausted (Dewar et al. 2000: 34; Trinder et al. 2014: 31–32; McKeever et al. 2018: 84).

One of the most controversial problems exacerbated by LASPO is the way that judges handle the process of cross-examination now that many more parties are unrepresented. The categorical exclusion of private family law means that perpetrators often appear as LIPs unless they have resources to fund their own legal representation. For some time after LASPO, when it came to Final Hearings or FFHs, this left them in a position where they were expected to conduct their own cross-examination of victims and any relevant witnesses. The implementation of the Domestic Abuse Act 2021 brought a long-awaited[15] statutory ban on direct cross-examination between alleged perpetrators and victims in family law cases, but this was certainly not straightforward. Prior to this, mechanisms to prevent cross-examination of victims by perpetrators were limited to judicial case management practices. Although PD12J recommended that judges should be prepared 'where necessary and appropriate' to conduct the questioning on behalf of parties, research demonstrated that this varied significantly in practice. Some judges would take control of the questioning process to protect victims, for example by approving questions in advance, or relaying the questions on behalf of the LIP (Corbett and Summerfield 2017: 16–18). However, other judges expressed unease about impairing either the traditional role of judicial neutrality or the 'right' of LIPs to conduct the cross-examination themselves (Trinder et al. 2014: 70; Corbett and Summerfield 2017: 15–16). As a result, direct cross-examination in these cases was regarded as 'routine' (All Party Parliamentary Group on Domestic Violence 2016: 4).

In 2017, Part 3A of the Family Procedure Rules (FPR3A) and Practice Direction 3AA (PD3AA) were introduced to tackle the way that the family court was lagging woefully behind the criminal justice system in terms of its ability to recognise and support vulnerable parties (Judiciary of England and Wales 2015).[16] These procedural provisions require judges to consider the potential vulnerability of parties and facilitate any measures that might support them to participate. This might include, for instance, special measures like screens, video links and

[15] The statutory prohibition of direct cross-examination was originally proposed under the Prison and Courts Reform Bill 2016–17, which fell due to the dissolution of Parliament in 2017. It was then re-proposed as part of the Domestic Abuse Bill 2017–2019, which fell due to the proroguing of Parliament in 2019. Finally, it was introduced under the Domestic Abuse Act 2021, s 61 which amended the Matrimonial and Family Proceedings Act 1984, Pt 4.

[16] In criminal hearings, direct cross-examination between alleged victims and perpetrators is statutorily prohibited under the Youth, Justice and Criminal Evidence Act 1999, s 36.

separate waiting rooms to help victims participate. PD3AA also requires the court to consider whether the questions to be put in cross-examination should be agreed in advance, and whether it would be appropriate for the judge to take over responsibility for putting questions to the witness. Nevertheless, research studies continued to reiterate concerning trends, with several victims continuing to report that they had been directly questioned by their abusers (Birchall and Choudhry 2018: 24–27). Although there are positive judicial attitudes to the use of special measures such as video links and screens, there is often inconsistent access to special measures, due to limited availability of resources within courts themselves (Corbett and Summerfield 2017: 24–26).

The family court process is therefore no stranger to initiatives, reforms and judicial guidance that seeks to address these problems and better support those who raise allegations of abuse. Compliance, however, appears to be an enduring problem. FFHs are still rarely ordered, and problematic stereotypes and understandings of domestic abuse continue to prevent effective responses within hearings (CAFCASS and Women's Aid 2017: 8–10; Lefevre and Damman 2019). The enduring nature of these problems was comprehensively acknowledged in a pivotal report published by the Ministry of Justice a decade after LASPO was first proposed (Hunter et al. 2020). This report, frequently referred to as the *Harm Panel* report, was compiled by a panel of domestic abuse experts who drew together existing research studies with data from family justice professionals and victims of domestic abuse who had used the family court. The scale and depth of this report meant that it was remarkably influential, in that the government was persuaded to invest in several major initiatives (Ministry of Justice 2020). In terms of future research, this included commitments to undertake reviews of several major aspects of family court hearings, three of which are most crucial for LIPs in these cases. The first is to provide a baseline understanding of how judges currently implement PD12J in family hearings (2020: 17). The second is to explore whether judges appropriately strike a balance between the benefits of contact and acknowledging the relevance of abuse to those contact arrangements (2020: 4). The third is to understand the extent to which judges make use of 'barring' orders[17] which can limit a perpetrator's ability to make consistently vexatious applications to the family court (2020: 11). In addition to these reviews, the government has also committed to piloting a more investigative (less adversarial) approach to family court proceedings, as well as trialling integrated domestic abuse courts (IDACs) which will address family and criminal matters in parallel (2020: 4). Only a matter of months later, the Court of Appeal handed down a crucial judgment that set out further guidance for judges in the family court in light of the *Harm Panel* report. This judgment emerged from four conjoined appeals in relation to FFHs where domestic abuse had been improperly addressed by judges.[18] Importantly,

[17] Children Act 1989, s 91(14).

[18] *Re H-N and Others (Children) (Domestic Abuse: Finding of Fact Hearings)* [2021] EWCA Civ 448.

this judgment clarified how crucial it is for judges to broaden their understanding of domestic abuse, particularly in terms of how coercive control may play out in future arrangements for children. It is hoped that this will offer some interim direction for judges while the family court awaits the outcomes of the government's reviews.

While these developments, in combination with the introduction of the statutory ban on cross-examination, are hoped to provide authority which may clarify judicial inconsistency and patterns of non-compliance, the family court still has a long way to go to address the deep-rooted cultural attitudes and misconceptions concerning domestic abuse in family cases. In the meantime, these problems will continue to intersect LIPs' experiences of the family court process in cases involving allegations of abuse. During my interviews with LIPs, for instance, these issues clearly underpinned many of the perceptions and interactions of the 12 who reported that they had represented themselves against an abusive ex-partner. Their contributions are therefore particularly vital for unravelling the specific ways that the system is responding to the distinct but fundamentally connected challenges of LASPO and domestic abuse reform.

IV. COVID-19 and Family Justice

Just as the implications of LASPO were starting to become apparent in research and practice, the family justice system was faced with another transformative moment: the COVID-19 pandemic. In early 2020, governments across the globe were forced to impose restrictions on our interpersonal interactions and use of public services to limit the spread of the virus. Beyond obvious concerns for public health and the importance of protecting vulnerable individuals, this also had serious consequences for the ways that the public began interacting with law and legal institutions. The closure of several industries meant that many individuals began experiencing financial precarity for the first time, and with necessitated social isolation came an increase in the level of legal need related to issues like employment, housing, and social welfare entitlements (Law Centres Network 2020; Creudzfeldt and Sechi 2021; Newman et al. 2021).

The pandemic's influence on family law problems is difficult to quantify precisely, but there is emerging data which suggests that COVID-19 is likely to have induced an increased demand for support in both the short and long term. In the short term, there was a clear and urgent increase in the prevalence of domestic abuse since March 2020, when the first national lockdowns were announced in England and Wales. In the first month alone, calls to the National Domestic Abuse Helpline spiked by 50 per cent, and visits to the Refuge website increased by an enormous 400 per cent (Refuge 2020). This suggests an increased number of post-separation legal issues, as more people are prompted to leave abusive partners. These issues are likely to also be more complex to resolve, given the inappropriateness of mediation for couples where there are power imbalances and allegations of domestic abuse. For already-separated couples, there were more re-emerging disputes over children, as school closures, isolation rules, and travel restrictions all created confusion and conflict within existing parenting arrangements.

In the longer term, the pandemic may also mean that several family disputes are stored up until a moment of increased social stability. Generally, people refrain from making major life changes when they are already under conditions of stress and uncertainty. This means that there is likely to be an increase in the number of family disputes in the years after the pandemic as people delay their decisions to separate. At the same time, the unique circumstances of the pandemic have forced many couples into making major relationship commitments. With lockdowns and strict limits on socialising across household bubbles, many couples decided to accelerate decisions to begin cohabiting together to avoid the alternative of not being able to see each other or living alone in isolation. Feeling rushed into isolating together as a household may strain some relationships, again causing more disputes to emerge later down the line (Fraser 2020).

During the pandemic, law firms and the advice sector were forced to rapidly close their offices, transition to home working, and find ways to support their clients by providing advice virtually or via the telephone. This task was far from straightforward – in addition to the challenges of arranging sufficient technology for home-working and balancing caring responsibilities, lawyers and advisers have also reported that there has been an enormous amount of hidden labour involved with trying to continue working within a justice system that continues to rely heavily on hard-copy paperwork and face to face meetings (Byrom et al. 2020: 22; Denvir et al. 2022). The additional time and workload associated with the shift to remote working has reduced their already-limited capacity to offer pro bono advice to people experiencing family breakdown. There are also specific concerns about the kinds of population groups that are engaging with advice services remotely. Emerging research indicates that those seeking advice in this format are often those who are experiencing legal problems for the first time, who present with at least some resources and a degree of confidence about how to ask for support (Denvir et al. 2022). Although dealing with a large demand for support across different areas of law from this 'new legal need', services have noted a distinct absence of their traditional client groups. These groups are those with limited resources, who would typically present in person at advice services as and when they need assistance. These groups are those most likely to struggle to maintain contact via email or telephone because they have inconsistent access to technology, unpredictable or chaotic schedules, or require additional support with translation (Creudzfeldt and Sechi 2021; Newman et al. 2021). It is potentially more likely, therefore, that there will be a particular increase in complex family disputes among certain population groups as problems escalate due to pandemic-related barriers to seeking help at an earlier stage.

The family court itself initially suspended in-person hearings in response to the pandemic and began to conduct some hearings online via web platforms and telephone. Under the assumption that public safety measures would be short-term, the initial position of the judiciary was that remote hearings should only be used for urgent matters and that most family hearings should be postponed. The logic was that remote hearings were unlikely to be appropriate for contested applications concerning children because of the challenges to determining the welfare of relevant children in this format. However, given the unexpected and rapidly changing context of the pandemic, judicial guidance was frequent, uncertain, and inconsistently implemented by different courts across England and Wales. In some areas, hearings were adjourned for any case involving a contested application or the need for parties to give evidence or participate in cross examination, but in other areas, all such cases continued (Byrom 2020; Byrom et al. 2020: 19; Clark 2021).

For hearings that did go ahead, legal professionals, court staff and the judiciary were faced with the challenge of trying to make court hearings work effectively without the familiar rhythms of the courtroom. As Byrom et al. note, a chronic lack of investment in the courts and tribunals service over the years preceding the outbreak of COVID-19 meant that the court system was poorly prepared for the sudden demand to conduct large scale remote hearings (2020: 24). For legal professionals, the initial shift to remote hearings meant a need to source appropriate equipment, such as a second screen that would allow them to view relevant documents and court bundles at the same time as the other participants in the hearing. A lack of centralised planning for the platforms that should be used for remote hearings and who should bear responsibility for inviting participants to hearings meant that the roles and responsibilities of hearing participants was often inconsistent, with lawyers themselves sometimes having to host video calls and manage participants because courts in some regions did not have access to the appropriate technology or administrative support (Ryan et al. 2020a: 24). These logistical issues not only had workload implications for professionals involved, who needed to find technological workarounds to meet their obligations during proceedings, such as communicating with their clients via instant messaging or text instead of relying on the ability to pass messages or have a quiet word that comes with physically sitting next to each other in the courtroom. Remote hearings also posed threats to long-affirmed privacy rules, with some reports of participants due to appear at a hearing dialling into platforms early, and accidentally joining the end of earlier hearings which overrun past their expected finish time (Ryan et al. 2020a: 15).

The shift to remote hearings can therefore be understood as a radical disruption to the traditional roles and responsibilities that are integral to the 'full representation' model on which the family court process continues to rely, even after LASPO. Court hearings are characterised by a host of material, temporal, and cultural traditions which dictate the order in which matters are discussed, draw parameters that distinguish 'legally relevant' knowledge from people's lived experiences, and ultimately give legitimacy and authority to the decisions that are made in the court environment (Rossner 2021). The transformative impact of the COVID-19 pandemic on the spatial power of the courtroom will be discussed in more detail later in this book, but for present purposes, it is important to understand that the shift to remote hearings has had a significant impact on the ways that legal professionals and judges engage with the court process. Importantly, this shift has also had several implications for how LIPs may experience the family justice process.

While the true impact of remote hearings on LIPs' experiences is still unfolding, emerging evidence suggests that the pandemic has had at least three distinct implications. First, in the initial stages of the pandemic, LIPs faced uncertainty concerning whether their hearings would proceed or be postponed. Second, remote hearings are likely to pose significant barriers to participation for many LIPs, given the requirements of access to technology and expectations of digital literacy. Third, emerging data suggests potential concerns about the extent to which LIPs perceive remote or hybrid family hearings as satisfactory or legitimate.

In the initial stages of the pandemic, a common view among the family judiciary was that it would be difficult to effectively run remote hearings involving LIPs. Given that legal professionals were reporting difficulties assisting LIPs even before the pandemic, the judiciary and lawyers alike were concerned about the impossibility of keeping order during remote hearings if LIPs speak out of turn, do not provide relevant information, or do not engage fully with the process. There were also concerns about confidentiality – without a representative to provide them with clear guidance on court expectations, it would be almost impossible to ensure that LIPs did not record or have other people around them who might listen in on a confidential hearing. More importantly, from an access to justice perspective, even when remote hearings include video for participants, it is much more difficult for judges and lawyers to pick up on non-verbal cues that suggest a LIP is struggling to keep up with proceedings, or whether they are becoming overwhelmed and need to take a break (Ryan et al. 2020a). For pragmatic reasons and concerns about access to justice, therefore, hearings involving LIPs were disproportionately postponed during the initial stages of the pandemic (Byrom et al. 2020: 19–21). This was an understandable response to a very challenging situation, but its effect must be viewed in light of the fact that LIPs are already those who are squeezed by the looming barriers to legal advice and support since LASPO, as well as the long-standing neoliberal policies which construct their reliance on the court process as a signifier of personal deficiency. As an already-strained family justice system rushed to preserve its processes, LIPs were once again bearing the brunt of the fall-out, with pandemic-related postponements meaning that their cases were initially left unresolved and their problems disproportionately at risk of escalating into even more serious and complex issues.

From June 2020, it was accepted that postponement was no longer an adequate solution for these cases, and that remote hearings would need to become a more commonplace feature of the justice system in the longer term (McFarlane 2021). From this point, some courts began to open at reduced capacity and family hearings were to run in a variety of formats, ranging from entirely remote, to hybrid (with some participants attending remotely and some in-person), to fully attended hearings. The new normal for family justice, therefore, is to be a process that incorporates hybrid and remote hearings. Both formats have created new technological challenges for lawyers and the family court as they struggle to ascertain the accessibility and functionality of different devices and to adapt proceedings in a way that can effectively accommodate lay court users. This has been far from straightforward. For instance, while video hearings are perceived by all parties as by far the most satisfactory way to facilitate remote attendance, these hearings are also far more susceptible to technical difficulties, as they require greater bandwidth from all participants. In particular, the connection and equipment requirements for these hearings often exceed the resources available to lay court users, especially LIPs (Ryan et al. 2021). During the midst of the pandemic, Ryan et al. (2020a: 28) noted that lay users frequently joined remote proceedings via mobile phones and expensive mobile data plans, struggled to find quiet spaces to join hearings due to limited space at home and balancing childcare, and sometimes found themselves dropping in and out of their hearings due to connection issues. Concerningly, this report noted that sometimes these dropouts would go unnoticed by other participants, leaving lay users feeling unimportant or unheard within proceedings. Technology, in terms of both Internet connections and access to appropriate equipment, may render hearings more accessible and efficient for some individuals, but clearly also operates as a barrier to participation for others. Although the effectiveness of technology appeared to improve as time progressed, success or difficulty with technology is nevertheless likely to play a significant role in how LIPs experience their family court hearings, as well as how they think and feel about the family justice system more broadly.

Even when technology works perfectly well, there are also likely to be a range of different experiences and perceptions of hearings with an online component. For instance, remote attendance may create additional barriers to participation in hearings. Emerging evidence suggests that remote hearings are often shorter in length (Byrom et al. 2020; Ryan et al. 2020b; Clark 2021). On one hand, this suggests that issues can be more concisely and efficiently addressed in a virtual format. On the other hand, shorter hearings mean less time to explain procedures and principles to LIPs, or less capacity to allow open discussion of issues to which they may substantially contribute. Given that LIPs are frequently unfamiliar with the roles, customs and norms that underpin (even online) hearings, they may find it much more difficult to ask for things to be repeated or explained, or to inform other participants that they do not understand or follow what is happening in proceedings (Ryan et al. 2020a: 12). Importantly, LIPs do not have a representative with whom to prepare before the hearing or process it afterwards, so misunderstandings and confusion are likely to become further entrenched without bookended support.

Another factor which is particularly important in family law cases is the degree of empathy that can be translated into this online context. Evidence suggests that remote hearings are perceived by legal professionals as impersonal or even transactional. Professional respondents to Ryan et al.'s study (2021) reported that such hearings felt very far removed from the usual practice of family law, which normally involves a great deal of trust-building and holistic support. One respondent noted that it might sometimes only become apparent to legal professionals that a lay user is distressed when the audio of a hearing picks up the sounds of their sobbing (2021: 19). Consequently, many parents who participated in that study reported that they felt unsupported during their hearings, even if they had legal representation (2021: 24). This problem is likely to be exacerbated for LIPs, as they do not have an advocate to keep an eye on them during proceedings, and other legal professionals in their hearings may be unable to identify non-verbal cues that a LIP is distressed, confused, or in need of support.

In contrast, misunderstandings or misconceptions about remote hearings may also affect how legitimate and serious proceedings appear to LIPs. In Byrom et al.'s study (2020: 67) responding legal professionals reported that the lack of a physical courtroom, and the formality that comes along with the procedures and customs that occur within that space, made a difference to how LIPs behaved in their hearings. Some suggested that LIPs were more likely to be 'disinhibited', speaking out of turn, or even seeking adjournment on the basis that a remote hearing would be an inferior alternative to the 'day in court' that some LIPs expect when they commence family proceedings. Survey data from Clark (2021)'s study suggests that this may sometimes depend on whether remote hearings are conducted with video, which is reported to encourage fuller involvement in hearings, and therefore less incentive to feel the need to assert themselves in this way. Nevertheless, taken together, this emerging evidence indicates that while some LIPs may feel excluded and silenced within online hearings, others may be more inclined to overstep procedural constraints, or even feel that the significance of their hearings is undermined. These oppositional experiences are unsurprising, given the range of different reasons that people may end up in the court process in the first place. As discussed, some people are forced to engage with proceedings as LIPs due to applications being made against them, whilst others are self-representing due to a broader mistrust of lawyers and the legal system. The task of ensuring meaningful participation for this diversity of LIPs in the family law process has always been complex, and these experiences indicate how this complexity may be even more exacerbated in an online context.

Invariably, efforts to respond appropriately to the demands of the COVID-19 pandemic have been compromised by the reality that the family court is still reeling from the impact of LASPO. Delays, for instance, have not only been attributed to adjournments, technology issues, or reduced communication between parties, but also to the fact that the system itself was already coping with constraints on resource and capacity (Ryan et al. 2021). This further reiterates the urgency of the question: where does family justice go from here, and what role do LIPs have to play within it? What is known is that remote hearings are here to stay in at least some capacity. In October 2021, the President of the Family Division set out his view that decisions about hearing format should not be formally dictated but rather left to judicial discretion (McFarlane 2021). The logic is that a discretionary approach allows hearings to be adapted to the individual circumstances of each case, with an understanding that parties should physically attend any hearings where an important decision may be taken. In disputes over children, this might include any of the hearing types, from FHDRAs and DRAs to FFHs and final hearings, depending on the case concerned. How this will operate in practice, however, is unclear. Although legal professionals have identified that the views of lay court users should be an important factor in deciding the format of a hearing, these views often differ between parents and professionals, with parents more likely to prefer in-person hearings, and professionals incentivised by the convenience and efficiency of remote hearings, where appropriate (Ryan et al. 2021). This raises broader questions about how the different perceptions, understandings and experiences of LIPs will be accommodated, given the burgeoning post-LASPO pressures facing the family court.

V. A Turning Point for Family Justice

This chapter has mapped the various policies, events and debates that have shaped the current state of family justice. In doing so, I have attempted to demystify the complexity of this landscape and illustrate the ways that this is likely to facilitate certain kinds of experiences for LIPs engaging with the family justice system. For instance, I have explored how and why LIPs have so frequently been blamed for being too ready to take their cases to court, and placing too much strain on the family court, legal professionals, and the public purse. Here, I have demonstrated that reliance on the family court has been constructed as individualised failures on the part of citizens, which in turn creates a variety of tensions and challenges for the relationship that LIPs have with the family justice system.

The implementation of LASPO has marked a significant turning point for this system. In many ways, it has marked the end of family justice in the sense that it has finally closed off the accessibility of support and resolution options for many parents and has delivered the last blow to many of the services that comprised the remaining advice sector. LASPO has also fundamentally compromised the capacity of the family court as it struggles to support an increased number of LIPs who are arriving with more severe and diverse needs and circumstances. However, by exacerbating these problems to such a degree, LASPO has also created a new era of family justice in which scholars, practitioners and policymakers are finally united on at least one thing: that the current relationship between LIPs and the family justice system is unsustainable, and that it is time to find new solutions and instigate longer term change.

The impact of LASPO has also been augmented by other intersecting issues and debates which must be accounted for. The enduring failures of the family court in terms of responding to domestic abuse as well as the ongoing ramifications of the COVID-19 pandemic for the family court process, are both crucially interwoven with the impact of LASPO. It is vital that we take the time to unravel and acknowledge the distinct but connected nature of these issues. This is because dealing with the issues of domestic abuse or the COVID-19 pandemic in isolation from each other and the broader post-LASPO context would limit the transformative potential of any proposed reforms. It would be all too easy to oversimplify either of these issues by divorcing them from the systemic and deep-rooted problems amplified by LASPO and conceptualising them as isolated crises that can be redressed through straightforward statutory reform.

By exploring the cumulative nature of these problems, we can begin acknowledging the ways that they each might be better understood if we explicitly examine them from the perspectives of LIPs themselves. The purpose of this book is to draw directly upon the experiences and perceptions of LIPs to demonstrate why their voices should be central to the debate about what comes next after LASPO. While this will be firmly rooted in empirical evidence regarding LIPs' experiences and interactions, this evidence will be analysed through a comprehensive theoretical framework. In the next chapter, I draw together multiple analytical tools that will subsequently be used to gain a deeper understanding of how LIPs' experiences are framed not only by the tumultuous political context outlined here, but also by broader structures of inequality that permeate the family justice system.

3

Conceptualising Litigants in Person

This chapter considers how LIPs and their relationship with the family justice system might be conceptually understood. Theorising this relationship is as equally important as gathering empirical data about LIPs' experiences of the process. This is because, put simply, how we think about LIPs matters. Even the language used to describe LIPs is significant. As Hunter et al. (2002: 7) note in the Australian context, different terms carry different sorts of implications about their experiences and needs within the family court. On one hand, 'self-represented litigant' implies a degree of choice on the part of the litigant representing themselves. On the other hand, 'unrepresented litigant' denotes the disadvantage that comes with lacking legal representation.

'Litigant in Person' is a more neutral term, simply describing the fact that the party is appearing in person. Nevertheless, LIPs are frequently categorised and conceptualised in different ways. Sometimes, LIPs are conceptualised as being outsiders to the justice system in need of adaptation. Other times, they are regarded as a homogenous population with uniform support needs. Increasingly, they may even be perceived as a threat to the traditional functions of the court process. Each of these different understandings is underpinned by a particular set of ideas about what role LIPs could and should have within the family justice system, as well as the extent to which the system itself is obliged to adapt to support them.

By exploring the different ways that LIPs have been conceptualised within existing research and policy, this chapter reflects upon the opportunities and limitations of different theoretical approaches for understanding LIPs, their needs, and their relationship with the family justice system. Ultimately, it sets out an analytical framework that will be used to understand LIPs' different experiences and perspectives throughout this book.

I. Tensions in Family Justice Research

Across the literature on self-representation, several researchers have devised different categories or typologies of LIPs. These are useful for understanding the broad range of motivations and circumstances that crosscut this population of court users, as well as how these may manifest differently in the relationships that they have with the family justice system.

In the Australian study discussed above, Hunter et al. (2002: 103–05) identified a spectrum ranging from 'serial or vexatious' LIPs with a 'flagrant disregard for the family court as an arbiter of family disputes', to 'procedurally challenged' LIPs who were relatively competent but struggled with various aspects of court procedure, to LIPs who were entirely overwhelmed, disproportionately vulnerable and most likely to end up abandoning their cases, who could only be described as 'vanquished' by the family justice system. These broad categories have been reiterated, developed, and refined by subsequent studies. For instance, Trinder et al. (2014: 24) also observed several LIPs that might be described as procedurally challenged or vanquished. While some vexatious LIPs were noted, they were relatively infrequent. In addition, these authors acknowledged a new category: the '(apparently) competent' LIP, who appears articulate and calm when observed within a court hearing, but in fact struggles to comply correctly with court procedures and frequently makes errors when preparing paperwork (2014: 33). This category of LIP demonstrates that even those with high levels of education and professional experience, who might have been expected to fare well in the court process, nevertheless struggled to navigate the procedural requirements expected of them.

As explored in the previous chapter, experiences of self-representation are likely to be even more diverse following the influx of new LIPs that came with LASPO. Based on her small-scale study, Barry (2020: 419–420) contributes yet another typology of LIPs who are self-representing in the post-LASPO context. Here, LIPs were conceptualised as falling into three categories. 'Self-reliant' LIPs are those who make a conscious choice to forgo legal assistance and conduct their own research (usually online) due to a mistrust of lawyers, but nevertheless struggle with paperwork and procedural requirements. 'Competent' LIPs are those who have been represented previously in the process and are relatively aware of procedural requirements as they are able to replicate the earlier work of their lawyer. Finally, 'new uninformed' LIPs are those who have never been involved in court proceedings and found themselves lost within the process with little idea of where to seek help. These new categories are indicative of the increased diversity of circumstances in which people are now self-representing now that private family law has been categorically removed from scope even for those on the lowest incomes. They also reflect the impact that the fragmented post-LASPO landscape of advice is having on experiences of self-representation. An increased reliance on online sources of information and unbundled legal services, as well as difficulty finding any sources of help at all, are all tenets of this landscape which inevitably shape the extent to which LIPs can prepare for hearings and navigate the process once they arrive at court.

These various LIP typologies are indicative of the different kinds of experiences that people may have when they interact with the justice system and its various processes. Although they each denote varying strategies and degrees of competence among LIPs, a common feature across all identified categories is the difficulty that comes with a general unfamiliarity with the legal system. In short, studies suggest that all LIPs – regardless of circumstance or motivation – struggle to use the court system without the assistance of others who are familiar with its processes. This is a crucial starting point from which we can begin to ask questions about what LIPs need, and how those needs might be addressed.

These questions are linked to underlying tensions within socio-legal and family justice research, which tends to focus on policy-relevant issues and is often geared towards making a real-world impact. For example, socio-legal researchers recognise the importance of producing evidence that can be used to argue for short-term policy changes that can bring about tangible improvements for people when they interact with law (Maclean 2015b). This can be seen within self-representation studies, where researchers have frequently made recommendations about the specific forms of assistance that may be provided for LIPs to improve access to justice and ease the pressure on the justice system.[1] The impetus to produce valuable evidence, however, exists in tension with the importance of being more broadly critical of the systems that frame experiences of law. For instance, others have critiqued how the justice system itself functions, both practically and culturally, to exclude and marginalise LIPs rather than to accommodate them.[2] Such arguments make the case for more meaningful and long term change. Such systemic reform would require a wholesale cultural and procedural shift in the way LIPs are understood and conceptualised within the legal system, which accounts for wider structures of inequality, as well as the extent of damage that has been caused to the infrastructure of advice and support by LASPO and previous reforms. Without this, research that seeks to address some of the problems faced by LIPs risks relying on an overly simplistic 'deficit model' of understanding the relationship between LIPs and the family court, which rests upon the assumption that LIPs are deficient in some way (such as lacking knowledge, skills or experience) and that the problems they face can be resolved by remedying these deficits (Hunter 1998). This book is underpinned by a recognition that both short-term and long-term goals are important. Without broader theoretical critique of the family justice system, the potential impact of short-term empirical evidence about the challenges LIPs face will inevitably be limited. In turn, without this short-term evidence, such critique will achieve very little in terms of meaningful change. Nevertheless, both endeavours must be underpinned by a critical focus on the institutional culture of the family court itself.

This chapter will draw four theoretical approaches together into an analytical framework which will be used as a lens to examine LIPs' experiences throughout this book. Each of these approaches contributes distinct theoretical and analytical tools for examining the experiences of LIPs in a way that can speak to both short and long-term goals. First, the framework is rooted in a commitment to exposing the diversity of LIP perspectives that are typically marginalised within the justice system, drawn from intersectional feminist legal scholarship. Second,

[1] See, eg: Trinder et al. 2014; McKeever et al. 2018.
[2] See, eg: Leader 2017.

this commitment is operationalised through a Bourdieusian theory of social class, which provides conceptual tools for tracing the broader structural effects of inequality, disadvantage, and difference that shape and frame experiences of this system. Third, vulnerability theory is used to examine how the legal system itself is implicated in these processes of marginalisation, and to shed light on the responsibilities that exist between state institutions and those who rely upon them. The final component of the framework – Actor-Network Theory – is rather different. Instead of providing tools that work to reveal these structures, this approach provides an analytical strategy for exploring the specific and material ways through which this context plays out for different LIPs in the family court process.

By bringing together theories from different traditions and disciplines, it is possible to look beyond law, and find innovative and critical tools with which to expose, understand and explore the experiences shared by LIPs, and to relate them to broader structures of power within society. It also provides the opportunity to move away from traditional ways of thinking about the legal system and its processes as inviolable, and instead begin to challenge assumptions about how LIPs are positioned by those processes – both in terms of short-term measures to address the challenges LIPs face within this system, as well as longer-term systemic and cultural change for the purposes of reconceptualising the relationship that they may have with the family justice system.

II. Marginalised Perspectives

Existing literature already demonstrates that LIPs are a diverse population comprising people who are self-representing in a variety of different circumstances, especially after the LASPO reforms. It would therefore be illogical and limited to assume that their experiences, perceptions, and support needs, are even vaguely uniform. A solid starting point for thinking about the relationship that LIPs have with the family justice system, therefore, is to commit to doing research in a way that is open to exposing and exploring this diversity of LIP perspectives.

To this end, feminist theory, and particularly feminist legal scholarship, is an instrumental resource for exposing and scrutinising the hidden complexities of the ways in which people engage with law. It encompasses a broad and diverse literature which offers a range of insights into how law or legal systems may operate to marginalise, exclude, or disadvantage women. Rather than describing a uniform approach to studying law, a feminist approach encompasses several different perspectives which are united by their underpinning objective of revealing and developing understandings of the conditions of women's lives and suggesting how these conditions may be improved (Smart 1989; Bridgeman and Monk 2000: 7). This rich history of feminist work has helped to achieve a great deal of substantive legal and political reform. It encompasses liberal claims for formal equality within law, radical calls for more focused attention on the relationship between sexual difference and oppression, understandings of how men and women are constructed differently based on their gender presentation, and the specific ways in which law unevenly reinforces and reproduces these constructions (Barnett 1998: 5–8).

A feminist lens offers an alternative perspective from the narrower focus on institutions, structures, and laws, by exposing and exploring the complicated and diverse realities of women's lives, and how they are produced by and within such structures. For example, within family law, feminist legal scholars have drawn attention to the gender-specific harms that law can perpetuate or even facilitate through legal concepts and statutes. Since family law tends to be designed around the idea of a 'non-gendered, non-differentiated legal subject', this scholarship argues that law frequently fails to acknowledge the complex network of regimes and discourses that regulate the possibilities and opportunities available to wives and mothers during relationships or the process of family breakdown (Hunter 2013; Thompson 2015; Barlow et al. 2017). This lens of critique is broad enough to include other structures and institutions that interact with law, such as the family, the labour market, or the tax and benefit system, which all form the backdrop to a society structured in a way that omits the concerns and realities of women's lives (Diduck and O'Donovan 2006; Conaghan 2013: 103). To this end, feminist legal theory provides a means of challenging ideas that are presented as objective, rational or impartial, by exposing the perspectives, experiences and understandings that are otherwise omitted from current understandings or debates.

There are two main tenets of feminist legal theory that can be used as analytical tools to explore the experiences and perceptions of LIPs. The first is the feminist commitment to asking questions about the world that seek to expose hidden and marginalised perspectives, traditionally referred to as asking 'the woman question' (Bartlett 1990: 837). In practice, this involves questioning, identifying, exploring and understanding the implications of practices that otherwise appear to be neutral or objective, and reflecting on how dominant understandings may compare to the lived realities and experiences of those affected by such practices. Family law in particular draws enormous legitimacy from the idea that it can provide an objective, impartial or even common-sense intervention into people's personal lives. However, a key benefit of looking at law through a feminist lens is to understand that this is by no means impartial – in reality, law draws understandings together from multiple disciplines, and the supposed objectivity of law is predicated upon its capacity to selectively recognise certain aspects of people's lives whilst deeming other aspects irrelevant.

To provide an example of how this selective recognition omits certain perspectives and experiences, we can look to the legal concept of 'best interests', which is central to private family disputes concerning children. This legal concept is constructed and interpreted within a context of psychological and emotional factors, which is not just 'legal', and which is inherently gendered (Diduck 2000: 253–54). The approach taken posits the interests of parents and children as conceptually separate, and as a result, assessments of best interests are frequently criticised for failing to incorporate the realities of mothers' lives, especially where domestic abuse is concerned (Fineman 1996; Hester 2011). Barnett (2000: 141), for instance, argues that the law has constructed a 'space' between contact disputes and domestic abuse, and professional attitudes have shifted to fit around this space. An important effect of this is that without a proper consideration of the relevance of domestic abuse to decisions about contact, mothers who resist contact are inevitably constructed within legal discourse as irrational and unreasonable. At the same time, this discourse has the effect of erasing the relevance of any violence perpetrated by fathers, and instead presents fathers who seek contact as 'safe family men'. In practice, law is capable of recognising a broad range of legitimate factors in constructing this legal concept, but the specific construction that is used and applied is one that results from a particular moral and ideological choice about what aspects of parenting should be recognised and promoted (Barnett 2000: 148).

Further, these decisions about which factors are legally relevant are often justified by reference to abstract principles such as equality or justice, which in turn make it far more difficult to use these principles as a basis for rectifying law's limitations (Hunter 2008). For example, traditionally feminist concerns of equality have frequently been co-opted to further non-feminist agendas, such as the claim that encouraging self-sufficiency and reducing eligibility for legal aid is a way of promoting the agency and autonomy of parents on relationship breakdown (Wallbank 2014). This claim fails to recognise the broader inequalities which characterise the conditions of people's lives, and this sort of selective recognition of legally relevant family issues has the effect of reducing other aspects of family problems to emotional and selfish disputes which are invariably private, and not of major concern or relevance during the decision-making process (Smart and Neale 1999).

Applying this commitment to the issue of LIPs and the family court means challenging the inaccessibility of court procedures by seeking to expose and amplify alternative understandings of the court process. Specifically, this means focusing more closely on how LIPs may perceive and respond to the challenges they face within this process and interrogating the implications of how the family court process operates, rather than simply focusing on LIPs' inability to meet these requirements. For example, lawyers often take on additional work during semi-represented hearings by extending assistance to LIPs, and this can make a hugely positive difference to the conduct and progression of cases and prevent them escalating unnecessarily (Maclean and Eekelaar 2012; Trinder et al. 2014: 62). This does not, however, mean that lawyers are always positively perceived by LIPs. Rather, evidence suggests that LIPs may be keenly aware of the power imbalance that exists between them and the lawyers they face, and this can lead to negative views of lawyers who might take advantage of them during the court process. Existing studies have already indicated that negative views of lawyers or perceptions of their own vulnerability may deter LIPs from entering into productive negotiations, due to fear of being pressured into disadvantageous agreements (Moorhead and Sefton 2005: 172–73; Trinder et al. 2014: 45–50; Lee and Tkacukova 2018). There is some evidence that this may be even more difficult after LASPO, as lawyers are becoming more cautious about the possibility of LIPs making complaints against them, and more are expressing a preference for conversations to take place 'on the record' instead of outside the courtroom (Ridley 2014; Richardson and Speed 2019: 141).

While it may be tempting to attribute these problems to LIPs failing to appreciate the ways in which professionals are trying to help them within the process, LIPs' perspectives are crucial to assessing the accessibility of the system. This is because these perceptions are indicative of the extent to which LIPs feel that they have been able to access justice and meaningfully contribute to the decision-making process (Tyler and Ho 2002: 54–57; Zimmerman and Tyler 2009: 480; McKeever et al. 2018: 67). Exposing and exploring hidden LIP perspectives is important not only for understanding the diversity of LIPs' needs, but also for reflecting upon how LIPs evaluate their experiences. In turn, this allows an appreciation of their potential implications for the trust that people have in the family court process (Zimmerman and Tyler 2009: 485).

The second tenet is the way in which modern feminist scholarship, particularly that geared towards achieving legal and political reform, is attentive to the different structures of inequality that shape people's lives and advocates an intersectional understanding of their experiences.[3] The idea that multiple forms of oppression or marginalisation can intersect and produce specific experiences of disadvantage has provided an important resource for feminist legal theory: despite traditionally focusing on the experiences of women, it is not limited to examining the impact of law on women. Rather, feminist scholars have argued that a feminist approach can and should be used to expose and explore the implications of multiple different and overlapping structures of inequality, such as gender, race, and class, which all work together to frame the conditions in which people experience society.

A feminist approach which is intersectional, therefore, seeks to expose the *complexity* of experiences that are omitted from law and legal practice, by telling stories that account for diverse experiences – including but not limited to gender – and resisting the temptation to explore just the aspects of people's lives that the law determines to be relevant or important (Conaghan 2013: 12–14). Bringing the intricacies of everyday life to the fore in this manner usefully challenges the legitimacy that law derives from its supposed objectivity, and further complicates our understandings of the lives of those who are governed by its rules and processes (Conaghan 2009). Through the concept of intersecting structures of inequality, we can locate law within its historical, social, and ideological context, trace how it operates to serve only particular interests, and create the space for 'oppositional meanings' to emerge (Bartlett 1990: 857; Barnett 2000: 132). In doing so, we can interrogate how legal discourse may operate to exclude the experiences

[3] The use of intersectionality as an analytical framework has emerged from the foundational work of Kimberlé Crenshaw. See, eg: Crenshaw 1989; 1991. It has since been taken forth by feminist scholars in relation to a broad range of issues, see, eg: Ashiagbor 1999; Grabham 2006; Conaghan 2007; Grabham et al. 2009.

and perspectives of a broad range of people who are differently affected by other inequalities, which may intersect in ways that cannot be disentangled (Conaghan 2009: 74). However, it is essential that the oppositional meanings produced through research do not only reflect those of particular groups, but instead allow an insight into the complex range of understandings, definitions, and experiences which are omitted from law.

The feminist commitment to exposing intersectional perspective is therefore a particularly useful starting point for thinking about how to understand LIP experiences, because it provides a means of exposing the complex range of social positions, circumstances, and inequalities – including, but not limited to gender – which may frame the experiences and perceptions that LIPs have when they use the family justice system.

III. Inequality, Disadvantage, and Difference

Moving beyond this starting point, it is useful to reinforce a feminist approach with other theoretical tools that can be used to trace the ways that LIPs' experiences are related to the broader structural context of society. By asking questions that not only expose the diversity of possible experiences, perceptions, and understandings among LIPs, but also interrogate the processes by which those experiences become marginalised, it is possible to 'build an account of the world as seen from the margins, an account which can expose the falseness of the view from the top and can transform the margins as well as the centre' (Hartsock 1990: 170–1).

On this basis, the feminist commitment to exposing marginalised perspectives can be reinforced by a Bourdieusian theory of social class, which can extend our understanding of how different forms of structural inequality may shape these perspectives. This is because Bourdieusian theory provides theoretical tools that can be used to understand the broader structural context of difference and inequality which frames the experiences that LIPs may have within the family justice system. It can therefore be used as a means of extending and deepening our understanding of LIPs' experiences of the family court, by helping us to acknowledge that those experiences do not exist in a vacuum – rather, any disadvantages that they may face in the court process are invariably related to wider experiences of inequality within society.

While there are several theoretical options for understanding inequality within society, a theory of class is particularly important. This is because there are clearly established links between economic inequality and the likelihood of experiencing legal problems. In terms of family law specifically, relationship breakdown is a process in which the socio-economic position of the individual is transformed, and which frequently coincides with or triggers other legal issues such as housing, immigration, and welfare issues (Pleasance et al. 2006: 55–56, 75; Pleasance and Balmer 2014; Pereira et al. 2017). Additionally, the ability to access quality legal services has always been more challenging for those with fewer economic resources. However, this is not simply a case of whether someone can afford to pay for good quality advice or representation. Rather, the ability to navigate the various aspects of the family justice system also requires other kinds of resources, such as knowledge about the options available, capability to locate assistance, as well as the time and skills required to make meaningful use of these options. Taking legal action therefore requires a host of socio-economic resources which are not evenly distributed throughout society. As a result, it is common for people to lack the resources to cope with the costs of resolving family law problems (Genn 1999: 168–69; Pleasance et al. 2006: 30, 53). Despite this, law and legal scholarship has not traditionally accounted for inequalities such as class.

Acknowledging the role of socio-economic position is even more important in the post-LASPO context. As discussed in chapter two, LIPs are required to navigate a fragmented network of advice and support now that most people are now categorically excluded from accessing any funded advice or representation. However, this is exacerbated by the fact that LASPO coincided with a host of other reforms to state-funded support which were implemented by the same government administration.[4] According to the Joseph Rowntree Foundation (2022: 10), approximately 22 per cent of families across the UK are recognised as living in poverty. Families with children have always been at greater risk of financial insecurity, but this is now playing out against a context of increased housing costs, precarious employment conditions and weakening state support. For example, before 2013, there had been a significant reduction in the number of families living on these low incomes due to steady levels of state support through the benefit and tax credit systems. However, since 2013, these statistics have started to reverse as these forms of support have been the targets of austerity measures (Joseph Rowntree 2022: 41). An increasing number of people – particularly lone and working parents – are therefore contending with circumstances in which they have limited access to the vital economic and social resources which enable them to participate fully in society. The LASPO reforms therefore have an important class dimension because this has not only withdrawn legal aid for most cases, but it has also not accounted for how the effects of austerity measures are likely to further compound the ability of people to navigate the legal system.

To understand the relationship between LIPs and the family justice system, it is therefore helpful to draw on a theory of class which can be used to provide an insight into how socio-economic inequality may frame experiences of this process. Bourdieusian theory is particularly useful for this task because it provides three central concepts which can be used as tools to explore the ways in which inequality is reproduced through culture – capital, field, and habitus.

Economic capital, as it is conventionally understood, is a resource that can be exchanged for benefits or used as a means of influence. However, for Bourdieu,

[4] See, eg: Welfare Reform Act 2012.

capital also comes in three additional forms – cultural, social, and symbolic. Cultural capital refers to the skills, knowledge, and dispositions that people gain during their life, the form of which depends on the interactions and experiences they have within society (Bourdieu 2005: 211). Similarly, social capital refers to the social networks that people can draw upon for support during these interactions and experiences. Therefore, both forms of capital are accumulated through life experiences – they differ according to the people that an individual has met and formed connections with, as well as what they have learned, been exposed to, and taken interest in throughout their lives. In practice, both function as tangible resources which can be exchanged or used to gain advantages in different contexts. Symbolic capital, however, operates slightly differently. This type of capital refers to things like authority, reputation, and prestige, which can easily be used to accrue other forms of capital. Education is an important example of symbolic capital, because it is something that can be exchanged for other forms of valuable capital in a variety of different contexts (Bourdieu 1986: 55; 1987: 812). By distinguishing between these different kinds of resources, it is possible to understand how people from different social origins have different opportunities and possibilities available to them. However, rather than just signifying differences between people, the concept of capital can be used to expose the different value that is attributed to different kinds of capital within society.

This leads to Bourdieu's second concept – field. Bourdieu argued that society is made up of several overlapping fields which all have their own practices and hierarchies of value. If capitals are synonymous with wealth, then fields are the marketplaces in which those capitals are spent and exchanged. Through the notions of capital and field, it is possible to appreciate that class is more nuanced than economic disadvantage. While employment and income are useful markers of inequality in society, focusing on these alone does not give a full insight into how people may experience disadvantage within specific contexts like the legal system. As McKenzie explains:

> … class has value attached to it. It can be read on the body through the way you walk, talk, or the clothes you wear. It can also be read through what you do, where you go, and what you enjoy in life (2016: 25).

Within each field, therefore, capitals are assigned value which determines how they can be used and the extent to which people can succeed in each context. In this sense, fields are sites of competition in which people struggle against each other to establish their 'cultural competence' within any given arena (Bourdieu 1984: 86–87). In other words, the capitals that are useful within one field may be completely different from those that are valuable in another.

However, there are some kinds of capital – such as the skills and confidence that may come from a university education – which are valuable across several fields. McKenzie provides a useful illustration of this through her study of a Nottingham council estate. Here, she describes the ways in which local dialect and certain clothing brands were privileged as valuable cultural markers within the local community, even though they were actively de-valued and stigmatised outside of this context. People who accumulated and displayed these markers were able to assert power and authority within the confines of this field, but then lost those advantages when they attempted to engage with other fields which were characterised by different hierarchies of value. In McKenzie's example, those who enjoyed advantages within the council estate were ultimately limited in their broader interactions with other fields, because their capital was not symbolic capital; it had no 'exchange value' outside of that context (2016: 30–31).

This raises an important point about the historical dimension of privilege, and the ways in which people with certain kinds of capital can travel easily between different fields, and others cannot. The opportunities to access, accumulate and use those capitals which are widely valued are by no means open to everyone. Rather, the distribution of symbolic capital follows broader patterns of how resources are distributed within society. This is because the hierarchies of value which work to structure fields are by no means neutral. In practice, Bourdieu argues, there are overlaps between fields relating to law, politics, and economics, because the holders of symbolic capital across each of these fields have 'kindred world views' (1987: 842). In other words, those who hold power within society generally have a greater capacity to continually influence the shape and structure of official fields, and inevitably do so in their own interests.

In relation to law, Bourdieu (1987) extensively discussed that one way of doing this is by privileging unique practices and hierarchies which characterise the 'juridical field'. Here, he explains that law is a field with its own culture. By culture, he means an underpinning set of protocols and assumptions, as well as its own internal social, psychological, and linguistic codes which all frame the way that law is practised and negotiated but are never specifically recorded or acknowledged (1987: 806). For example, valued capitals in the juridical field include knowledge of and familiarity with legal rules, as well as specific ways of behaving and communicating which are perceived as authentic to law. These unique forms of cultural capital enable those who are initiated in law to 'explore and exploit the range of possible rules and use them effectively as symbolic weapons to argue a case' (1987: 827). Similarly, within the juridical field, certain forms of speech and written text have greater meaning and value than they do outside of this context. For example, when giving legal judgments, the act of speaking has the specific power of making something true. Additionally, the written formalisation of text in a court document gives those words power in ways that would not be possible if they were simply said aloud (1987: 809–10).

While an obvious barrier to using the family court without a lawyer is the reality that LIPs rarely have access to legal knowledge, some evidence suggests that most problems that they experience relate to a lack of familiarity with procedure and customs of the court process. Sandefur (2010) has gone as far as to suggest that the positive impact that lawyers make to court hearings can be largely attributed to their procedural knowledge. Rather than their legal expertise, it is therefore the *familiarity* that lawyers have with the juridical field which enables parties to navigate relationships with legitimacy and achieve better outcomes. In this sense, the value that is placed on juridical capital within the juridical field has a distinctly exclusionary effect for those who have not been initiated through legal education and training. In theory, the legal system is an arena where people can contest different arguments and versions of truth, but the elasticity of law is realistically only open to those who know how to appeal to its recognised and valued rhetorical devices (1987: 827). These exclusionary practices enable the juridical field to set its own parameters of what is 'legally' relevant and important, and to dismiss and devalue other skills and perspectives (1987: 828–29).

This provides an extremely useful understanding of how and why law operates in a way that is blind to difference and structural inequalities like gender or class. By discounting these important differences, the authority and legitimacy of law can be derived from the supposed objectivity of legal rules and practices. However, through Bourdieu's theory, it is possible to expose that this is by no means objective – rather, the juridical field operates to selectively recognise certain capitals, and to discount capitals which do not fit neatly into the structure of this field. He described this as a form of symbolic violence because it is imposed on those who have little choice about whether to accept or reject these hierarchies of value (Bourdieu 1987: 812). Through the concepts of capital and field, therefore, it is possible to understand how broader patterns of inequality within society have the potential to shape experiences of disadvantage within specific contexts like the legal system.

Bourdieu's final concept is the habitus. The habitus is the internal mechanism through which people accumulate different kinds of capital and develop their own sense for which capitals are useful for them when they engage with different fields. It is a useful concept for understanding the subjective ways in which people interpret their own position within the structure of different fields and respond to experiences of disadvantage. Taken together with capital and field, the concept of habitus requires researchers to consider how people perceive the context in which they find themselves, and how their responses can in turn further shape their experiences. Returning to McKenzie's example, for instance, residents of the council estate were able to invert the dominant narrative and create their own alternative structure of value within the confines of the local community, even at the cost of facing disadvantage when they engaged with other fields. From a methodological perspective, this is also a useful way for researchers to reflect on the challenges associated with reaching marginalised communities. Savage (2015), for instance, draws on Bourdieusian theory to explore the reasons why disadvantaged and marginalised groups may be less likely to participate in research than others in the first place. In doing so, he emphasises that it is important for researchers to remember that when people recognise the odds against them, they can be tempted to withdraw from the struggle altogether (2015: 333). The habitus can therefore provide an important insight into the subjective ways that people themselves perceive the legal system: not only how LIPs may respond when they are faced with aspects of the family justice system, but also into how LIPs may perceive the legitimacy of that system if they have already experienced disadvantage in relation to law, state institutions, or even within society generally.

Taken together, Bourdieu's concepts can be used to reinforce the feminist objectives of exposing the hidden narratives of law as well as the implications of law's blindness to inequality and difference. In relation to socio-economic disadvantage, they can be used to demonstrate that people can be prevented from participating in certain fields not only because of a lack of economic resources, but also by hierarchies of cultural value, which deny people appropriate recognition within certain contexts. However, this is not to say that a lack of cultural recognition is always dependent on a lack of economic resources. Fraser (2008: 10–16) argues that although this is inherently linked with economic inequality, there are many other ways in which people can be oppressed or disadvantaged based on who they are, and their status within other structures in society, like gender and race (2013: 193–4). Although Bourdieu did not explicitly discuss this, the flexibility of his concepts means that they are useful for addressing other structures of inequality besides class because they account for the historical reiteration of both unequal outcomes and the processes by which these outcomes are produced (Sommerlad and Sanderson 1998: 29, 37).

Sommerlad and Sanderson (1998: 17), for instance, argue that the juridical field facilitates a culture which is specifically exclusionary to women. In their work, they use the concept of field to demonstrate how legal rules fail to account for structural constraints like caring responsibilities or other social arrangements which disproportionately affect women. As such, the inequality that women experience across society is constructed as irrelevant within the juridical field (1998: 2). Additionally, through the concept of capital, they explore the ways in which women can be ascribed certain characteristics based on their gender presentation, which are then devalued within the juridical field. In their work, capitals associated with femininity or motherhood were ascribed to women by others in the field, and these were then undermined, misrecognised, and devalued in ways that those held by men were not (1998: 28–29, 37–38). The task of extending Bourdieusian concepts to address other forms of disadvantage has been taken forward by a new generation of Bourdieusian researchers (Burke et al. 2016: 1). Approaching these concepts from very different academic backgrounds to Bourdieu, these scholars have been able to develop concepts like 'black cultural capital' and drawn links between the habitus and the concept of 'respectability' to address the ways in which structures of value are racialised and gendered as well as classed (Skeggs 1997; Rollock 2007; Wallace 2016; McKenzie 2016).

In this sense, Bourdieusian concepts can be used to understand how specific structures of inequality can be reiterated over time, and each produce unique experiences of disadvantage which are related to, but manifestly different from, the disadvantages which stem from socio-economic inequality. However, what these concepts cannot do is provide an understanding of how these different inequalities intersect with each other, and how this makes experiences of disadvantage even more complex. In other words, what is also needed is an understanding of how categories like class and gender work *together* to produce unique experiences of disadvantage. To this end, it is useful to explicitly draw Bourdieusian concepts together with the feminist ideas discussed above and use them in an intersectional way. This enables us to move beyond talking about categories like gender, race and class as if they are mutually exclusive. Instead, an intersectional application of Bourdieusian theory provides an imperative to 'complicate our understanding of the social dynamics of inequality' by embracing the complex and overlapping ways in which these categories may operate (Grabham et al. 2009: 13). In doing so, it is possible to recognise not only the cumulative ways in which people may be affected by different structures of inequality, but also the unique and complicated ways in which individuals experience disadvantage in relation to their different social positions.

IV. The State and the Family Justice System

So far, I have drawn together theoretical tools that emphasise the importance of exposing marginalised perspectives and which aid the task of understanding structures of inequality that frame those perspectives. Thus far, this framework can help us to appreciate the unequal effects that stem from specific structural categories, as well as how these may differ from person to person. However, it is also useful to go further and consider how the legal system itself may be implicated in experiences of disadvantage.

This leads to the third component of the framework – vulnerability theory. Although the concept of vulnerability has been explored extensively by philosophers and political scholars (Goodin 1985; MacKenzie et al. 2014), this theory has most prominently been developed in relation to law by Fineman (2008; 2011; 2017). The basis of Fineman's vulnerability thesis is that using approaches like Bourdieu's theory in an intersectional way does not go far enough to provide a full picture of disadvantage. Instead of attempting to map the intersections between different forms of inequality, she argues that it is more useful to understand disadvantage through a lens of vulnerability. Under this view, disadvantage is not only related to structural categories, but also to the extent that the state and its institutions operate to provide citizens with appropriate support.

The basis of this approach centres around the idea that legal culture and discourse is designed around the 'liberal legal subject'. Through this, the subject of law is always presumed to be able to function fully, autonomously, independently, and responsibly, without the need for state support or intervention. This construction does not take account of the different ways in which people experience disadvantage or rely on one another or the state for support at various points in their lives (2008). It is this legal and political logic of self-sufficiency which has informed several reforms to family law and legal aid policy in recent years, such as increased emphasis on mediation and the stigmatisation of people who need to take their family cases to court. It has also provided a justification for the way in which legal aid was reformed under LASPO – by reserving legal aid only for the 'most vulnerable' citizens, the government has constructed most people as self-sufficient and responsible for resolving their own family law problems.

In this way, vulnerability theory shares a clear epistemological foundation with feminist theory, which seeks to expose law's blindness to difference and experiences of structural inequality. However, through vulnerability theory, Fineman argues that researchers should move away from this categorical approach to inequality, and instead consider how the liberal legal subject might be replaced with the 'vulnerable subject' (2011). The vulnerable subject, she argues, more accurately reflects the extent to which we are all in need of support at various points during our lives, and the ways in which we are all dependent on others within society for the resilience to be able to cope with particular circumstances of hardship or avoid them altogether. To this end, the vulnerable subject acknowledges that vulnerability is a universal and constant part of being human – we are all vulnerable to disadvantage, but we have differing levels of resilience to cope with the situations that we face within society (2017: 147–48). Further, the state of vulnerability fluctuates – it is not a fixed characteristic that can be neatly assigned to certain categories or groups of people but can be exacerbated or facilitated by different contexts and experiences.

The vulnerable subject therefore provides an opportunity to consider what law and state institutions might be like if they were not designed around the liberal legal subject but were instead structured in a way that accounts for the inherent and inevitable nature of vulnerability, as well as the responsibility of state institutions to go some way to ameliorating that vulnerability. Therefore, instead of focusing on the individual and their different identity categories, this approach directly emphasises the important role that institutions themselves may play in mitigating the effects of inequality or facilitating experiences of disadvantage. There is already a vast amount of literature that suggests LIPs face challenges because of how the legal process works. Before court, LIPs consistently experience difficulties complying with paperwork requirements, often struggling to understand legal terminology or translate their problems into the categories used within forms (Dewar et al. 2000: 45; Moorhead and Sefton 2005: 131–32; Williams 2011; Trinder et al. 2014: 36–42). These requirements are often experienced as exclusionary barriers even for LIPs with high levels of education, due to the specialised nature of legal language and administrative customs within the court process (MacFarlane et al. 2013: 58–60; Trinder et al. 2014: 24). Additionally, within court hearings, LIPs struggle with 'legal' tasks which require specialist training and experience, such as advocacy and cross-examination (Trinder et al. 2014: 70). The task of reimagining what this process might look like if it were instead designed around a vulnerable subject, therefore, also provides an important opportunity to challenge the construction of 'most vulnerable' which has been used in LASPO policy, by exposing the different and diverse ways in which people may be vulnerable to disadvantage within the legal system, because of the way that the system itself operates.

This approach reinforces the theoretical tools already assembled from feminist theory and Bourdieusian theory, because it means that we are not limited to understanding disadvantage through class or identity categories. Instead, it enables an openness to other fluctuating and situational ways in which people may experience disadvantage *because of how the legal system itself operates*. As an example, much of the literature on self-representation discusses the prevalence of vulnerable characteristics among LIPs as a means of indicating the different ways that they may be disadvantaged within the court process. However, vulnerabilities are also often inextricably tied up with or even facilitated by experiences of the court process (McKeever et al. 2018: 48). Interviews with Citizens Advice advisors demonstrate that the experience of self-representation itself can exacerbate or trigger mental health issues, have a detrimental impact on physical health, and place individuals in financially precarious positions due to the costs involved and the requirement to miss work for court hearings (Citizens Advice 2016: 16–18). These are not only pre-existing problems that LIPs bring into the court system, but rather are indicative that the system itself may operate to make these problems worse, or sometimes even be a key factor in causing them. It is not enough, therefore, for researchers to simply expose the diverse range of LIP perspectives which are omitted from law and legal discourse, or to relate these experiences to wider structures of inequality. It is additionally and equally important to question the very process by which these dominant definitions, practices, and understandings are formulated in the first place.

This is because our resilience is not simply linked to the social positions we are born into, but rather derived from the relationships we have with state institutions, and the extent to which they provide us with support and resources (Fineman 2017: 143). The kinds of resources that institutions might provide citizens range from physical and material resources which determine quality of life, human assets such as skills and abilities through education and employment opportunities, and social relationships and networks (Fineman 2016: 22–23). In this sense, vulnerability theory runs parallel to Bourdieusian theory, because it emphasises the important ways in which specific contexts like the legal system have an important role in determining the prospects of those who attempt to succeed within it. Whether through providing people with different levels of resilience or attributing different kinds of value to their capitals, it is the structure of the legal system itself that produces experiences of disadvantage. However, where vulnerability theory departs is where it emphasises that institutions have an underpinning *responsibility* to rectify these inequalities and ensure parity of participation.

This is something which Fineman argues is not possible through an intersectional use of social theory. Importantly, she argues, focusing on categories of identity like gender, class, and race as a means of understanding disadvantage 'distorts our understanding of a variety of social problems and takes only a limited view of what should constitute governmental responsibility' (2016: 15). This highlights a conflict between vulnerability theory and the other approaches in this framework, but not one that is irreconcilable. This criticism of an intersectional approach is not unfounded. In fact, many feminist scholars have argued that by focusing on these categories, research can have the unintentional effect of further masking the important role of the legal system in producing those disadvantages. By focusing on categories which relate to individual circumstances, researchers may in practice simply be 'supporting the law's propensity to classify' (Grabham 2009: 186). For example, in their investigation of the legal aid system in Australia, Hunter and De Simone (2009: 161–62, 169–76) found that identity categories were only one part of women's experiences of disadvantage. Rather, disadvantage was overwhelmingly attributable to the institutional context of the legal aid system – the eligibility guidelines and practices of different legal aid offices, as well as the matters raised in legal aid applications were all issues that cut across identity markers.

Nevertheless, vulnerability theory alone would not be able to provide the valuable insight into the effects of inequality which have been outlined so far in this chapter. So far, both Bourdieusian and feminist approaches provide means of unravelling the significant implications of historically reiterated structures such as gender, class, and race. For instance, in justifying their focus on gender-based disadvantage within the legal system, Sommerlad and Sanderson (1998: 4) explain that gender is a 'principal determinant' in the experience of women as a group, due to the history and significance of this category. To this end, it is important to be conscious that any reforms or interventions which are employed to support some LIPs may in practice have the effect of producing disadvantage for others in different social positions. Therefore, by taking all three of these approaches together, it is possible to account for the complex effects of inequality, whilst *also* considering how people may be disadvantaged because of the ways that institutions operate. Further, a strength of using these theories together is that it not only enables exposition of marginalised experiences of law, but also enables reflection on how the legal system is implicated in those very processes of marginalisation.

V. Material Manifestations of Disadvantage

Together, the three approaches outlined so far provide an array of conceptual tools for interrogating the relationship between LIPs and the family justice system in a way that accounts for the nuanced and complex context of inequality and disadvantage that frames their experiences. The final component of the framework – Actor Network Theory (ANT) – is rather different. Instead of providing tools that work to reveal these structures, this approach provides an empirical means of exploring the specific and material ways through which this context plays out for different LIPs in the family court process.

Despite its name, ANT is best understood as an analytical method that can be used to explore social arrangements, rather than a theory through which to understand or explain them. It was developed within the field of science and technology studies and is commonly attributed to the work of Latour (2005), though it has been more recently taken forward by other scholars who have adapted its tenets (Law 2004; Cloatre 2013). Taking inspiration from the scientific tradition, ANT is an approach which advocates examining social arrangements on a micro scale – paying attention to seemingly small moments and documenting the detail of how people and objects are arranged in those moments.

There are two central tenets of ANT. The first is that everyone and everything is both an actor within a network, and a network in and of itself. The second is that actors can be both human and non-human. The family court, for example, can be understood as one actor within the network of the family justice system or even the legal system. However, if analytically useful, it can also be examined as a network which can be broken down into its own constituent actors: LIPs, judges, lawyers, as well as courtrooms and paperwork. In turn, these actors can also be deconstructed and examined, and there is no limit to how far any object of analysis can be broken down into its constituent parts. By breaking a network down, it is possible to explore in detail the relationships between its actors, and specifically trace *how* certain actors can influence others and shape the network. While some actors may be able to translate the objectives of others into those that mirror their own, others may have difficulty negotiating some of these relationships (Buzelin 2005: 196–97). For example, the success of a LIP may depend on their ability to make use of courtrooms and paperwork, to convince judges and lawyers, or even the ability of others in the process to recognise and respond to their needs. Since 2017, FPR3A and PD3AA have provided guidance to assist judges in identifying vulnerable litigants and aiding them where their participation is likely to be diminished by way of their vulnerability. However, these provisions are premised upon recognising litigants with particular characteristics, such as mental health problems, disabilities, and domestic abuse. They do not extend far enough to recognise that LIPs often face difficulties participating in the court because they are unfamiliar with the legal context. Therefore, ANT is extremely useful for unpicking exactly how LIPs may face specific problems at various stages of filling out paperwork, navigating court buildings, and constructing legal arguments, where their success depends on their relationships with other actors. Taking an ANT approach to this project involves carefully documenting the interactions that LIPs have with different aspects of the court process and paying specific attention to the material detail of those interactions.

In this sense, ANT requires researchers to describe the material manifestations of social arrangements, as well as the detailed process by which social arrangements come to be (Cloatre 2013; 2018: 659; Baiocchi et al. 2013: 330). This commitment of ANT has been particularly useful for socio-legal researchers who are interested in unravelling how law operates within society (Cloatre 2013; Cowan and Carr 2008; Hunter 2016). As I have highlighted through Bourdieusian theory, the legal system is often conceived as an arena with its own culture, assumptions, codes, and practices. These all operate as internal sources of legitimacy for the juridical field but are never specifically recorded or acknowledged (Bourdieu 1987: 806).

Socio-legal scholarship is already well-attuned to the value of providing detailed accounts of legal culture as a means of challenging these underpinning assumptions and drawing attention to how law is understood and experienced (Ewick and Sibley 1998). However, it is the combination of this commitment to detail with an attentiveness to materialism which distinguishes ANT from other approaches and makes it a particularly useful tool for examining the experiences that LIPs have of the family justice system (Cloatre 2018: 659).

The materialist focus of ANT means that it asks questions about how non-human actors can play important roles and have significant effects for social arrangements. For example, Riles (2000; 2006) uses ANT to explore the role that documents play within the legal system. Legal documents, she argues, have the power to foreclose important and contentious debates. A document can be used as a means of rendering complex discussions as 'a matter of settled history'. This is because the act of recording something in a document erases any record of the oral discussions that took place to produce that document. In this sense, she argues, documents are artefacts of a prior struggle, which themselves provide sources of further authority which can be drawn upon at a later stage by those who were able to influence the record in the first place (2006: 76–8; 83). By tracing the specific role of the document within law, therefore, Riles is able to disrupt our thinking about how law operates – how it is able to function and reinforce itself.[5] Focusing on the micro scale through ANT therefore also means having to re-engage with the very nature of law as a social category, discipline, institution, and label. Importantly, and in alignment with vulnerability theory, this ensures that the family justice system itself is subject to critical scrutiny, in terms of the extent to which it is able to accommodate the diverse range of LIPs coming before it after LASPO. Rather than conceiving of law as something which is already made, ANT requires researchers to provide a detailed account of law in the making – *how* specific interactions and relationships work together to produce outcomes like disadvantage (Cloatre 2018: 657–8; Levi and Valverde 2008: 822).

Taken together, the tenets of ANT therefore require researchers to avoid taking social arrangements for granted, and instead to scrutinise the relationships that make those arrangements possible. In a way that clearly overlaps with feminist objectives, ANT is underpinned by a commitment to a 'bottom-up' approach to understanding social arrangements. However, by advocating that those social arrangements should be examined in such an empirical way, ANT is epistemologically and ontologically distinct from all three of the other theories in this framework. While the other three theories all provide different resources for understanding how disadvantage may relate to structural inequality and difference,

[5] This is further reinforced by the work of other non-ANT scholars who focus more generally on the materiality of law. These researchers have emphasised that the power of law is exercised not only through material objects and physical environments but also through spatial and temporal dimensions. See, eg: Jacob 2017; Mulcahy 2010; Grabham 2014; 2016; Mulcahy and Rowden 2020.

ANT has traditionally been critical of these kinds of theoretical explanations. For ANT theorists, using social theory to frame research findings is to take a shortcut – to treat inequality as an explanation for disadvantage, rather than to see disadvantage as an effect of a social arrangement that needs to be explored (Baiocchi et al. 2013: 336). It was on this basis that Latour (2005) originally went so far as to argue that social theory such as Bourdieusian theory should be 'jettisoned'.

This is an important criticism of how researchers may use sociological theory. For instance, focusing on the importance of structural inequality carries a risk of analysing LIP experiences with a pre-supposed view of what those experiences are going to be like, and potentially erasing marginalised perspectives by translating their accounts into academic terms like capital and field, without scrutinising the detail of how disadvantage comes about. However, this criticism of social theory is also a key weakness of the ANT approach. By advocating a flat ontology, in which researchers may only explore what they find during their empirical investigations, ANT does not pay attention to the deeper and historically reiterated structures of inequality that provide the context within which these social practices unfold. In this sense, ANT may be interpreted as rejecting analyses which account for categories such as gender or class, or the historical dimensions of these structures. This scepticism of social theory has been heavily criticised. Feminist scholars in particular have argued that without a theoretical understanding of the ways in which macro structures and categories have historically reiterated arrangements of inequality, it is impossible to fully understand the relationships and interactions which take place on a micro scale (Cloatre 2018). By focusing only on the interactions that happen on the ground, ANT risks being 'an apolitical strategy that effectively effaces the violent histories and embedded power imbalances that constitute social relations' (Cloatre 2018: 653). In other words, while ANT theorists may criticise structural approaches for explaining without describing, ANT is also at risk of describing without explaining (Levi and Valverde 2008: 822). Failing to take account of structural context when analysing the experiences of LIPs would prevent broader thinking about potential meaningful and long-term change within the family justice system.

Reconciling structural and anti-structural approaches is not an easy task. Nevertheless, it is possible to use ANT in a way that is sensitive to this structural context for two reasons. First, it is possible to use ANT without adhering to anti-structuralism. This is by no means simple, but it is possible to use these approaches concurrently by following the example of other scholars who have explicitly rejected the anti-structuralist ontology which underpins traditional ANT approaches. As ANT has been applied in multiple disciplines, researchers have confronted these important 'blind spots', and instead recommended using ANT as a set of sensibilities which can be used more productively than traditional applications of Latourian ANT. For example, within law, Cloatre has most prominently mitigated these blind spots by taking the benefits of ANT's micro approach, whilst rejecting ANT's scepticism of structural theory. She argues that it is instead far more progressive to draw ANT together into theoretical frameworks with other theories that provide a proper account of how power and inequality operate on a structural scale (2018: 660). In doing so, Latour's view of social theory has often been resigned to 'classical' or 'purist' forms of ANT, and is generally regarded as at best problematic, and at worst dangerous (Levi and Valverde 2008: 811; Cloatre 2018: 653, 658).

Second, rejecting anti-structuralism does not mean that ANT's concerns about theory are discounted. Instead of 'jettisoning' theory, researchers are encouraged instead to use ANT as a broad set of sensibilities which can be used as pragmatic guides through which to 'orient' social theory (Law and Singleton 2013: 485–86). Cloatre has described this method of using ANT 'as a matter of care' (2018: 660–61). As discussed so far, these sensibilities include an attentiveness to the relational and material nature of social arrangements, as well as *how* particular social arrangements come to produce effects like disadvantage (Baiocchi et al. 2013: 335). By using ANT in this way, concepts which have classically been used to 'explain' social relations, become instead the very substance of what needs to be explained through a renewed attention to the micro-connections that form entire social arrangements (Cloatre 2018: 653). Although it is unlikely that he would have embraced ANT, Bourdieu himself was a core advocate of the idea that researchers should be open to different approaches. He recommends, for instance, that researchers should 'mobilise all the techniques that are relevant and practically usable, given the definition of the object' (Bourdieu and Wacquant 1992: 227). Similarly, as part of the next generation of Bourdieusian scholars who have developed and refined his concepts, Atkinson explains that this task involves working both with and against Bourdieu, and that researchers should not be afraid of deviating from his work when the research demands it (2011: 344). Instead of undermining the structural understandings I gain from the other theories, it is possible to use ANT as a resource for asking more questions about how disadvantage is experienced on the ground, rather than closing down questions about how that disadvantage is rooted in broader structures of inequality.

ANT – used as a sensibility – can therefore be combined with the structural theories in this framework in a way that actually elevates feminist concerns and objectives, because it helps researchers reflect on the constructed nature of knowledge, including their own role within the research process. In producing an account of the different kinds of experiences that LIPs may have within the legal system, ANT indicates the importance of remaining open to experiences which do not fit with the ideas that underpin structural theories. Even more importantly, ANT can be used in a way that holds researchers accountable to using theory in a way that helps to gain a deeper understanding of the experiences that LIPs have in the family justice system. It is also a means of reflecting on how these theoretical tools influenced the methodological and analytical decisions taken by scholars, and the implications of these for the usefulness of the research that is produced. Interpreting ANT in this way and combining it with other theories therefore means that it does not have to be an apolitical strategy. Rather, it can be used to elevate the inherently political nature of the questions asked by the other three theories in this framework.

VI. A Theoretical and Empirical Enquiry

At the beginning of this chapter, I argued that how we think about LIPs and their relationship with the family justice system matters. However, what also matters is how certain forms of knowledge and different perspectives are received. There is no shortage of cross-jurisdictional empirical evidence to demonstrate the variety of procedural, legal, and cultural barriers that LIPs face when they engage with the family justice system. There is also no shortage of evidence about how long-standing problems with the legal aid scheme, the accessibility of legal advice and support or the continued political emphasis on mediation may contribute to these barriers. In fact, the implementation of LASPO has been accused of flying in the face of the vast amount of existing evidence at our disposal (Barlow et al. 2017: 205).

The challenge, therefore, is to find a way of informing the trajectory of future reform both in the short-term and in the longer-term. There is unlikely to be sufficient political will to fully invest in state-funded legal advice and representation to the extent that would sufficiently address the problems which have characterised the legal aid scheme since its implementation, let alone to expand investments even further to understand and address the additional challenges posed by the COVID-19 pandemic.[6] There is also the possibility that continued clashes with government over funding for welfare services may be counter-productive, as it may in practice facilitate further cuts. For example, Harris (2015) warns against condemning initiatives like the exceptional funding scheme rather than working with government administrations on how to improve it, for fear of it being abolished entirely.

Nevertheless, there are opportunities for marginalised accounts of the family justice system to be instrumental in bringing about both short-term and longer-term change. First, in the post-implementation review of LASPO, the government indicated its openness to improving the evidence base on LIPs, explicitly acknowledged that LIPs require more support than is currently available, and that more was needed to enable the justice system itself to function with increased numbers of LIPs (Ministry of Justice 2019a: 26, 153). Secondly, the Ministry of Justice also appears to be willing to lead significant change specifically in respect of domestic abuse, with renewed commitments to addressing the long-standing failures of the family court's response to these litigants. While these examples fall far short of an open call for change, these are important examples of opportunities that may be maximised to make meaningful improvements to how LIPs interact with the family justice system. Importantly, these opportunities are not only short-term. Rather, it is possible that the aftermath of LASPO provides the scope to reorient

[6] In fact, the government has explicitly indicated their unwillingness to consider reinvesting in legal services as a solution, by stating 'access to a lawyer is not always the correct or most affordable answer' (Ministry of Justice 2019a: 35).

conversations about the family justice system in a way which incorporates the voices of those who have been directly affected by legal aid reform and highlights the extent to which vulnerabilities are experienced within the court process as it currently operates. This provides an important and timely opportunity to draw together a theoretical and empirical understanding of what the relationship between LIPs and the family justice system is like, as well as to consider how this process could and should be adapted in the longer term to be more accessible to the range of people now making use of it, and what kinds of support and advice people in different circumstances require when they do (Trinder et al. 2014: 119–20; McKeever et al. 2018: 204).

The framework of theoretical and analytical approaches drawn together in this chapter provides two purposes. First, it establishes the lens through which LIP experiences will be explored throughout this book. Each approach contributes distinct resources for understanding how LIPs are positioned differently in relation to broader inequalities within society, and how this may manifest in specific experiences of disadvantage when LIPs attempt to navigate and participate in the processes that underpin the family justice system. Second, it demonstrates the importance of drawing together theoretical and empirical tools to undertake an inquiry that is capable of speaking to both of these short-term and long-term goals that tend to characterise socio-legal research.

Drawing all four of these approaches together is by no means a simple task – there are several moving parts which work together in different ways. It is therefore understandable and common for researchers to shy away from this kind of challenge. As Davies (2017) explains, within the discipline of law, there is a deep-running preference for an 'aesthetic of coherence'. Arguments and findings are naturally more convincing if they present logical conclusions and do not draw attention to other elements that do not quite fit. But, she argues, there is 'no logical reason for theory to insist upon purity and neatness, especially if it means excluding or foreclosing the intrinsic complexity of its objects …' (2017: 4–5). Moreover, there are important benefits of working with different approaches which ask slightly different questions about how inequality, difference, and disadvantage may play out for LIPs within the legal system. Embracing complexity and working through and with the tensions between these approaches is itself productive, because this ultimately also requires critical engagement with each of these theories, as well as an attentiveness to the political implications of which voices and accounts are relied upon when we talk about LIPs and the family justice system and make arguments for meaningful change.

4

Navigating the Family Justice System

During their time in the family justice system, LIPs are expected to navigate a unique and arguably disjointed role within court proceedings. This is because the family court process is premised upon a full-representation model, which assumes that parties come to court with the benefit of both advice and representation. Under this model, different court users perform prescribed roles which each make distinct contributions to the overall court process. For the system to function effectively and efficiently, each court user is required to perform their role. The presence of LIPs disrupts this normal functioning, because they are expected to simultaneously play the roles of both client and lawyer, and other professionals are often forced to adapt their own roles in order to mitigate the delays and problems that stem from LIPs' lack of familiarity with the legal system. Existing studies have noted that, as a result, LIPs face not only intellectual, practical, and emotional challenges when they come to court, but also 'attitudinal' barriers from others within the system (McKeever et al. 2018). Even though most LIPs do not fit the profile of an over litigious or disruptive litigant, LIPs are frequently regarded with trepidation because of the way that their presence frustrates the normal workings of the family court (Trinder et al. 2014: 50).

The full-representation model has endured despite the reality that there have always been a consistent proportion of LIPs within the process, even before LASPO. In practice, this means that LIPs are expected to navigate a complex web of unfamiliar norms, rules, customs, and expectations that are integral to the continued functioning of the family justice system in its present form. Some of these requirements are explicit, such as the definitive procedural rules and legal principles that govern how a case should be managed and by which criteria decisions should be made. Others are more surreptitious and relate to unspoken assumptions and understandings about the ways that things are done within the legal context, such as accepted social hierarchies between different court users, or cultural expectations about how different court users should behave in legal spaces.

Drawing on the experiences shared by LIPs during interviews, this chapter will explore some of the ways that LIPs may respond when they are faced with navigating different kinds of rules and customs. Starting with the more explicit rules of the family justice system, it will consider how LIPs fared when they were faced with the challenge of navigating the procedural rules that dictate how their dispute is handled within the family court process. Under the current model, the success of this process is heavily dependent on lawyers conducting a significant amount of preparatory work before hearings. This means that LIPs are expected to pre-empt and respond appropriately to court documents, as well as understand how these relate to the overall objectives of the court process. Building on this, the chapter will then move to discuss the ways that LIPs may engage with the legal norms that govern decision-making in family disputes. Here, I draw upon LIPs' experiences of feeling excluded within the legal system due to their lack of specialist legal knowledge and explore how this exclusion occurs. Finally, the chapter examines the ways that LIPs may perceive and respond to the more illusory assumptions that underpin the legal system. While these unspoken rules are frequently difficult to identify and describe, during interviews it was clear that these rules manifested in material ways during court hearings. Here, I draw upon LIPs' descriptions of the physical environments that framed their court proceedings to explore their perceptions of the social hierarchies and cultural expectations that underpinned their interactions with others in the system.

This is by no means intended to be an exhaustive account of the different ways that LIPs may travel through the family justice system, nor a comprehensive picture of the different kinds of procedural, legal, cultural, or social norms that frame those experiences. Nevertheless, by exploring these key examples, it is possible to draw together an understanding of how LIPs face a multifaceted range of challenges when they are expected to navigate an unfamiliar family justice system in which they do not have a clearly defined role.

I. Procedural Requirements

The family justice system is underpinned by clear procedures and processes. These procedures dictate the different roles that people play within the system, as well as the scope, format, and order in which family problems are considered and decisions are made. This requires court users to behave in specific ways at particular points in time, to prepare for different stages of the court process as necessary, and to follow the agreed structure for how family matters should be discussed. Family court procedure therefore ultimately rests upon the assumption that court users are familiar with the *way things work* in the family court. For lawyers, judges, and family justice professionals who play their roles in court proceedings day in and day out, these requirements provide an important framework through which their work is structured and organised. However, these procedures are not designed with lay participation in mind – rather, the family justice system continues to assume that lay court users will be assisted by a legal professional who can guide them through the process.

Procedural requirements and norms can therefore be understood as potential mechanisms of disadvantage for LIPs within the family justice system, in two ways. First, in terms of the ways that they navigate the system through playing the role of their own representative. Using Galanter's (1973: 4) distinction between 'one shotters' and 'repeat players', it is possible to appreciate that repeat players' frequent engagement with the legal system comes with various advantages and benefits, such as the experience to know how and when to take risks, apply pressure to the other side, and where there is scope to bend the rules. In other words, repeat players can 'play the litigation game differently from [a one shotter]'. One shotters lack this all-important familiarity with the system and how it works and, as such, are termed 'have-nots' to indicate the disadvantage that they face within the legal process when considered alongside repeat players. While Galanter's distinction was intended as a means of drawing comparisons between the different kinds of parties that may come to court to litigate, it is also a useful way of appreciating that LIPs are frequently isolated within the procedures of the family court, and often positioned as the only 'have-nots' in a process otherwise occupied by repeat players.

Second, this disadvantage manifests through the procedural distinctions that exist between lay clients and legal professionals. In her theatrical analysis of magistrates' courts, Carlen (1976: 49) argues that legal professionals 'systematically present their coercive devices as being nothing more than the traditional, conventional and common-sensical ways of organising and synchronising judicial proceedings'. Those who regard the court as a workplace therefore have a more comfortable understanding as well as a degree of control over its rules, rituals and routines, whereas defendants – who are both subject to and object of these rules – must navigate them through a 'fog of mystification' (1976: 54).

The dual role that LIPs occupy within family proceedings requires them to navigate procedural rules from the position of a lay court user, without the advantages that come with frequent engagement with the legal system. The presence of LIPs is therefore disruptive to these agreed procedural norms, because they often do not pre-empt and navigate these procedural requirements in the manner expected. In particular, the effectiveness and efficiency of the family court process hinges upon parties conducting pre-hearing preparations. In advance of court hearings, parties and their representatives are expected to compartmentalise different aspects of their family breakdown and narrow down disputed issues. In respect of these issues, they are required to prepare and organise submissions, collate relevant information, and complete required paperwork. This unseen preparatory work is crucially important because this is what largely determines the substance and outcome of each hearing – as Trinder et al. (2014: 35) note, 'much of the work on a case occurs before the courtroom'. Pre-hearing preparations are arguably even more crucial for LIPs, because while they may be forgiven for procedural errors within hearings, a failure to prepare the evidence and paperwork may make it impossible for their cases to continue. This is evident across existing studies from both before and after LASPO, which have indicated that LIPs frequently face difficulties when it comes to filling out court forms and preparing paperwork. Consequently, LIPs disproportionately experience delay, application rejections, and additional expense in having to resubmit their paperwork or have their hearings adjourned (Dewar et al. 2000: 43–45; Moorhead and Sefton 2005: 131; MacFarlane et al. 2013: 60; Trinder et al. 2014: 36–40).

Researchers across multiple jurisdictions have long advocated the need for court paperwork to be more accessible to lay users. Studies have recommended that legal systems should employ standardised forms which avoid complex language and legal jargon, especially when cases are likely to involve LIPs (Zorza 2009: 68; MacFarlane et al. 2013: 58–60; McKeever et al. 2018: 104–05). In England and Wales, court proceedings concerning disputes about children are initiated via a C100[1] form. This form can be completed online and contains minimal reference to legislation. As such, it could be argued that the form is relatively user-friendly in comparison to other court forms and documents. During interviews with LIPs, however, experiences with the C100 appeared to suggest that avoiding legal jargon may not sufficiently mitigate the barrier of procedural familiarity.

> I mean, I didn't need to ask an awful lot of advice; the forms were quite direct and to be honest I felt like, without being unsympathetic to anybody else, you'd have to be a bit of a div[2] to not understand what the forms were saying.
>
> **Cheryl**

> I was filling out an application that made no sense, using words that made no sense that I didn't understand, with something at the top of the paper that said C100 which doesn't mean anything. And then underneath, it has three or four instances where you can use that to go to court … remember, the same form is given to Mum's solicitor – if you have a team of solicitors, they're filling these out on a daily basis and you're scratching your head … on question one.
>
> **Chris**

Twelve LIPs made applications using the C100 form, and seven reported during interviews that they found it difficult to use. Cheryl and Chris appeared to have very different experiences of reading and interpreting the C100, and their contrasting experiences provide a useful insight into why some LIPs may face challenges when preparing paperwork.

Chris explained during our initial conversations that he was dyslexic and that he often struggled to understand written information unless it was explained to him verbally. Initially, Chris' application was rejected and returned to him for containing errors and insufficient detail. Cheryl, on the other hand, had been able to make use of a specialised form assistance service offered for free by a local family law firm in her area. Through this service, she was guided through the form and did not face any error-related delays. Though it cannot be drawn conclusively from these interviews alone, one interpretation of this is that the language and the requirements of the forms may have been easier for Cheryl due to her solicitor's familiarity with family court paperwork.

To understand how and why this familiarity might make such a difference, it is useful to consider these different experiences through a Bourdieusian lens.

[1] See: www.gov.uk/government/publications/form-c100-application-under-the-children-act-1989-for-a-child-arrangements-prohibited-steps-specific-issue-section-8-order-or-to-vary-or-discharge.

[2] Regional British slang meaning 'idiot' or 'unintelligent person'.

While Bourdieu wrote extensively about the forms of capital which are unique to the juridical field, he also drew attention to certain forms of capital which are valuable across fields – symbolic capital (1986: 55). This concept is useful for appreciating the ways in which several fields operate according to broadly similar hierarchies of value, because they all privilege skills which tend to be accumulated in similar life trajectories. For example, further and higher tiers of education tends to provide individuals with opportunities to develop skills such as written eloquence or a wide vocabulary, which are both useful across fields like law and politics (Bourdieu 1977: 842). These capitals, therefore, are important symbolic resources which can be drawn upon to navigate things like bureaucratic paperwork and forms. Although the C100 may not contain many references to statute, it nevertheless embodies the symbolic markers that characterise the legal system as a distinct space with which familiarity is preserved for certain social groups. Written proficiency and the ability to draw upon and understand complicated forms of language are therefore important prerequisites for navigating court forms. However, the opportunities to accrue these capitals are disproportionately classed, and therefore may be out of reach for several LIPs who are coming to court from underprivileged socio-economic backgrounds, especially after LASPO.

These different experiences expose the procedural barriers that may inhibit LIPs' ability to do preparatory work. They also indicate that these barriers may be experienced unevenly, and disproportionately by those with learning difficulties, limited degrees of literacy, or those for whom English is not a first language. Kate, for instance, was from Eastern Europe. Although her spoken English was fluent, she explained that during her time as a LIP she would ask her English friends to help her understand the paperwork she received from court. For Kate, barriers to engaging with court documents were not related to the language used, but rather the complex sentence structures that are commonplace within the documents that come from the family court. This aligns with the concerns of existing research which indicates that understanding court forms is often difficult, especially for those with language barriers (De Simone and Hunter 2009: 256). In her linguistic analysis of applications for financial relief on divorce, Tkacukova (2016: 441–42) has highlighted the significance of specific syntactic constructions used in court forms – for example, subordinate clauses such as 'if' and 'once', and double-negative determinants such as 'other than' and 'unless'. Family court paperwork often employs these linguistic devices due to the need to capture a large range of potentially significant information from court users, and use this to manage cases within the system as appropriate. Despite being free of legal jargon, court documents are likely to act as barriers to those who are unfamiliar with the family justice system because they are designed with specific procedural objectives in mind. For those who do not have prior experience with this procedure, it is difficult to appreciate why information is presented and collected in these unique formats.

Traditionally, procedural barriers have been mitigated through the provision of legal aid-funded lawyers who can use their familiarity with the system to guide, coach, and represent lay clients throughout these processes, or at the very least, give self-representing clients advice about what to expect from court procedures. Court procedures therefore depend on these professionals to bridge the gap between lay clients and the legal system. However, the gradual erosion of eligibility that has taken place during the lifetime of the legal aid scheme, combined with the continued political emphasis on mediation and stigmatisation of those reliant on lawyers or the family court, mean that LIPs have frequently struggled to access either advice or representation. Arguments in favour of preserving access to legal advice are often centred upon the value of expert advice for giving LIPs accurate understandings of their legal positions as well as realistic expectations for the possible outcomes of their cases. However, advice is also a crucial means through which LIPs can gain understanding of how the family court process works, better enabling them to navigate procedural expectations. In their study, Trinder et al. (2014: 23, 36) noted that LIPs who were able to access advice from a solicitor before their hearings had less difficulties with court paperwork, a better awareness of possible outcomes, and were more likely to appreciate distinctions between legal and moral notions of justice.

The presence of LIPs in the family court is often understood as problematic for the procedural efficacy of the court process more broadly. Put simply, the delays, errors and gaps that emerge when LIPs are required to navigate an unfamiliar set of procedures are disruptive to the agreed roles that are traditionally played by other court users, including judges, lawyers, and court staff. This has always been a problem for the family court, but concern among the legal professions about the impact of LIPs is even more significant following the LASPO reforms (Bevan 2013). Given the fact that most people are now categorically excluded from legal aid for private family law issues regardless of their socio-economic backgrounds, there are now likely to be many more people attempting to navigate unfamiliar procedural requirements when they engage with the family justice system. In fact, emerging evidence suggests that there are now significant numbers of LIPs arriving in court having accessed limited or even no advice at all (Lee and Tkacukova 2018). Problems related to procedural compliance are therefore likely to be even common after LASPO, causing significant delays and disruption, as well as an enormous amount of additional work for others in the family court process.

The continued reliance on professional expertise, combined with the assumption that this expertise is freely available to those who need to use the family court, was problematic long before the LASPO reforms. By maintaining procedural barriers, the family court process positions LIPs as exterior to the normal running of the family justice system instead of facilitating a role for them as legitimate court users. In other words, procedural barriers do not exist for LIPs because they do not have legal representation, but rather because of how the court process is designed and how it continues to function.

II. Legal Norms

While procedural rules dictate the format and means by which family disputes are managed, the decisions made in the family court are underpinned by a nuanced legal framework, comprising statutory principles and a rich history of case law. Far from imposing bright-line rules, family law is intended to be interpreted flexibly, in a manner that is responsive to the specific and unique needs of different children and families (Dewar 1998). During court hearings, a key part of lawyers' role is to negotiate how these legal norms should be interpreted and applied in relation to the families involved in proceedings. Due to the specialist nature of legal vocabulary and knowledge, LIPs are not privy to these legal norms. In fact, self-representation studies have consistently emphasised that LIPs struggle to distinguish between information that they feel to be important and information which is legally relevant to their hearings (Moorhead and Sefton 2005: 155–56; Trinder et al. 2014: 71). Frequently, this has a negative impact on the outcomes of cases, with LIPs frequently struggling to participate in negotiations, and sometimes abandoning cases entirely when they cannot understand the rules and standards that are used to dictate the outcomes of their hearings (Hunter et al. 2002: 103; Moorhead and Sefton 2005: 221).

Law derives its authority and legitimacy from the idea that legal rules and norms exist as separate, even elevated, from the rest of society. Language and specialist forms of knowledge are key tools with which this illusion is maintained (Illich 1977; Ewick and Sibley 1998). However, as discussed in chapter three, feminist scholarship has made a great deal of progress in exposing how legal rules are not objective, but instead comprise political choices that account for only certain realities and subjectivities. Through a Bourdieusian lens, this understanding is deepened. The juridical field does not simply privilege symbolic capital such as written and oral eloquence or education, but also actively constructs its own specialist forms of capital which can only be utilised by those with legal training. Given that many LIPs are those who are now excluded from legal aid regardless of their economic resources, it is even more likely that disadvantage within the legal system is shaped by experiences of broader class-based inequality. This is because those from particular socio-economic backgrounds are not only excluded from opportunities to accumulate symbolic capital that may have transferable value within the juridical field but are also disproportionately less likely to find themselves with opportunities to gain the specialist forms of capital which are unique to this field. In practice, this means that LIPs not only face barriers in terms of their ability to participate in and influence the course of conversations about governing legal norms, but often may be excluded from these conversations altogether.

When describing their experience of court proceedings, LIPs frequently expressed difficulty understanding what was happening during their hearings when judges and lawyers would discuss the law in relation to their case.

For instance, all 17 LIPs who faced legal representatives in semi-represented hearings explained that the 'legal' conversations that took place between these professionals were difficult to understand, and that they felt excluded from discussions which centred around references to things like statute or case law.

Legal norms were therefore a key facilitating factor in the segregation of LIPs from other court users within proceedings. Further, LIPs with learning difficulties and mental health problems may be specifically and disproportionately affected by this exclusion.

> There is a mask over their conversations – something is happening on a higher level that you aren't allowed to know, and you can't control.
>
> **Gary**

> They would talk among themselves in legal-type language, and I was just sat there waiting for it to be translated, but you don't know what they said at first, or if they're saying all of it to you.
>
> **Grace**

Gary explained at the beginning of his interview that he had learning difficulties and was also suffering with depression. Although he required additional help with paperwork throughout his time in the court process, this did not affect his ability to understand things which were verbally explained to him in lay terms. Nevertheless, Gary explained that professionals would often talk between themselves for portions of his hearings, and these discussions would only be explained to him after they had been concluded. Similarly, Grace had various learning difficulties which meant that she needed additional time to process and respond to verbal information. This meant that in addition to the exclusionary effects of legal terminology, she also frequently struggled to understand what judges and lawyers were discussing when they spoke quickly or not clearly. Both experiences are indicative of inconsistent understanding as to the kinds of accommodations that LIPs may require in order to follow these conversations, particularly where there are mental health problems or learning difficulties.

Traditionally, litigants would have lawyers advocating on their behalf who could contribute to these discussions as well as translate the content of them. In the absence of a lawyer performing this role, LIPs experienced hearings as segregated into 'legal' and 'lay' discussions, in which there were some conversations dedicated to the use of legal forms of knowledge, and others which were made accessible to them through being translated into lay terms. The consequence of this was that some conversations themselves were rendered entirely inaccessible for Grace and Gary, and that they had to wait for judges to subsequently translate these conversations into lay terms which they could process and understand. For Grace in particular, this often meant waiting for written summaries of information which were provided after the entire hearing had concluded.

In this scenario, LIPs' lack of knowledge means that they are regarded more as lay clients without representation, instead of representatives in and of themselves.

Although it is encouraging that judges respond to LIPs' needs by explaining the content of these conversations, the fact that LIPs cannot contribute to these conversations first-hand is likely to be a significant barrier to their ability to effectively participate in all aspects of their hearing. Conversations are constructive linguistic processes, in which knowledge and propositions are exchanged between parties and shared understanding and meaning is created (Coulthard and Johnson 2007). As Grace explains, when she was only presented with the conclusion of these conversations, she was excluded from being a party to that process of exchange and contributing to or understanding the reasoning that led the judge and lawyer to reach that conclusion. This is even starker for individuals who may have additional difficulties understanding verbal communication and are not recognised as in need of specific accommodations beyond translation into lay terms. Further, exclusion from legal conversations facilitates a sense of disadvantage among LIPs because it prevents them from contributing their perspectives and experiences to negotiations about how the law should apply to their circumstances, which in turn can lead to mistrust of the legal system and those working within it (Tyler 1990: 154–55; Leader 2017: 199).

Interestingly, the problems stemming from these divisions between 'legal' and 'lay' conversations in hearings did not appear to be experienced in the same way by LIPs who were facing other self-representing parties.

> What was really helpful was that she talked through the law in her head out loud. So, even though she did occasionally talk to the assistant in jargon, for the actual hearing she would be, like, reading through everything and recapping everything but doing it out loud and verbally with us.
>
> **Fiona**
>
> The judge actually said things like, 'Are you clear on this?', and 'Do you need to say anything else?', which was really good compared to when his lawyer was there, purposefully using as much legal jargon as possible – he was a right ass.
>
> **Sarah**

The majority of LIPs were able to draw upon experiences of both semi-represented and unrepresented hearings during their interview. Although all LIPs reported that they struggled with understanding legal terminology, concepts and principles when they arose, five – including Fiona and Sarah – had very positive experiences of judges explaining relevant law to them during unrepresented hearings. For Sarah, this experience was specifically contrasted with the hearings where she had faced a legal representative.

Research by Citizens Advice (2016: 40) indicates that in cases without any legal advocates, hearings can lack structure and judges are required to intervene more often. For example, in Trinder et al.'s (2014: 62–63) study, researchers found that in cases where neither party was represented, judges would often take a 'fully inquisitorial' approach. This would involve actively helping LIPs to communicate by steering their contributions and coaching them through the hearing. While this generally worked well and parties were typically satisfied with this approach, the researchers noted that this approach placed significant demands on the judge, to the extent that this approach may be unsustainable in the context of long case lists and limited time for judges to prepare for each hearing. It is possible, therefore, that without lawyers, the judges described by these five LIPs had little option but to take a 'fully inquisitorial' approach.

Here, it is helpful to draw upon the ANT approach in order to understand the ways in which legal norms were experienced differently in the absence of lawyers. As discussed in chapter three, a useful tool provided by ANT is the ability to consider networks such as the family courtroom as an active collection of actors working together to produce this network. The removal of legal advocates as key actors within this network means that inevitably, actors within it must relate to each other in different ways in order to produce this network. Fiona, for example, explained that mentions of law were still present in her case – the judge would use legal language when talking to the court professionals present – but from her perception, most of the hearing was conducted via conversations which involved both her and her ex-partner. Sarah also experienced a shift in approach from her judge for the one hearing in her case where her ex-partner was unrepresented, and specifically attributed this change to the absence of his lawyer. Without a legal advocate using the language and references that she found unintelligible, she also perceived her judge to be more accommodating, and that particular hearing to be more inclusive. A significant difference in the experiences of these LIPs appeared to be temporal – rather than having to wait for professionals to finish a 'legal' conversation before it is translated, the absence of legal advocates meant that the hearing involved a continuous translation of knowledge and process.

These contradictory interpretations of the conversations which took place during hearings indicate that in the absence of legal representatives, LIPs may feel that 'legal' aspects of cases are more accessible. It also suggests that legal norms, when rendered inaccessible, can potentially operate as a key exclusionary factor for LIPs during hearings. While it may not be surprising that legal knowledge is inaccessible to lay court users, the juxtaposed experiences of semi-represented versus fully-unrepresented hearings presented here indicate that the current attitude of isolating LIPs in a bid to protect them from legal knowledge they are unlikely to understand, may actually exacerbate the disadvantage that stems from not knowing or understanding these legal norms. Unrepresented hearings are often categorised as the most chaotic, but the perceptions of these five LIPs indicated that the absence of an opposing advocate meant that they felt more included in the discussions which took place during hearings, and were left feeling that their judges had helped them to engage with the law. For them, the absence of a legal professional for the judge to converse with effectively limited the extent to which legal forms of knowledge and specialist language could be overtly used to exclude them in proceedings.

At this point, it is useful to connect the experiences of these LIPs with a broader point about the role of legal norms in family law disputes. While this finding raises clear concerns about the navigability of legal norms, it is important to avoid assuming that delegalisation of family justice is an appropriate way to address these concerns. While LIPs clearly expressed a preference for hearings that centred around lay language and clear reasoning instead of legal language, they nevertheless recognised that law and specialist forms of knowledge still governed the decisions made in their cases. Further, the problems faced by LIPs were not related to the presence of legal norms but the way that these norms had the effect of excluding them. This is a crucial distinction, and it relates specifically to the way that family justice system itself operates. This distinction is all the more important in the post-LASPO context because of the ways that LIPs are often stigmatised for relying on formal mechanisms of family law and the reality that there is very limited political appetite for any initiatives or reforms that might make legal norms more accessible to lay individuals.

III. Physical Environments, Social Hierarchies and Cultural Expectations

So far, I have explored how the family justice system can be understood as a context that is rendered unfamiliar and inaccessible to LIPs because of the specific procedures and specialist forms of knowledge that are used. However, using the family court also involves navigating a complex web of cultural and social norms, such as accepted hierarchies between different court users, and cultural expectations about how different court users should behave and relate to each other within the process. These are often much less overt than legal and procedural expectations because they comprise unspoken but ingrained professional understandings and customs. They include things like knowing how and when to speak or where to stand during proceedings, to being able to pre-empt how others will act and permissible options available for responding to them. While experiences of the family court process are formally dictated by a framework of legal and procedural principles, there are also myriad implicit rules that govern the gaps. Navigating these rules is all the more complicated for LIPs who, by virtue of their unique dual role in the process, do not have the understanding of cultural norms that comes with frequent engagement with the legal system, nor fit cleanly into customary professional hierarchies.

As explored throughout this chapter, LIPs' perceptions of exclusion or disadvantage in this system are inextricably connected with the fact that they are outsiders who are unfamiliar with this context and the way that it works. Although social and cultural norms are difficult to identify and articulate, one way in which these unspoken conventions clearly manifest is through the different physical environments that frame LIPs engagement with others in the family justice system. Carlen (1976: 50) explains that 'the rules of spacing and placing … define the specific territorial rights and duties of those designated as occupiers of particular social space'. While legal professionals are legitimate occupiers, LIPs are imposters with neither a prescribed place of their own, nor experience of the obligations or possibilities that exist in relation to other court users. Many LIPs have never experienced courtrooms before. In Leader's (2017: 160) study, she noted that LIPs would often base their expectations on examples like courtroom dramas, which was frequently inaccurate and led to experiences of intimidation when courtrooms were not as they expected them to be. This is reiterated by Moorhead and Sefton (2005: 164–65), whose findings suggest that LIPs often experience distress or even 'emotional turmoil' when they attend hearings and are expected to 'cope with the unknown'. To this end, Citizens Advice (2016: 46) have emphasised the benefits of offering LIPs the opportunity to familiarise themselves with the setting of their hearing beforehand.

The intimidation and distress that LIPs may experience when navigating unfamiliar environments are therefore frequently related to the unspoken social and cultural norms that characterise those spaces, such as how people can and should behave and interact with each other. What makes these unspoken customs and expectations all the more unpredictable is that there is broad inconsistency in what these physical environments look like. During interviews, it emerged that LIPs attended their hearings in two different kinds of locations, depending on the capacity and resources of the courthouse to which their case was assigned: the first being a traditional courtroom, and the second a meeting room or judge's chamber. While six LIPs consistently attended traditional courtrooms for their hearings,[3] 17 found themselves attending hearings across both location types depending on the availability of rooms and judges on the day.[4] Each of these environments came with different cultural expectations as to how LIPs should behave and exist within these spaces, and facilitated different kinds of social relationships between LIPs and other court users.

The layout of hearings, for instance, can significantly influence how court users perceive each other and their own role within proceedings. Traditional courtrooms dictate precise formats for how court users are positioned in relation to each other. This had important implications for 10 LIPs who faced lawyers in semi-represented hearings. These LIPs explained that they were expected to stand in the space on the front row which would traditionally have been reserved for their own lawyer.

> His barrister would sit at the front, and cos you've not got one, you stand next to him, and that – straight away, he's got someone with experience in front of him like a shield, and you're just up there at the front alone.
>
> **Edie**

[3] Of these six, two attended a self-contained family court located in repurposed historic buildings, which meant that their hearings were held in older, more traditional courtrooms. Four attended newer Civil Justice Centres, in which hearings were heard in contemporary, modern courtrooms designed according to the same layout as traditional courtrooms. For a historical account of courtroom architecture in England and Wales, see: Mulcahy and Rowden 2020.

[4] These 17 interviewees attended hearings in combined courts, which is the most common type of courthouse in England and Wales. These courthouses are designed to host family, county, and magistrates hearings all in one building. Availability of rooms and judges was therefore more variable in these courthouses depending on the demands in other areas. See further: Mulcahy 2010.

Through an ANT lens, it is possible to trace how the physical arrangements of a traditional courtroom may actively mediate relationships within proceedings. Edie's placement alongside the lawyer is a conscious retention of the physical arrangements that underpin fully represented hearings. These arrangements can be understood as markers of the cultural and social norms that typically characterise these proceedings, because they draw implicit distinctions between the active role that lawyers are expected to play in advocating, negotiating, and participating with other professionals, and the passive role that lay court users are expected to play. In a semi-represented hearing, one of these 'active' actors is absent, and the lay court user without representation is no longer able to fulfil their expected role of passivity. Stepping into their lawyer's shoes is therefore a material disruption to these norms, and this can have a significant impact on how LIPs perceive their relationships with others, as well as their own disadvantage. Rather than placing her on an equal footing, this arrangement made Edie feel isolated and exposed within hearings. Specifically, she felt disadvantaged by the impression that the judge would hold her to the same standards as the lawyer, despite their different expertise and experience. Tacitly, therefore, retaining the cultural norms of the traditional courtrooms gives rise to certain implications about the legitimacy of LIPs' role within proceedings, and risks contributing to the sense of disadvantage that many LIPs experience when trying to navigate the legal and procedural norms of the family court process.

The cultural distinctions between different court users were also generally evident when LIPs described the dynamics they had with judges in traditional courtrooms.

> The judge sits higher at the front, and we sit lower, like paupers. He has nearly half the room, and we're all in the other half of it … which I felt was just a bit disrespectful. You have to remember that when people like me are self-representing, it's daunting enough, and it almost distracts you from the main reason you're all there.
>
> **Maxine**

Seven LIPs referred explicitly to ways in which the physical prioritisation of judges within these spaces conveyed a sense of separation between them and other court users which was daunting. Maxine explained that having to look up at judges, who were often positioned on raised platforms in sectioned-off parts of the courtroom, made her feel disrespected within her hearings.

Many sociological approaches have recognised the ways in which materiality and the physical organisation of space can reflect the power and dominance that operates within particular environments (Lefebvre 1991; Massey 2005). In particular, use of structural elevation within courtrooms is a common way of bestowing judges with 'spatial dominance' which is symbolic of their authority within the legal system (Carlen 1976: 50; Mulcahy 2010). However, drawing upon ANT is particularly useful here to appreciate how these physical arrangements might actually mediate the relationships between actors. The seniority of the judge, and the ways that lawyers are expected to relate to them, is implicit in the ways that traditional courtrooms are arranged. Positioning judges on raised platforms, with a larger division of space, or with their own entrances to the courtroom are all common markers of respect and authority that the judge is supposed to embody as the adjudicator of the hearing. These distinctions can also be understood as material manifestations of cultural and social differences between different court users. For example, the fact that Maxine referred to herself as like a 'pauper' is indicative of the way in which these physical arrangements may reiterate class differences between judges and LIPs. In Leader's (2017: 149) study, LIPs frequently commented on class-based differences between themselves and legal professionals, such as tone, behaviour, and accents. Similarly, in Lee and Tkacukova's (2018) survey, LIPs also provided examples of judges where they were described as 'posh' or 'out of touch'. Given that the legal system already operates in an exclusionary way by privileging symbolic and juridical forms of capital, class is therefore an important factor in how LIPs perceive other actors, and the environment in which those interactions take place can also play an important role in mitigating or exacerbating those perceptions of difference. For Maxine, the elevation of the judge was not simply a reflection of their authority but amounted to disrespect for 'people like [her]' who are self-representing.

While traditional courtrooms often served as material manifestations of the cultural and social norms that characterise family proceedings, these norms were less explicit when hearings were held in meeting rooms or judges' chambers, which have fewer traditional manifestations of legal authority such as raised flooring, divisions of space, or judicial dress. Holding proceedings in these spaces is common practice, with 10 LIPs describing experiences of being called into small office rooms with the judge for their hearing. Four of these LIPs commented specifically on how much they preferred these environments over traditional courtrooms.

> We had about four up in the big court, but [judges'] chambers are just like going into an office room, which is perfect, because it's much more comfortable. It feels like you're gonna get down to it, it's more like a meeting. It's when you get into that bigger space, you're more like, getting told what to do.
>
> **Grace**

For Grace, smaller rooms which were not constrained by the prescribed physical arrangements of 'the big court', were not only less intimidating but more productive and accessible for her. This aligns with MacFarlane et al.'s (2013: 72) finding that less division of space within courthouses can contribute to LIPs having more positive perceptions and experiences of self-representation. Additionally, it builds upon Moorhead and Sefton's (2005: 122) argument that LIPs who do not attend hearings may be intimidated by traditional court formats – as they explained, 'the grander the building, the more it made them nervous'. However, what Grace's comparison adds is an understanding of how and why meeting rooms themselves may actually be more comfortable.

In respect of Bourdieusian notions of capital and the interpretative process that occurs through the habitus, Grace's comparison of judges' chambers to office rooms indicates that the format of these rooms was, at least to a degree, recognisable and familiar to her. As discussed in chapter three, individuals who are exposed to particular fields and become familiar with the kinds of behaviours and capitals which are privileged within them, can become more attuned to this process of value attribution and therefore more 'omnivorous' in their use of capitals for success in those contexts (Bennett et al. 2009: 177). Through the habitus, familiarity can lead individuals to perceive themselves as having greater chances of success within particular fields. While LIPs have limited experience of the legal system, many have previous experiences of attending meetings in offices. For example, Grace and four other LIPs were also involved with social services and the Child and Family Court Advisory and Support Service (CAFCASS).[5] A further three were also simultaneously navigating the administrative processes involved with applying for welfare and housing support from local authorities. Although hearings were stressful and often problematic for LIPs in other ways, the hearings that were held in meeting rooms were often perceived as a continuation of this ongoing experience of attending meetings to resolve the issues related to their family breakdown. This idea that hearings were perceived as more accessible when they were held in meeting rooms may therefore be related to the ways that these spaces do not have obvious physical arrangements that denote cultural constraints and social expectations, such as intimidating and often class-oriented hierarchies between judges, lawyers, and LIPs. Rather, the fact that these office-like spaces were similar to other experiences that LIPs had when dealing with administrative aspects of their lives went some way towards breaking down the illusion that the family justice system is a distinct and inaccessible space in which LIPs are typically discouraged.

Despite most LIPs preferring these spaces to traditional courtrooms, this was not a consistently held view, with two LIPs explaining that meeting rooms were not appropriate for the serious nature of the issues concerned in their child arrangements proceedings.

> It doesn't matter to me; I want the i's dotted and the t's crossed. It should be. You're dealing with children, not someone who owes someone money. It should be the most professional place you've ever seen in your life, but it isn't.
>
> **Chris**
>
> It's a hard one, because I don't know if a small room gives enough clout to the importance of what's being discussed. The issues are life-changing, it seems a bit – you know, a discussion around a table?
>
> **Edie**

While the physical representations of social hierarchies and the cultural power of judges and family law were intimidating for most LIPs, these arrangements

[5] CAFCASS is a non-departmental public body in England established to promote the welfare of children involved in family court proceedings. In Wales, there is an equivalent body known as CAFCASS Cymru.

provided Chris and Edie with assurance that their problems were being taken seriously. However, subsequent hearings in courthouse meeting rooms and judges' chambers left both feeling that the process itself lacked professionalism, which they believed undermined the serious issues at stake in their cases.

This reiterates existing research which has already noted the importance for LIPs of feeling as though they are being taken seriously within their proceedings (McKeever et al. 2018: 173). However, to understand these different interpretations, it is again helpful to consider the different circumstances in which individuals bring their cases. In the lead up to court, Edie and Chris had both experienced various incidents of conflict and misconduct in relation to CAFCASS officers and support workers. While it cannot be drawn conclusively, this may offer some insight as to why they may have felt particularly vulnerable to further unprofessionalism in the courtroom. For some LIPs, culturally accepted rituals and customs may be incomprehensible but are nevertheless part of an 'orderly display of justice' (Carlen 1976: 50).

Taken together, this suggests that there is a diversity of possible ways in which LIPs may engage with the social and cultural norms that underpin the family justice system. For most LIPs, 'crude assertions of authority' within physical environments are exclusionary signifiers of social hierarchies or the cultural distinctiveness of the legal context (Mulcahy 2010: 9). For others, these material manifestations may actually provide a sense of formality that extends legitimacy and official recognition to their family disputes, even if not to their own role within proceedings.

Of course, the ways that LIPs navigate cultural norms and social hierarchies within family courtrooms are now likely to be even more diverse following the outbreak of the COVID-19 pandemic. In chapter two, I set out some of the barriers associated with the shift to remote and hybrid hearings that was necessitated after March 2020. Access to technology and connectivity issues for LIPs are perhaps the barriers most often raised within debates about post-pandemic access to justice, given that a significant minority of the UK population are digitally excluded.[6] Beyond this, there are several other challenges, including increased difficulty for judges and lawyers to ensure that LIPs sufficiently understand what is being discussed, are not distressed or upset during hearings, or even to keep order within proceedings when they are no longer structured by the routines and customs that are inherent to the design and functioning of physical courtrooms.

The move towards remote hearings can therefore be understood as a radical disruption to the traditional roles and responsibilities that are integral to the full representation model (Rossner 2021). Hearings involving elements of remote participation are likely to come with their own manifestations of social

[6] According to the Local Government Association (2021), an estimated 11.7 million (22 per cent) people in the UK are without the digital skills needed for everyday life; 9 million (16 per cent) are unable to use the internet and their device by themselves; and 3.6 million (seven per cent) are almost completely offline.

hierarchies and cultural norms. Although it was not possible to draw on any direct experiences of remote hearings from LIPs during interviews, given the contrasting experiences discussed so far, it is possible to appreciate that this will have a kaleidoscopic range of both positive and negative implications for LIPs. For some, the absence of physical indicators like prescribed layouts, raised flooring or grand displays may be a welcome shift to court proceedings which are more egalitarian and less intimidating. For others, this may only bolster concerns about the professionalism, legitimacy and urgency of proceedings.

These contrasting experiences are likely to be extremely prevalent among cases involving allegations of domestic abuse. During interviews, the 12 LIPs who had self-represented against abusive ex-partners had unique experiences of physical courtrooms, with intimidation and distress a defining feature of both traditional courtrooms and meeting rooms.

> He's behind his barrister obviously, which means he's on the row behind me, which is really weird, because he's looking at the back of your head which is really unnerving. He just stares at me every time and it's really quite intimidating.
>
> **Ama**

> It was a tiny room, just two seats next to each other behind a table. I moved my chair to the side of the table to be further away from him and feel a bit more in control. I couldn't say what I wanted while I was right next to him like that.
>
> **Joan**

For Ama, the layout of a traditional courtroom led her to feel exposed to intimidation by her perpetrator. This interpretation was reiterated by four other LIPs who discussed this environment, and the ways that being alone in the courtroom meant they were subjected to non-verbal intimidation strategies, where perpetrators were able to stare or smirk at them during hearings. At the same time, six LIPs including Joan raised that meeting rooms and judges' chambers were also locations of intimidation, because they were forced to sit in close proximity with perpetrators.

Thinking about this through ANT, it is possible to understand that these different interpretations and experiences of hearing locations are shaped by the physical arrangements of meeting rooms. For instance, the social dynamics and cultural underpinnings of courtrooms are evident in the ways that LIPs described the furniture and arrangements as well as their proximity to others in these rooms. While Ama felt trapped in her ex-partner's eyeline within a traditional courtroom, Joan was able to manipulate aspects of the material environment in order to feel more safe. However, the fact that Joan had to do this in the first place indicates that neither of these layouts were set up in a way that was sensitive to the dynamics of abusive relationships.

When cases involving allegations of abuse reach the family court, it is crucial for judges to have a supervisory presence within hearings. However, as discussed in chapter two, research has continually demonstrated that judges and legal professionals often have limited awareness of the coercive and subtle ways in which abuse can be perpetrated, despite improvements to the definition of domestic abuse contained within PD12J. As a result, Birchall and Choudhry (2018: 23–24) explain that victims are often placed in frightening and dangerous situations including having to sit next to perpetrators, due to family court professionals not understanding the dynamics and impact of abuse. This is reiterated by the experience of these LIPs, who felt unable to rely on judges to recognise these experiences of intimidation in either location.

Under FPR3A, judges are expected to consider the relevance of domestic abuse to litigants' ability to attend hearings 'without significant distress'. However, judges may not recognise that such distress may actually be facilitated, or at least exacerbated, by the layout of hearings. For example, Corbett and Summerfield (2017: 26–28) specified that according to the judges who participated in their interviews, 'larger rooms were seen to be beneficial in putting distance between uncooperative parties'. In practice, larger courtrooms – although they were often seen to be inappropriate for child arrangements cases – were used as a case management tool to encourage parties to 'behave better'. However, the judicial perspectives discussed by Corbett and Summerfield centre mostly around the importance of courtroom format for ensuring that parties do not disrupt proceedings, rather than ensuring the protection of the vulnerable witnesses concerned in those cases.

Despite the myriad challenges associated with an increased use of remote hearings, the side-lining of physical courtrooms may in practice have transformative potential for the extent to which victims can be protected during hearings. Emerging research, for instance, suggests that for many victims, the ability to join hearings remotely from a safe location allowed them to maintain crucial distance from their perpetrators (Ryan et al. 2020a: 17; Ryan et al. 2021). Yet, the effectiveness of this as a protection strategy nevertheless continues to hinge on the practices of legal professionals and judges. In a virtual environment, there is ambiguity as to how hearings should be managed. During the early stages of the pandemic, this was compounded by a lack of certainty and unfamiliarity with remote methods. This led to extremely problematic scenarios, such as victims and perpetrators being left alone together on the same phone line while they waited for judges and lawyers to dial in for their hearings (Ryan et al. 2020a: 14). Additionally, even when entrance to remote hearings is staggered, there are enduring concerns for some victims about using video calls because of the risk that perpetrators may scrutinise their background for information about their location (Ryan et al. 2020a: 17).

In some regards, the COVID-19 pandemic provides significant opportunities for the family court to manage hearings in a way that is more attentive to the needs of victims while they engage with the process. However, it is important to acknowledge that the shift to remote participation does not eradicate the cultural norms and social dynamics that underpin family court hearings (Rossner 2021). Rather, it is likely to amplify and refracture these into an even more diverse range of possible experiences. Using domestic abuse as an example, I have explored how victims may face varied barriers and challenges across different physical and remote environments. Rather than eliminating the problems associated with physical hearing locations, therefore, the pandemic has only further augmented the need to re-examine the norms and hierarchies that LIPs must navigate when they are translated through these various environments. Judicial practices in physical courtrooms have centred around maintaining order within LIP hearings, and this continues to underpin professional concerns about LIPs potentially being more disinhibited within remote hearings (Byrom et al. 2020: 67). These environments therefore continue to be structured by the same norms and hierarchies that simultaneously marginalise the interests of LIPs and impose specific expectations on them about how they should behave. Consequently, while it is common for LIP-focused debates to centre upon how tangible procedural and legal rules may be reformed, such change is potentially meaningless without a proper understanding of how the unspoken cultural and social dynamics of the family court affect its navigability.

IV. The Full-Representation Model

This chapter has explored several different kinds of rules, customs and norms that frame LIPs' journey through the family justice system. While it can only provide a snapshot insight into the different kinds of norms that underpin the court process, this is nevertheless indicative of just how deeply the family justice system is rooted in a full-representation model. The assumption that parties come to court with full advice and representation underpins every aspect of the process, including the relationships that court users have with one another, the ways that conversations are negotiated, and the perceived legitimacy of decisions reached in this context. Despite the efforts of other professionals, this framework of rules and customs means that LIPs are faced with the challenge of refuting the full-representation assumption at every stage of the court process. As such, they are continually positioned as an external force which contravenes and disrupts the justice system, rather than as legitimate court users with a clearly defined role.

Further, LIPs are likely to respond in a variety of different ways when they are faced with the task of navigating exclusionary norms. By examining LIPs' experiences through different conceptual lenses, it has been possible to expose how responses are frequently mediated by broader structures of inequality which frame experiences of society, and compounded by the different resources and disadvantages that LIPs face in other aspects of their lives. In practice, this further complicates the task of accommodating LIPs within the current network of rules and customs that constitute the family justice system. While procedural leeway and guidance from judges or legal professionals is well intended and is likely to assist many LIPs, these efforts alone cannot account for the diverse range of support needs of LIPs, especially after LASPO. This kind of short-term flexibility also cannot address the deep-rooted cultural norms and social hierarchies that operate to isolate LIPs within the process. Further, the task of incorporating any of these accommodations into the current process invariably places greater burden onto already-strained workloads of those working in the family justice system.

The barriers that LIPs face when they are expected to navigate the family justice system are far from new. In reality, LIPs have always faced exclusionary norms and have always struggled to navigate a system premised upon a historically reiterated set of roles to which they do not belong. The last decade has, however, marked a period of significant change for this system. The LASPO reforms have facilitated major disruptions to the otherwise accepted norms that underpin the family court process, and this has only been further compounded by the effects of the COVID-19 pandemic. While the family court process may once have been perceived as an inviolable structure of procedures and rules, it is now forced to adapt on a daily basis – both in terms of guiding LIPs through court hearings, as well as adapting proceedings so that they may take place in virtual or hybrid formats. In many ways, these events have even further impaired LIPs' ability to seek support and participate in their hearings by further isolating them from sources of advice as well as court professionals. A great deal of further work is needed to build a stronger understanding of how LASPO and the pandemic have intersected and impacted LIPs' experiences of family justice. However, even at this early stage, it is possible to see that this has forced change within the family justice system.

5

Contributing to the Family Court Process

In the previous chapter, I explored some of the ways that LIPs may experience exclusion or disadvantage due to the different kinds of norms, rules, and customs that they must navigate throughout their time in the family justice system. While these governing rules come in a variety of forms, what underpins many of them is the way that they act to constrain how different court users are permitted to communicate within the process. By dictating when and how certain issues may be raised, what aspects of a family dispute are legally relevant, and who is permitted to discuss those issues within hearings, their combined effect is to limit and prescribe the ways that LIPs can talk about their family problems within proceedings.

Understanding how LIPs communicate with others and the extent to which they feel heard within the family court process is an integral part of understanding the kind of relationship that they have with the family justice system as a whole. In the criminal justice context, scholars have already identified that there is a striking connection between the perceived legitimacy of law or legal systems and how fairly individuals feel they have been treated by legal authorities (Tyler and Ho 2002). These scholars suggest that if a structure or system is viewed as unfair, then those who are disadvantaged within that system might reasonably respond by ignoring or defying the authority of legal decisions (Tyler 1990). While this scholarship has so far been primarily concerned with the acceptability of criminal sanctions, it also provides a useful starting point for considering the broader implications of LIPs feeling excluded or alienated within family court hearings.

This chapter is concerned with how LIPs communicate with others in the court process, and the extent to which LIPs are enabled to contribute to the proceedings that concern their family disputes. It begins by exploring LIPs' experiences of communicating with others in the process in three key respects: speaking in court, conveying information through paperwork, and asking and answering questions through cross-examination. Here, it explores the specialist mechanisms by which court users are expected to contribute information to the court process, and reflects upon the implications of expecting LIPs to communicate via prescribed formats and methods. Following this, it provides an insight into how some LIPs may respond to these constraints by finding other ways to ensure they are heard within the confines of oral and written court procedures.

I. Speaking in Court

Speaking in court is a key part of contributing to family law proceedings. Traditionally, hearings rely upon legal representatives to present concise, legally relevant arguments to a judge or panel of magistrates on behalf of their clients. Despite the increasing prominence of self-representation, these procedures have endured and LIPs are required to advocate their positions verbally, albeit with varying degrees of guidance and prompting from other professionals involved. However, self-representation studies have frequently identified that LIPs struggle to cope with advocacy, even if they generally appear confident elsewhere in proceedings (Williams 2011; Moorhead and Sefton 2005: 163; MacFarlane et al. 2013: 89–96; Trinder et al. 2014: 23). By exploring this requirement from the perspectives of LIPs during interviews, it was possible to shed new light on why and how LIPs may face these difficulties.

LIPs' descriptions of what it was like to speak in court appeared to be underpinned by two major challenges. First, LIPs experienced difficulty emulating the *performative* nature of speaking which is traditionally expected in the court environment. The requirement to convey information in this way was particularly problematic for those with certain learning difficulties and mental health problems. Second, this specialist format of advocacy often led LIPs to interpret advocacy as an *adversarial* task, which operated to further exclude and disadvantage them within their hearings.

Speaking in a court setting is often compared to a performance (Ramshaw 2013; Rossner 2021). Advocacy involves presenting a structured set of points or arguments with the objective of convincing an audience of a predetermined point of view. Six LIPs indicated that they felt uncomfortable speaking in court because it made them feel observed or scrutinised by others in the courtroom. Maxine, for instance, compared her proceedings to being on reality television to demonstrate the feeling that her performance was being evaluated by the judge in her case.

> It's like a circus act – you've got the judge there judging how well we're all performing, it's like the X Factor[1] … the barrister does this all the time, he's been put in situations like this loads of times, he knows how to act, but your performance is judged to the same standard.
>
> **Maxine**

In order to further explore this perception, it is useful to consider from a Bourdieusian perspective how speaking in court requires certain kinds of capital. Language, in terms of the words we use as well as how we put those words to use in different contexts, is inherently classed. This is because language is a device through which individuals can draw on different kinds of capital in order to convey meaning (Edwards 1976: 91–92). Legal advocacy allows a speaker the opportunity

[1] The 'X Factor' was a British reality television music competition, popular between 2004–2018.

to demonstrate both their symbolic capital – that is, vocabulary and grammatical patterns that they have accrued throughout their previous educational and professional opportunities – as well as specialist forms of cultural capital – words, terms and mannerisms that are unique to the juridical field. However, the way in which such linguistic skills are accumulated depends on the exposure and access that individuals have to specialist contexts like the legal system, as well as professional and social circles in which this kind of public speaking is practised.

This means that the requirement to cater a performance to the family court context is heavily geared towards those with prior experience of either the legal context itself, or related fields characterised by similar communication practices. It is therefore unsurprising that in quantitative comparisons between represented and unrepresented case outcomes, having a professional legal advocate for this stage of the court process has been found to make a 'spectacular' statistical difference to litigants' chances of success (Sandefur 2015: 924). The advantages that legal professionals have when they speak in court are related to both their ability to use language to evoke specialist forms of knowledge, as well as their ability to use the performative nature of advocacy to further convince their audience. For example, in Conley and O'Barr's (1998) linguistic study of courtrooms in the United States, self-representing individuals without legal training tended to present 'everyday' and 'relational' narratives when making submissions in court. In other words, LIPs in their study presented accounts conversationally, using reference points such as events or people, instead of the legal rules and principles which are commonly used in the court context. These conversational accounts also frequently lacked clear structure in comparison to the way that lawyers are used to constructing logically-sequenced arguments in advance. Even beyond legal technicalities and specialist forms of knowledge, the oral presentation involved in legal advocacy is nevertheless characterised by what Tkacukova (2016: 442) refers to as 'goal-oriented' narratives. By this, she means that speaking in court is a one-sided activity, in the sense that the aim is to *convey* rather than *exchange* information through monologue-style instances of speaking.

Research has already demonstrated that specialist legal knowledge and vocabulary can have the effect of preventing effective communication between LIPs and legal professionals (Moorhead and Sefton 2005: 214). There is evidence to suggest that many judges already recognise these challenges and adapt hearings to try and make advocacy easier for LIPs. For example, Leader's study (2017: 145) found that sometimes LIPs were told to 'tell their stories simply' or to 'just speak plainly and simply'. However, as she notes, this alone was not enough for LIPs to feel as though they were being enabled to participate. Rather, what is 'plain and simple' is likely to have different meanings inside and outside of the courtroom, and even when it does not involve using legal words, the task of advocacy still involves being coherent in a specifically 'legal' way. In essence, requiring LIPs to present points orally within court hearings is therefore implicitly still asking LIPs to meet 'significant, and often unclear, performative demands', even if legal professionals themselves do not realise that this is what the process requires (2017: 163).

The performative nature of speaking in court is likely to be particularly problematic for those with learning difficulties and mental health issues who may not be able to convey their points all at once. During interviews, 13 LIPs explained that they felt pressured because their time to speak was restricted to just one or two opportunities during hearings.

> Academically minded people work well under pressure, so my Mum could notice things and think under pressure. She was able to think on her feet, I can't, and all the other people you'll be interviewing won't be able to either.
>
> **Grace**

> When you come out of the courtroom, you're thinking of things you should've said or asked. When you're speaking the judge can interrupt you and ask you things, and make you lose your thread – I can't do that scattergun approach.
>
> **Ama**

Ama was contending with stress-related anxiety and depression, which often led her to feel panicked and unfocused during her court hearings. This meant that when she was invited to speak, she was frequently unable to remember everything she wanted to say, especially when she was interrupted for clarifications. Similarly, Grace's learning difficulties meant that she required additional time to understand things that had been said by the other party and respond to them effectively within her own submissions. Although they were not permitted to speak on their behalf, four LIPs explained that their McKenzie Friends were an invaluable source of support during this stage, due to the ways in which they were able to help them prepare and remind them of key points during the limited opportunities they had to speak. For example, when Grace was expected to present her position, her mother would help her by holding cue cards between them, which enabled her to stay on track and say everything that she had prepared, even if she was interrupted by the judge. While Grace and Ama experienced distinct challenges in other aspects of the court process, both felt impeded in their ability to effectively advocate for themselves because of the way that communication in the family court is constrained to these unfamiliar, performative formats.

This aspect of the court process, therefore, is particularly unsuitable for those who already struggle with verbal forms of communication. When court users present with mental health problems or learning difficulties, the family court is required to consider whether the participation of any party in hearings may be diminished by reason of vulnerability. In making this assessment, judges are expected to consider the relevance of 'mental disorders' to the ability of litigants to 'put their views to the court'.[2] This means that exceptions and accommodations can be made to assist LIPs, such as relying on lawyers to provide structure to proceedings or changing the order of conversations within hearings. However, it is inevitably difficult for the judiciary to use bright line notions of 'mental disorders'

[2] See: FPR3A and PD3AA.

to pre-empt situational conditions like anxiety, if they are not explicitly raised by LIPs in advance.

Further, while this guidance is well-intentioned, it cannot go far enough to mitigate the structural barriers that LIPs are likely to face when they are expected to speak in court. While judicial guidance is an important way of signalling to judges that LIPs may require additional time or support to convey their points during hearings, there is also value in critically reflecting on the assumed centrality of advocacy to the court process. The current practice of requiring LIPs to present their points verbally within hearings fails to appreciate that professional training is often required for effective advocacy, and also fails to accommodate LIPs' diverse range of communication needs. Additionally, treating advocacy as the default method of communication in the family court is likely to cause even further problems after LASPO, due to the increased numbers and diversity of LIPs who are likely to require additional support and accommodation.

So far, I have explored how the performative nature of advocacy may impair LIPs' ability to communicate in their hearings. However, it is also important to consider how these experiences may impact the perceptions that LIPs have of the courtroom dynamic. In particular, LIPs frequently interpreted the requirement to give formal submissions in court as a combative activity, where they were leading an assault on the other party's case. In describing their experiences of advocacy, five LIPs clearly conceptualised the process of speaking in court as adversarial.

> If you do good in your speech, you win. Simple. So I did, I kept fighting, because I haven't got any other options. I had to fight, because I had no one to fight for me like [ex] did, and that's my child, I had to fight for her.
>
> **Kate**

> I got a recommendation for a McKenzie Friend, who was fairly notorious. He's in prison now, but for me he was brilliant. He stepped over the boundaries quite a lot, he spoke when he wasn't allowed to, but I wouldn't have gotten through seeing [ex-partner] in court without him.
>
> **Fiona**

In addition to the political emphasis that continues to be placed on mediation, the family court process is also designed so that at every stage, parties can be encouraged and given every opportunity to settle or agree on an arrangement for themselves, if possible.[3] However, research has consistently found that for LIPs, there is a stark contrast between the settlement ethos of family law and the way in which family hearings are actually experienced (Dewar et al. 2000: 52–53; Moorhead and Sefton 2005: 163–64; Trinder et al. 2014: 72). These LIPs seemed to conceptualise the prospect of presenting their position in court as their half of a larger fight or a battle, which would be compared against the speech given by the other side, before a winner was decided.

[3] See: PD12B.

LIPs frequently used words and phrases such as going to 'fight' in court, and 'fighting' for children when describing their experiences of orally presenting their points and responding to the position advocated by the other side. Kate, for example, reasoned that in order to get the outcome she wanted in a hearing she had to perform well in her oral presentation, so that the judge would agree with her over her ex-partner. Similarly, Fiona appeared to equate success within hearings with the ability to assert her position authoritatively within hearings – specifically by overstepping the limitations that were placed on her opportunities to speak during hearings, such as speaking more than once. These experiences suggest that due to the way that hearings are traditionally structured around formal advocacy, LIPs may conceive invitations to speak in court as their sole chance to assert themselves during the hearing and convince judges of their position. Additionally, a significant aspect of convincing the judge that their position is correct, appeared to be a refusal to concede to any suggestions or arguments made by the other side.

Viewing this through a Bourdieusian lens, it is possible to consider the contextual factors that may contribute to shape these perceptions and interpretations of the advocacy process. Specifically, LIPs' understandings of what is expected from them are inextricably shaped by the kinds of resources that they are able to draw upon when they prepare for their hearings. For instance, according to Maclean and Eekelaar (2009), a major part of the role of a legal representative is to manage the expectations of their client, in terms of both potential outcomes of hearings and what to expect in the courtroom. Now that many LIPs may be unable to access this guidance, it is possible that the settlement ethos of the family justice process is increasingly lost. Additionally, as Moorhead and Sefton (2005: 163) explain, LIPs often have a 'social interpretation' of what constitutes a successful argument, which was described by a lawyer in their study as 'arguing over the back fence with the neighbour'. Both of these arguments suggest that without lawyers, LIPs may descend into more adversarial methods of advocacy, and thus further exacerbate conflict between themselves and cause further strain on the family justice system. While it would not be realistic within the current political context to argue that all LIPs should have access to lawyers in order to understand the settlement ethos of the family court, it may nevertheless be important to consider how their approaches to advocacy may be influenced by the other sources of information that they may draw upon in absence of legal advice. For instance, the interpretations of LIPs may instead be framed by the attitudes and approaches of others who they seek assistance from online or through McKenzie Friends.

As discussed so far, many McKenzie Friends have useful experience to offer LIPs – specifically for Fiona, this McKenzie Friend provided her with the confidence and protection that enabled her to face her abusive ex-partner in court. The benefit of this support should not be underestimated, particularly for survivors of domestic abuse who are likely to be even further impaired in their ability to advocate for themselves confidently and effectively in front of their perpetrators. Nevertheless, as noted in chapter two, there is also some evidence to suggest that professional McKenzie Friends may take advantage of the opportunity to appear in court in order to gain a platform from which to further their own agendas against their family court (Legal Services Consumer Panel 2014: 19; Trinder et al. 2014: 96–98; Smith et al. 2017: 21; McKeever et al. 2018: 93). For example, many individuals may choose to offer their services because they have their own 'axe to grind', following 'custody battles' of their own (Thomas 2016). In addition to the assistance that Fiona's McKenzie Friend offered with paperwork, therefore, he also played a vital role in making her feel as though she had asserted herself well within proceedings. However, the approach that he encouraged her to take may have meant that he also potentially hindered her ability to participate in other aspects of the process, as well as exacerbated the already protracted conflict that existed in her proceedings.

The current landscape of family law support, which has been intersected by both the LASPO reforms and the additional barriers that have since emerged as consequences of the COVID-19 pandemic, mean that many LIPs may increasingly draw upon alternative sources of help which perpetuate adversarial attitudes. This is particularly so when the format of court processes like advocacy are already designed in such a way that not only makes it more difficult for LIPs to communicate their points, but also engenders competition rather than negotiation. The potential consequences of this for LIPs is that they will be further excluded from the capitals and attitudes which are valued within the court process – openness to settlement, compromise, and negotiation. Instead of taking these approaches, these LIPs interpreted advocacy as an adversarial process, and experienced further disadvantage as a result of their being less willing to attempt to reach agreements or compromises during proceedings.

II. Using Paperwork to Communicate

Aside from speaking in court, the second key way that parties communicate with their judge and other professionals in their case is through the written paperwork that must be prepared, submitted, and shared via court bundles in advance of each hearing. In family court proceedings, court bundles may typically include a position statement setting out a concise summary of a party's main arguments as well as other documents that they have been directed to provide. For FFHs and Final Hearings, this bundle may also include a proposed list of questions to ask the other party or any witnesses during cross-examination. Research indicates that LIPs frequently struggle to collate and prepare these bundles, with LIPs' paperwork found to be commonly either incomplete or 'chaotic' (Trinder et al. 2014: 69).

In the previous chapter, I emphasised the different ways in which LIPs may struggle to navigate the procedural expectations that underpin legal documents and court forms. Even when legal terminology is minimised, the task of preparing a bundle is nevertheless a specialist activity which is difficult for uninitiated court users to execute effectively. Leader (2017: 168) notes that in attempting to follow instructions about what to include and what to prepare, LIPs only ever deal with the physical bundle, and are rarely privy to the significance of these documents within the wider court process. The experiences of LIPs reiterated these concerns, but also offered a valuable insight into how LIPs may perceive their court bundles as an important means of communicating with others in their hearings, especially if they faced the difficulties complying with the expectations of advocacy outlined earlier in this chapter. Further, these experiences offer specific insight into how and why some LIPs may actually *over* prepare their bundles in an attempt to mitigate the disadvantage they anticipated in other aspects of their hearings.

For all LIPs, both court bundles and the position statements within them were regarded as very important during the preparatory stages of the court process due to the ways in which they enabled communication with judges outside of the hearing.

> I think that made the judges like us more, or at least they were more patient with us generally, and helped us probably do better than some of the other LIPs that you might have spoken to. They were definitely relieved to have someone who had done all the right things, handed it all in on time, and put it all together neatly. One of the male judges said it was one of the best bundles he'd seen from a LIP, and we should be pleased with ourselves, which was nice.
>
> **Grace**

Aside from actually speaking in court, the bundle is the main way in which LIPs are able to communicate with judges, and as a result, ten LIPs talked about how important they felt the bundles were for making a good impression on their judge before the hearing. Grace, for example, felt that she and her mother had received recognition from judges in terms of their organisation, and that their success in this regard distinguished them from other LIPs.

Here, it is useful to return to the analytical tools provided by ANT. Specifically, the materialist focus of ANT means that it is useful for asking questions about how non-human actors can play important roles within social arrangements. Therefore, by scrutinising the detail of how court bundles are used by different actors within the court process, it is possible to gain a deeper insight into how this produces specific effects for the relationships between actors who rely on these bundles. The traditional role of the court bundle, for instance, is to convey information required by the judge for the purposes of the hearing. However, for LIPs, the task of preparing the court bundle provided the opportunity to influence and adapt this traditional role. Rather than simply a device through which to convey information, the court bundle was also a material means of presenting themselves in a good light to judges in advance of the hearing, so that when they came to directly interact with each other, this relationship would begin from a solid starting point.

A well-organised bundle, therefore, was a useful resource for Grace. While existing research studies indicate that LIPs may not always appreciate the procedural significance of the court bundle, this suggests that LIPs do nevertheless appreciate the significance of the bundle for the potential impact it can have on their relationships with their judges. Pleasing judges with organised bundles was identified as extremely important for almost half of LIPs, who were all keenly aware of the ways in which their written work could affect how they would be perceived once they arrived in the courtroom. However, attempts to present themselves positively to judges using court bundles did not always go to plan.

> I don't know if I did something to make them dislike me, I'm not cocky but I was prepared … It was like I got slandered for doing too much homework.
>
> **Catherine**

> One of the female judges scowled at me when I got there, saying she didn't have time to read it all and that I'd submitted too many papers.
>
> **Ama**

Nine LIPs explained that they had over-prepared their bundles, in that they had included far more than sufficient examples of information requested by the court. This aligns with the findings of earlier research, which has indicated that sometimes the difficulties LIPs face in preparing bundles can lead them to preparing too much information, as well as too little (Moorhead and Sefton 2005: 153; Trinder et al. 2014: 42, 64–65). The ability to gain positive recognition from judges through the court bundle is therefore contingent on the ability to be selective and concise when preparing this content. However, this precision is again dependent on the ability to be reflexive in the use of capitals such as familiarity with the conventions surrounding court bundles, and professional training in how to selectively use paperwork to evoke specialist knowledge, which is rarely accessible to LIPs.

Returning to the theoretical framework, it is possible to draw upon both ANT and Bourdieusian theory to reflect on how over-prepared bundles may actually serve to disadvantage LIPs in these arrangements. In her ANT analysis of legal documents, Riles (2000: 76–80) argues that a document can act as an artefact of a conversation, with the effect of effectively closing down other avenues of debate which are not immortalised within the final form of the document in question. While the court forms discussed in chapter four are an example of how documents may be used to constrain LIPs to providing only procedurally relevant information, court bundles do not have the same material constraints. Rather, they provide a less rigid format in which LIPs have a relative degree of control over the format and content. By understanding the significance that LIPs attributed to the court bundle as a means of impressing their judges, it is possible to understand how in the absence of access to field-specific capitals, many LIPs may provide as much information as possible in an attempt to appear organised and dedicated. However, as seen in Ama's case, a consequence of this is that due to the time constraints of the justice system, judges may not have time to read the whole bundle or are frustrated in their task of doing so in the depth required.

This suggests that the perceptions that LIPs have of their court bundle may differ from the reality of how bundles are received in court. In McKeever et al.'s (2018: 105–06) research, the authors found evidence that judges could sometimes resent the additional burden of work that fell to them as a result of failure of LIPs to provide the court with all the necessary paperwork. In a similar way, therefore, the experiences of Catherine and Ama suggest that over-preparation may also cause difficulties for relationships with judges. While it is unlikely that their judges considered Catherine or Ama not dedicated, if over-preparation makes the job of hearing a case more arduous, LIPs are unlikely to achieve similar aims of making a positive impression or influencing judges in the manner intended.

This reinforces and deepens Leader's (2017: 168) argument that a lack of understanding about the significance and role of the court bundle can mean that LIPs struggle to understand why their efforts are ineffective. However, it also sheds light on the ways in which LIPs may attempt to use court bundles as a tool with which to overcome aspects of the process which they perceive themselves to be disadvantaged for. For example, the position statement is the central focus of the court bundle, and all LIPs invested a great deal of effort into preparing their position statements for each hearing. In contrast to other documents requested in the court bundle, this was a document over which LIPs had total control and could use as a means of directly communicating with judges in writing.

> I write very well. I can speak very well as well, but when I write the statements, they're all solid, concise, they make the points that I want to make. I can compartmentalise it on paper, whereas in the court they want it presented in a way that they decide on the day, but I've not been to that law school class. Writing I can do very well, because I can get all my points across.
>
> **Ikraa**

> Well, you're in a nerve-wracking situation in court, and you've got allegations flying at you left right and centre, whereas you've just got more time to be calm and answer questions and get everything you want to say on the paper.
>
> **Sarah**

From Ikraa and Sarah's perspectives, the statement was an opportunity to convey their arguments in a context that was less emotionally charged, and in which they had some control over how they expressed themselves. This indicates just one way in which LIPs struggled to communicate effectively within the courtroom itself, but also suggests that they attempted to use the statement as a tool to mitigate the disadvantage they experienced in relation to the requirements of advocacy.

Thinking about this through Bourdieu's habitus, it is possible to understand that when individuals engage with unfamiliar fields like the legal system, they continually assess their own possibilities and opportunities within those contexts. This means that they subjectively recognise the way in which they are recognised by others, as well as how they may be able to respond to the requirements of the field in which they find themselves. Here, Ikraa and Sarah were pre-empting the vulnerability they anticipated that they were going to experience once they faced their ex-partners in the courtroom. They recognised that given the emotional nature of the issues at hand, they were unlikely to be able to draw upon capitals like eloquence and vocal authority in that environment. As such, they both exercised their abilities to make use of the capitals they had access to whilst outside this environment – high levels of literacy and written communication, as well as the time, distance and flexibility which enabled them to compartmentalise these emotions on paper. In addition to the ways that LIPs may try to use court bundles as a means of influencing judicial perceptions of them in advance of the hearings, some LIPs may also attempt to use the position statement to maximise the benefit of the opportunity to communicate via paperwork and mitigate the disadvantage they anticipated in relation to speaking in court.

Of course, the opportunity to use position statements in this way is unlikely to be an option for all LIPs. As discussed in relation to the barriers that some LIPs faced in understanding the language of court applications, many LIPs coming to court are likely to come from backgrounds characterised by low levels of literacy, and in which English as a second language is also disproportionately represented. The opportunity to predict and mitigate future experiences of disadvantage may therefore be out of reach for many LIPs, such as those with learning difficulties, who experience additional challenges using written forms of communication. Therefore, while the court bundle and the position statement may provide an opportunity for some LIPs, others may be limited entirely to their ability to advocate for themselves during hearings.

III. Asking and Answering Questions

The third way that parties may communicate with others in their hearings is if their case progresses to either a FFH or a Final Hearing, in which they are expected to engage in the process of cross-examination. The purpose of cross-examination is to enable parties to test specific elements of evidence from witnesses and expose weaknesses in the claims or position of the other side. Traditionally, this process would be managed to a large extent by legal representatives. Lawyers would typically be the ones undertaking the process of asking questions, and when it comes to parties being questioned as witnesses, legal representatives would prepare their clients for what to expect. In the absence of legal representatives, LIPs are frequently required to engage in this specialist and unique format of asking and answering questions without this support.

In terms of asking questions of the other side, LIPs explained that they struggled to think of what questions to ask the witnesses in front of them. In fact, most ended up struggling to ask questions at all.

> I think I was really prepared … I just pulled out the important bits of it, just like in the way barristers do, I made sure to get them to repeat all the good bits. But the judge kept picking me up, for saying statements rather than questions.
>
> **Catherine**

Instead of asking questions as a means of testing evidence and making new contributions to the information at play in her hearing, Catherine and seven other LIPs explained that they would repeat aspects of the case which they felt were the most important facts for the purpose of portraying their ex-partner negatively in court.

This aligns with the findings of previous studies, which have argued that regardless of the procedural assistance that might be made available to LIPs, there are some specialist tasks such as cross-examination, which LIPs simply cannot perform effectively, if at all. Trinder et al., (2014: 70) for instance, found that LIPs struggle with this questioning process in two main ways – first in formulating questions, and second, in keeping their questions to those which are legally relevant. In this study, the researchers found that judicial approaches to managing the process of cross-examination varied widely. For instance, while some judges would take complete responsibility for devising and delivering the questions, others would help LIPs to formulate questions, or give some guidance to LIPs about the topics that should be addressed. Some judges in this study took a 'sink or swim' approach, in which LIPs were offered no more assistance than that which would be available to a trained lawyer, and LIPs were rebuked for mistakes or straying off topic (2014: 71–75). Similarly, in Moorhead and Sefton's (2005: 183) research, the researchers found evidence of opposing barristers assisting LIPs with the format of cross-examination, often by acting as an intermediary or helping them to formulate questions. However, in their study, there was a general sense of anxiety among both judges and lawyers about the disruption this caused to the impartiality of judges and the position of represented litigants, which meant that there was not a uniformity of approach (2005: 184).

There are a range of ways in which judges may assist LIPs with the task of putting questions to witnesses. However, none of these eight LIPs mentioned any assistance that they were given by judges – in fact, three including Catherine explained that judges had criticised their questioning technique. It should be noted, of course, that Catherine's judge may have been attempting to help her by reminding her to ask questions rather than give statements. However, an important finding is that this was not perceived as help by Catherine. Rather, during our interview, Catherine was still of the position that she had prepared well and effectively emulated her ex-partner's barrister during her questioning.

To understand this further, it is useful to turn back to the theoretical framework. As discussed earlier in this chapter, the Bourdieusian notion of capital is an important and valuable means of understanding the class-based inequality that characterises particular forms of communication, because the ability to effectively cross-examine is again dependent on the extent to which individuals have access to particular skills and experience. While advocacy requires LIPs to have attributes such as the ability to give a single presentation which conveys all information in an authoritative and convincing manner, cross-examination requires LIPs to reflexively use these skills in order to actively deconstruct aspects of the other party's case. For instance, Tkacukova (2016: 445) explains that cross-examination provides a unique opportunity to reiterate one's own position through the device of another person, by eliciting specific responses from them. Cross-examination is distinctly asymmetrical, in that it follows a strict question and answer dynamic, which remains goal-oriented (Tkacukova 2010). The task of testing evidence through questions is therefore another example of a specialist and regulated form of communication, distinct from ordinary forms of conversation or confrontation that LIPs are likely to have encountered before.

While symbolic capital may be a useful resource through which LIPs are able to demonstrate oral eloquence, confidence with public speaking, and posing their questions authoritatively, this alone still does not mean that LIPs are able to pose questions in the legally relevant manner expected by the court process. As Trinder et al. (2014: 70) note, the ability to question effectively during the cross-examination process does not necessarily relate to intelligence, but rather 'legal nous'. The skill of legal questioning is not something that comes naturally even to those who are generally privileged within society. While some LIPs may have some experience of oral presentations such as those required in advocacy, the opportunities for individuals to engage in cross-examination style communication outside law is even more rare. Rather, this skill is developed through the specialist experience and training which comes from practising within the juridical field. The ability of lawyers to question effectively stems from the knowledge they have of governing legal principles, as well as their experience as to how individuals typically respond to different kinds of questions, and how to influence the narrative which is presented in order to fit with legalistic conceptions of 'truth' or 'fact'.

Through Bourdieusian theory, therefore, it is possible to appreciate that the oral procedures that underpin the family court process exist within a broader context of class-based inequality, where only certain groups of people have access to the advantages and opportunities which enable them to move fluidly between the requirements of having to give one-sided oral presentations during advocacy, and then adapt to this specialist means of questioning, in order to reinforce the same goal-oriented narrative by using the accounts of witnesses. By virtue of being excluded from this all-important legal knowledge and experience, Catherine was also excluded from understanding the precise ways in which lawyers typically succeed within the process of cross-examination. Rather than relying upon these capitals as a means of exposing weaknesses in her ex-partner's case, Catherine was only able to repeat parts of the hearing, and unable to use this process as a means of otherwise influencing the hearing. Additionally, LIPs who had difficulty posing questions like Catherine, did attempt to undertake cross-examination in a goal-oriented way – by pulling out the 'important' bits of a case, they attempted to reiterate their argument and work towards a conclusion which portrayed them in a better light than their ex-partner. Importantly, the requirements of this process, as well as the approaches that LIPs may take when attempting to cross-examine, may therefore in practice also perpetuate the adversarial attitudes and interpretations discussed so far in this chapter.

In terms of answering questions from the other side during cross-examination, six LIPs were cross-examined by opposing lawyers in semi-represented hearings.

All six explained that they struggled to answer questions for the purpose of defending their case and reinforcing their evidence.

> The last final hearing just happened so quick, and no one told me what was going to happen, like the whole format I just didn't know what to expect. I wasn't told beforehand that I would go into the box. If I knew, I would've sat there with my brain and not gone to pieces at the questions.
>
> **Edie**

> I was there giving evidence, and it was difficult because I didn't think about my answers, I was just honest in saying what I thought of him. But looking back now, if I had said it in a different way, that would have been fine. But because I was under pressure and scared, I didn't think then about how my answer would be used, and then it was all used against me.
>
> **Kate**

While existing literature focuses mainly on how effectively LIPs can make use of the questioning process, this finding allows an insight into how LIPs may perceive the answers that they give during this process. For instance, in reflecting on their experiences, both Edie and Kate felt that they would have been able to provide better answers if they had been able to access information about how the questioning format was going to work, or how their answers were going to be used by the other side.

In Corbett and Summerfield's (2017: 37) research, judges reflected upon the kinds of vulnerability that they felt were important and relevant to whether witnesses required special protections during the cross-examination process. Here, judges identified that learning difficulties can sometimes mean that a witness might need support – for instance, judges explained that they might remind a LIP to speak clearly, help them by breaking a question down to make it easier to understand, and taking breaks throughout the hearing. This is a positive indication that some judges may intervene to help some LIPs, and a suggestion that judicial understanding of vulnerability relating to these circumstances is broader than the narratives that have informed recent legal aid policy such as LASPO.

However, as discussed so far, effective cross-examination involves the use of specific capitals, including linguistic tactics, such as combining open and closed questions and employing pauses to emphasise particular aspects of the answers given. In the same way that LIPs struggled to make use of these tools during questioning due to the limited access and familiarity they have with this unique form of communication, they also appeared to struggle in predicting how lawyers would use these tools against them. Without access to legal forms of knowledge or the experience that is only available through legal education and training, LIPs are therefore also inevitably disadvantaged in their ability to *respond* to questions during the cross-examination process, because they may struggle to know what sort of answers will best support their case or at least prevent their cases from being undermined.

Kate spoke English as her second language. In giving 'honest' answers, Kate relied on familiar narratives and forms of expression when answering questions, in which she was limited not only to ordinary, non-specialist modes of conversation, but also excluded from the nuanced and complex ways in which lawyers are able to manipulate language and influence responses through the asymmetrical question-and-answer dynamic. This suggests that the current requirement for LIPs to answer questions without necessarily having had any prior guidance about the process, may disproportionately place individuals who do not speak English as a first language at a disadvantage.

Communicating via the cross-examination process is also particularly difficult for self-representing survivors of domestic abuse who are directed to participate in FFHs. Prior to the long-awaited implementation of the Domestic Abuse Act 2021, there were no specific provisions to prevent cross-examination between alleged perpetrators and victims of domestic abuse, even though this has long been statutorily prohibited in the criminal courts.[4] This means that mechanisms to prevent cross-examination by abusers have historically been limited to case management practices, spread across various practice directions and procedural rules.[5] Under these rules, judges are required to consider the potential vulnerability of parties and facilitate any measures that might support them to participate. This may include, for instance, special measures like screens or video links. They are also required to consider whether the questions to be put in cross-examination should be agreed in advance, and whether it would be appropriate for the questions to be put to the witness by the judge instead. However, despite these myriad guidance and procedural rules, judicial management of FFHs has always been inconsistent.

This consensus was reiterated by the experiences of the LIPs who spoke with me about their experiences of cross-examination in court before the Domestic Abuse Act 2021 came into force. Five LIPs who had made allegations of abuse explained that they were expected to cross-examine their perpetrators during hearings, and four were cross-examined by their perpetrators (one indirectly, three directly). Unsurprisingly, across all nine of these accounts, LIPs described the intimidation and fear that came with being re-exposed to their abusive ex-partners via the cross-examination process, even where special measures like screens had been made available. In addition, their accounts suggested that being forced to engage in cross-examination further impeded their ability to communicate within the court process. Traditionally, cross-examination is effectively executed through using closed or leading questions to coerce particular forms of responses from witnesses. This can be done by limiting or prescribing the possible responses a witness is able to give – similarly, by managing the speed of questions and length of pauses between questions, it is possible to emphasise certain aspects of the exchange and dramatically reinforce the flaws in their evidence and argument (Tkacukova 2016). However, in a dynamic where LIPs felt unsafe even sharing the same physical space as the other party, it was wholly unrealistic to expect them

[4] See further: ch 2, and judicial commentary in *Q v Q; Re B (A Child); Re C (A Child)* [2014] EWFC 31; *Re K and H (Children: Unrepresented Father: Cross-examination of Child)* [2015] EWFC 1 and [2015] EWCA Civ 543.

[5] See: PD12J; PD3AA; FPR3A.

to effectively test evidence using this style of communication. In this sense, the class-based and gendered inequalities discussed so far frequently intersected for victims who were expected to ask and answer questions in this format. Rather than an opportunity to strengthen their case and convey their points to the court, these nine LIPs conceived cross-examination as an experience to get through with as minimal emotional trauma as possible.

While the statutory ban on direct cross-examination provides welcome protection for victims who may find themselves self-representing in the court process, it should not be taken as a panacea for how abuse allegations are managed within the cross-examination process. In practice, there is still much work to do in terms of ensuring that cases involving allegations are actually directed to FFHs in the first place. It is also imperative that when cross-examination does occur, that judges do not disaggregate violent incidents from broader patterns of abuse when they arise during the questioning process (Barnett 2017). Finally, there is still a need to ensure that abuse established via the cross-examination process is genuinely considered relevant to child arrangements outcomes, rather than being extrapolated because it does not align with the 'pro contact' culture that has been found to frequently underpin decisions in the family justice system (Hunter et al. 2020; Barnett 2020). The prescribed format of asking and answering questions in the courtroom is likely to be an unfamiliar and intimidating means of communication for many LIPs, but is likely to be especially challenging for those contending with circumstances of abuse, who may struggle to convey important points and evidence through this process even when they are raised, given the deep-rooted cultural problems with the way that such allegations have historically been handled by the family court.

IV. Being Heard within the Family Court Process

So far, this chapter has explored three distinct ways in which LIPs are expected to convey information and contribute to their family court proceedings. Throughout each, I have emphasised that there are in fact a range of different barriers that are likely to prevent LIPs in various circumstances from effectively communicating with others in the family court. However, it would be overly simplistic to assume that LIPs are simply passive in response to these challenges. In practice, LIPs' experiences appeared to indicate that LIPs may consciously adapt their approach in order to be heard within the court process. For instance, those who anticipated difficulties communicating via verbal procedures like advocacy and cross examination frequently responded by channelling their efforts into communicating via their written paperwork. This suggests that LIPs may attempt to mitigate barriers to contributing to their proceedings by effectively trying to offset the disadvantages they face at different stages of the process. Unfortunately, this approach does not align with the procedural expectations of the court process, which dictate precise rules for how, when, and what parties can contribute to their hearings and communicate with others in proceedings. As a consequence, LIPs' attempts to convey information may be understood as disruptive to this traditional balance between verbal and written forms of communication, placing greater burdens on others in the process in a way that actually risked further impairing their chances of being heard within hearings.

For LIPs, these experiences frequently led to feelings of frustration. This was particularly true among the three LIPs who had university-level or professional qualifications, who each emphasised that communication with the court ought to have been manageable, given their levels of education and professional experience, but was in fact quite difficult.

> It's impossible to know what they wanna know. It was hard enough for me, a graduate, to try and get it right. Then, how does anybody who left school with no qualifications on their own get it right? And you know, they've lost their voice.
>
> **Catherine**

The concepts of capitals and field can be used to appreciate the different starting points that people occupy when they are required to establish their 'cultural competence' within a given context (Bourdieu 1984: 86–87). However, while symbolic capital such as written eloquence and a wide vocabulary may help LIPs to get as far as navigating paperwork and public speaking, this does not necessarily extend to understanding why and how the court process requires specific forms of communication at certain times. Rather, there is a limitation even to the value of symbolic capital when fields like law place the greatest value on capitals which are specific to that profession and environment. Specifically in relation to law, Bourdieu argued that cultural competence is demonstrated by drawing upon a range of internal rules and codes which are never explicitly recorded or acknowledged within the juridical field (1987: 806). This means that within this field, certain forms of language have greater meaning and value than others, and that there are specific ways of behaving and communicating which are perceived as authentic to law. However, the ability to access and use these understandings is restricted to those who have had the means and opportunity to accumulate these capitals through professional training and experience.

Education, and the symbolic capital that comes along with it, therefore does not appear to be a useful resource for the task of effectively conveying information during family court hearings. Despite Catherine having access to the advantages that come with symbolic forms of capital, such as professional experience of using paperwork, correspondence, and giving presentations, these advantages still could not fully substitute for the specific advantage that comes with being familiar with the complex and definitive modes of expression used in the legal context. This distinction between education and familiarity with the legal system was also an important conclusion drawn by Trinder et al. (2014: 24, 83) where researchers found that beyond the ability to navigate written and oral communication, there was no clear link between educational attainment and the ability to identify legally relevant issues, as even the highly educated and professional LIPs who participated in their study struggled to do so. The experiences of these LIPs therefore reiterate this finding and indicate that conveying information in this context is likely to endure as a problem for LIPs who are not legally trained.

The value of distinguishing between symbolic and field-specific capitals here, is that it is possible to appreciate that LIPs with access to higher education may have specific expectations about the barriers they are likely to face as a LIP. As Catherine explains, she entered the court process with specific expectations about the confidence and proficiency she would have in that space, and was left feeling frustrated and isolated when she found that, despite her skills and attributes, she struggled to be heard within her proceedings. Further, Catherine's question is extremely pertinent: how might LIPs respond when they do not carry this same sense of confidence or privilege into the court process? What might a LIP do if they anticipate disadvantage within the process, and want to ensure that they are heard within proceedings? A response which arose frequently during interviews, was that seven LIPs relied upon the services of McKenzie Friends who could support them to be assertive and confident within hearings. All seven of these LIPs explained that they had found a McKenzie Friend useful because of the barriers they faced otherwise in completing certain tasks on their own. Specifically, McKenzie Friends were described as important for helping them to either speak up in the courtroom or effectively prepare paperwork in advance of hearings. In practice, these McKenzie Friends were important resources through which these LIPs were able to overcome the constraints on communication that they experienced within the family court process, and ensure that they were heard within proceedings.

In chapter two, I explained that McKenzie Friends have always been an important resource for LIPs because they provide essential support by assisting with paperwork and providing emotional and practical support in the courtroom. McKenzie Friends have traditionally been friends, family or support workers, but as legal assistance became more limited in the decades leading up to LASPO, research has demonstrated that there has also been a gradual increase in 'professional' or 'fee-charging' McKenzie Friends, who may offer a variety of services beyond the traditional role of providing practical and emotional support in the courtroom (Moorhead and Sefton 2005: 57; Legal Services Consumer Panel 2014: 9; Trinder et al. 2014: 96; Smith et al. 2017: 5). Additionally, the role of McKenzie Friends has become increasingly more contentious after LASPO, because there is a suggestion that even greater numbers of LIPs will rely on McKenzie Friends for assistance in light of even more limited options for accessing advice and support, especially within child arrangements cases (Barry 2019: 70).

The complex debate surrounding McKenzie Friends hinges upon two powerful but opposing arguments. On one hand, the diminishing availability of legal aid and free advice means that the support that is provided by both free and professional McKenzie Friends may be vital for going at least some way to plugging some of the burgeoning gaps in advice and assistance, especially after LASPO (Barry 2019: 79). However, on the other hand, the services provided by McKenzie

Friends are unregulated and of variable and unpredictable quality (Legal Services Consumer Panel 2014: 21).[6] Further, as explored earlier in this chapter, there are a small minority of McKenzie Friends who may even attempt to pursue their own agendas or perpetuate damaging attitudes towards the family court through the cases of others, and it is inappropriate to expect LIPs to be able to distinguish between the form and quality of the services that McKenzie Friends may provide (Legal Services Consumer Panel 2014: 19; Barry 2019: 78).

Of the seven LIPs who relied upon McKenzie Friends, two were contending with mental health problems (Aly and Gary), one had learning difficulties (Grace), and four had a history of domestic abuse (Fiona, Sal, Beth, and Ikraa). In terms of the McKenzie Friends they relied upon, three were strangers who advertised their services online and charged fees, three were support workers, and one was a family member. Across their experiences, McKenzie Friends appeared to play an important role in mitigating the specific barriers that these LIPs faced to effective communication in the courtroom, both in respect of written paperwork and verbal procedures like advocacy. Instead of struggling to convey information through these different stages, these LIPs were able to draw upon the support of McKenzie Friends in order to maximise their opportunities to communicate.

First, those with mental health problems and learning difficulties attributed the value of their McKenzie Friends for helping them to express themselves in writing through their paperwork. As discussed earlier, Grace was contending with learning difficulties which meant that she needed extra time to process information. Within the court process, Grace was supported by her mother, who was treated as a McKenzie Friend for the purposes of providing Grace with essential support in the courtroom. However, her mother also assisted with all other preparations for court, and for all intents and purposes, they shared the experience of the court process together. Similarly, two other LIPs, Aly and Gary, had mental health problems which meant that they relied upon support workers to assist them with application forms and paperwork, in addition to attending hearings with them. Each of these three LIPs specified that they were particularly concerned about their ability to manage these preparatory stages, and that having McKenzie Friends was an important way of circumventing these difficulties.

Although this is only a small sample of LIPs who relied upon McKenzie Friends, this understanding indicates that there may be an important structural dimension to the ways that people may be motivated to seek help from McKenzie Friends. Research has already indicated the extent to which those living in poverty or with limited economic means also disproportionately contend with mental health problems, disabilities and learning difficulties (Joseph Rowntree 2022). In addition to limited access to economic resources, the strain of living on low wages and precarious employment is a major contributor to psychological stress and generally chaotic lifestyles. (Pleasence et al. 2006: 49). Given the way in which the

[6] But see: Smith et al. 2017: 18.

majority of people have been excluded from legal aid eligibility, these characteristics are likely to be even more prevalent among LIPs after LASPO. As discussed in chapter one, one implication of LASPO is that LIPs are likely to include even greater numbers of those on extremely low incomes, and those with mental health problems and learning difficulties (Trinder et al. 2014: 102–05). Further, the experience of self-representation itself can often exacerbate or trigger mental health issues, particularly given the costs and stress involved in going through the court process (Pleasence and Balmer 2014; Citizens Advice 2016: 16). Taken together, this is likely to mean that people in these or similar circumstances are likely to face even greater difficulties when it comes to completing court forms and preparing paperwork. For these individuals, McKenzie Friends are an essential resource of support for complying with the requirements to communicate certain aspects of their case via prescribed written formats. In particular, having a McKenzie Friend was useful for helping these LIPs to express themselves in writing, using confident language and diverse vocabularies, and ensuring that judges would be aware of all information perceived to be integral to their case.

The newly diverse range of circumstances in which people are now self-representing may therefore mean that there is an increased demand for McKenzie Friends, particularly from people with mental health problems and learning difficulties who may face specific difficulties during the preparatory stages of the court process. This reflects the findings of Smith et al. (2017: 35) who found that a minority of professional McKenzie Friends pitch their services at precisely these clients – those on low incomes, with mental health problems and several other intersecting problems. However, this in turn emphasises existing concerns about the potential consequences when individuals with mental health problems or learning difficulties instruct McKenzie Friends who provide agenda-driven or poor-quality support. As Barry (2019: 79) has indicated, inadequate support can have a detrimental impact on the mental health of clients. Therefore, it is possible that people with these characteristics are not only more likely to instruct McKenzie Friends, but are also more likely to be vulnerable to the potential dangers that come with the variable and unregulated services that McKenzie Friends may provide.

Second, in addition to the ways that people with mental health problems and learning difficulties may be motivated to rely on McKenzie Friends, the experiences of four LIPs who had experienced domestic abuse suggested that there may also be a gendered dimension to the use of McKenzie Friends to support communication in the family court.

> He helped me to submit all my paperwork, made loads of phone calls, made sure I had all the evidence I needed. He even spoke to the social worker for me when I couldn't stand her anymore.
>
> **Fiona**

> Take someone with you. Honestly, just take me – you'll be scared if it's your first go, but I'm not scared anymore. I've helped a couple of women at my group since then, and they just need someone to sit them down and tell them when to speak up and when to shut up.
>
> **Sal**

Here, Fiona describes the help she received from the McKenzie Friend that she came across within a public Facebook group. Before her hearings, he would support her in terms of completing paperwork, negotiating the conversations she was expected to have with family law professionals, and even contacting public offices in order to obtain documents required for the court bundle. For Fiona, her McKenzie Friend was a vital source of guidance, which was especially valuable because he provided her with continuous support which encompassed all of the tasks she was required to do before court and involved him taking over control of when and how these tasks needed to be completed. Most importantly, this meant she was able to avoid communicating directly with family law professionals and her ex-husband in advance of court hearings.

Fiona's experience reiterates the argument that, particularly after LASPO, some McKenzie Friends may stray into the realm of charging fees in exchange for more non-traditional services, such as those relating to advice-giving and acting as quasi-representatives during hearings (Legal Services Consumer Panel 2014: 26; Hunter 2017). It shows that McKenzie Friends may overstep the traditional boundaries of the McKenzie Friend model by providing services relating to all preparatory stages of the court process from application to negotiating with family law professionals outside of the courtroom. However, it also suggests that the use of professional McKenzie Friends may relate to broader, gendered experiences of inequality. Research has already highlighted the gendered ways in which fathers may provide assistance to other fathers through the capacity of McKenzie Friends, and how this often involved perpetuating negative attitudes towards mothers and the family court, to the detriment of the father involved in the case (Legal Services Consumer Panel 2014: 19; Barry 2019: 77). However, the experiences of these four LIPs suggest that there is also an importantly gendered dimension to the ways that mothers may rely on McKenzie Friends. Specifically, victims of abuse may perceive McKenzie Friends as not only beneficial, but essential for mitigating the difficulties that they expect to face when trying to communicate with others throughout the court process, especially when expected to communicate with an abusive ex-partner. In effect, having someone to communicate on their behalf meant that these interviewees were able to be more assertive in their dealings with the court and the other side than if they had been on their own.

Victims of domestic abuse frequently have limited access to economic and social capital after they leave abusive relationships, and are also disproportionately likely to be contending with other legal problems at the same time. They may also be at risk of further intimidation and control from perpetrators, especially when the court process itself requires them to communicate with each other. The Legal Services and Consumer Panel (2014: 19) have already indicated that LIPs may choose McKenzie Friends over lawyers in some circumstances because they are perceived to provide greater emotional support. This insight extends this to suggest that, in practice, McKenzie Friends who take control of contacting other parties and managing the preparatory stages of court hearings may be extremely important for victims who may otherwise struggle to convey information via the verbal procedures expected in the family court, and who may rely heavily on the emotional support of another person with the confidence to – as Sal says – encourage them to 'speak up' when necessary, or even speak on their behalf.

However, it is also possible to see how victims may face particular risks if they seek help with this from inappropriate sources. For instance, two LIPs who were self-representing against their abusive ex-partners paid for professional McKenzie Friends, and their experiences were indicative of the specific ways in which victims in particular may feel pressured into instructing professional McKenzie Friends in order to gain protection during their time in the process.

> My McKenzie [Friend] was late and then walked me to the cashpoint. I was scared that if I didn't give him the extra cash, he wouldn't come with me to the hearing, but I needed him there.
>
> **Beth**

The appeal of having someone to negotiate with other parties on their behalf and to shield them from their ex-partner during the process may mean that victims are at greater risk of exploitation, especially if they are contending with limited options after LASPO. Beth, for example, was also contending with simultaneous difficulties of gaining access to economic resources which were largely still controlled by her husband. With her limited finances, she instructed a McKenzie Friend who agreed to help her for a set fee. However, she explained that he would ask for additional money at crucial points, such as immediately before hearings, with the threat of withdrawing his support if she did not pay more than the original agreement.

While some fee-charging McKenzie Friends only ask for reasonable costs such as travel, others may charge unpredictable and unregulated amounts of money to support LIPs (Legal Services Consumer Panel 2014: 13–14; Smith et al. 2017: 25–26). Despite the increased level of need for advice and support after LASPO, there are still important apprehensions about the appropriateness of individuals charging potentially vulnerable LIPs for a range of services which may be of variable and unknown quality. If anything, the fact that LIPs are likely to have more limited options after LASPO exacerbates these concerns, because many people may have nowhere else to turn for help with specific aspects of the court process.

The consensus of existing literature is that these 'rogue'[7] McKenzie Friends constitute only a minority of those who advertise their services (Smith et al. 2017: 22). However, the suggestion that McKenzie Friends may be specifically sought out by victims of abuse could mean that they may be at particular risk of encountering these professionals. Additionally, for these LIPs, it may be more complicated than simply being able to distinguish between the quality of the services provided by McKenzie Friends. Beth was aware that her McKenzie Friend was exploiting her

[7] This term is often used to describe professionals who 'unscrupulously exploit clients for personal gain, or otherwise engage in wholly inappropriate conduct'. See: Smith et al. 2017: 21.

financially, but her need to avoid facing her perpetrator alone was so significant that she felt she had no choice but to comply with his demands for extra money. McKenzie Friends may therefore be an important resource for mitigating the barriers that victims face when they try to contribute to their hearings. However, relying heavily on McKenzie Friends may also exacerbate these difficulties if the support they provide is not adequate or if they form part of the minority of professionals who may take advantage of LIPs in these circumstances.

An increasing reliance on McKenzie Friends may therefore be incredibly positive given the limitations of other resources, especially for those with mental health problems, learning difficulties, or circumstances of abuse, who may specifically struggle to contribute to the court process, due to the prescribed ways that they are expected to communicate at particular stages. As demonstrated by the experiences of LIPs discussed here, McKenzie Friends may provide an important resource for enabling LIPs to convey their points when they may otherwise have not been heard within proceedings. However, it is also important to appreciate that people in these circumstances may in turn be disproportionately at risk of accessing inappropriate or inaccurate support, if they are motivated to actively seek and provide support and advice from McKenzie Friends. This is likely to be even more complex after LASPO, with not only a diverse range of professional and free McKenzie Friends offering support to LIPs, but also a newly diverse range of LIPs with low incomes and higher proportions of mental health problems, learning difficulties, and domestic abuse. It is also likely to be even further complicated by the COVID-19 pandemic, which has invariably increased the significance of social media and the Internet as sources of information for LIPs, and the likelihood that they may seek assistance from McKenzie Friends in these online spaces (Tkacukova 2020). Nevertheless, these experiences are broadly indicative of how LIPs may respond in order to be heard within the family court process, and how the constraints of verbal and written procedures may operate to suppress LIPs' ability to contribute to hearings.

V. Changing the Conversation

The reality that LIPs experience barriers to contributing to the court process is far from surprising. The purpose of the legal process is to isolate relevant matters from complex family disputes, and to provide a means by which solutions can be reached in relation to those issues. The legitimacy and perceived fairness of those solutions rests upon the consistency of the method by which they are reached. However, it is impossible to maintain consistency in a context where the majority of cases involve LIPs. As many research studies have demonstrated, LIPs are frequently unable to translate their experiences into specialist or legal terms, and struggle to understand what information is required and when it should be volunteered. This can often lead to LIPs fostering feelings of frustration, when they are unable to communicate the parts that they feel to be important and are left with the impression that others in the court process do not value their contributions (Leader 2017: 144–45). Each court case that was described to me during interviews came with a chaotic and emotional context which had built up over several years before they began self-representing. In some interviews, these stories took hours to tell, and several breaks for cups of tea and tissues. When LIPs find themselves in the family justice system, they are faced with the task of extracting the legally relevant aspects of these experiences and translating their lives into stringently prescribed written and oral formats.

Nevertheless, it is not productive nor realistic to suggest that LIPs should be allowed to talk at length about their problems in the courtroom or produce entirely unregulated written accounts of their disputes. There are other family justice processes, such as mediation, which are more suited to helping parties to improve their communication and working through their issues together. The role of the court process is to provide a necessary safety net through which the family justice system can intervene to support those cases in which effective communication between parties is not possible or perhaps even unsafe. This means that court proceedings, to a degree, must always regulate the kinds of contributions that can be made to proceedings and govern the ways that court users communicate with each other, in order to ensure that appropriate outcomes are reached and that there is fairness and safety within proceedings.

There is, however, an important need to rethink the full-representation assumption that underpins communication within the family justice process. Prescribed oral and written procedures mean that many LIPs are faced with barriers to communicating even those aspects of their case that the court deems to be relevant, especially after LASPO where support is more limited, and LIPs are coming to court from a newly diverse range of circumstances. This not only undermines the value of those procedures, but also risks compounding negative perceptions of the justice system, where LIPs leave the court process feeling that they have been unable to contribute, that what they have said has been ignored, or that they had to 'fight' to be heard. As demonstrated throughout this chapter, many LIPs are not passive in their response to feeling excluded from court hearings. In practice, they are likely to respond in a variety of ways, depending on their circumstances. Some may channel their efforts into preparing extensive written bundles in order to allay their anxieties about not being able to speak up during oral procedures like advocacy and cross-examination. Others may conceptualise opportunities to speak in court as their chance to challenge the arguments of the other side and come out as the 'winner' in the eyes of the judge. Some may even draw upon the assistance of McKenzie Friends in order to ensure that they are heard within proceedings, which can either aid or impede these efforts, depending on the motivations and capabilities of those they rely upon. In each of these scenarios, the court process is undermined, because disruption of these oral and written procedures can impair the efforts of other professionals, and the further entrenchment of adversarial attitudes is unproductive for the objectives of reaching appropriate outcomes.

The ways in which people respond and react to legal authority are based significantly on their subjective assessments of how they are treated within legal processes. This in turn affects their willingness to accept the constraints of the law, as well as the perceived fairness of legal decisions (Tyler 2003: 283–84). It is therefore not only important to ensure that individual LIPs are able to contribute the information that is relevant to the outcomes of their cases, but also to ensure that LIPs feel that they have been listened to, even though they do not have a lawyer to speak on their behalf. Supporting LIPs to communicate effectively within court proceedings is therefore crucial for a sustainable family justice system. As others have already argued, experiences of alienation in the legal process can be mitigated when there is an open line of communication between LIPs and other court professionals (McKeever et al. 2021). The complexity of providing this support, however, lies in the fact that LIPs have a range of different support needs. This is even further complicated by the ways that communication requirements may be translated into virtual and hybrid formats as a consequence of the COVID-19 pandemic. As Rossner (2021) argues, while some elements of hearings have been transformed with the move towards remote hearings, there have nevertheless been concerted efforts among professionals to translate many of the rituals of the courtroom into virtual contexts. In reality, the more structured nature of video calls combined with a lack of non-verbal cues and interpersonal contact may only reiterate the procedural constraints on communication during the family court process.

There is no simple fix through which the requirements surrounding advocacy, paperwork, and cross-examination can be adapted in order to be accessible to lay court users. Rather, what is needed is a process that can be responsive and flexible to the diversity of circumstances in which LIPs may need to communicate. Most importantly, this requires the family justice system to shed the implicit expectation that parties come to court prepared to convey relevant information in particular formats at designated times, and instead start to reconsider how the process may properly start to account for the different kinds of court users that are relying on the safety net of the family justice system.

6

Finding a Role in the Family Justice System

The lack of a clearly defined and legitimate role for LIPs lies at the root of almost all of the experiences explored so far throughout this book. The full-representation assumption that characterises the family court process starkly underpins the journey that LIPs take through the family justice system, by imposing explicit and implicit parameters around how LIPs can and should participate in their family court proceedings. As emphasised in earlier chapters, LIPs are required to orient themselves within a complex and sometimes unspoken framework of rules and norms which have been designed with lawyers in mind. In response, some LIPs may try to forge a role for themselves within their court proceedings by attempting to navigate these rules with varying degrees of success. Others may attempt to find a role for themselves by trying to evade or work around these constraints, by trying to maximise their efforts in some stages of the process in order to offset the disadvantages they face in other stages.

The effectiveness of these efforts is in part down to the circumstances and resources of individual LIPs, with some LIPs being more able to draw upon privileged skills and knowledge necessary for either navigating prescribed rules or identifying margins of flexibility within them. However, the ability to play a meaningful role within proceedings also hinges significantly on the relationships that LIPs have with other individuals in the family justice system. On one hand, productive and positive relationships with judges and opposing lawyers can help LIPs to play an active role in proceedings, such as through genuine opportunities (and encouragement) to communicate their needs, raise concerns, and to feel that both have been meaningfully addressed. On the other hand, unconstructive relationships characterised by misunderstandings or mistrust may lead LIPs to either constructing an adversarial role for themselves or resigning themselves to playing the role of passive observer within their own hearings.

The purpose of this chapter is to bring to the fore the implications of LIPs' omission from the family justice system. It explores the extent to which LIPs are able to play a meaningful role in the court process, reflects upon the kind of roles that LIPs do play within this process, and how this relates to the role that they are expected to play by others. It will do so by tracing the different kinds of relationships that LIPs may have with other participants, considering judges, legal professionals, and other LIPs in turn. It emphasises the crucial importance of each of these relationships for meaningful participation, before turning to consider what this means for how LIPs conceptualise their own role within the family justice system.

I. Relationships with Judges

Within the family court process, judges are of integral importance to the role that LIPs can play. From making directions for reasonable adjustments, to adapting the course and format of proceedings, the judge or panel of magistrates presiding over a family court case hold significant power in facilitating available support for LIPs and determining the environment in which a LIP may participate. However, the relationship between LIPs and judges is not only influenced by what judges can offer in terms of material assistance. Another significant – but more elusive – factor affecting these relationships is how LIPs perceive judges. For instance, in highlighting the potential implications of social and cultural norms for LIPs in chapter four, I drew upon Maxine's observation of judges' physical positioning in courtrooms. Here, it was noted that judges are often seated on elevated flooring, with a clearly demarcated section of the room, and that this physical manifestation of judges' seniority and power within this space may in practice evoke sentiments of disrespect and unfairness for LIPs. The perceptions and expectations that LIPs have of judges are therefore also crucial factors in defining the relationships that exist between them. This was evident across interviews, during which LIPs frequently raised dissatisfaction with their judges for not listening enough, not responding or helping them enough, or making directions that LIPs perceived to be against their interests. While it is inevitable that, to an extent, judges are described more negatively by those who were dissatisfied with their case outcomes,[1] during these conversations it was nevertheless possible to identify two main challenges that continuously underpinned difficult working relationships between judges and LIPs.

The first is that LIPs were often disappointed when judges did not arrive at hearings with a full and detailed understanding of the case and the information contained in the court bundle. This builds upon some of the problems explored in chapter five, in that this was perceived by LIPs to significantly affect their ability to contribute to proceedings, especially for those who faced more difficulty when faced with the task of speaking in court. The second is that LIPs were frequently mistrustful of judges when they observed them engaging in collegial or friendly interactions with opposing lawyers. This relates more broadly to the ways that unspoken social and cultural norms can appear mysterious and alienating to those

[1] This is an inevitable limitation of producing accounts based on retrospective experiences of the court process. Feminist research in particular is highly attuned to the ways that participants' perspectives, views, and understandings are invariably influenced by subsequent events and even the social, psychological, and emotional process of describing experiences during interviews. See generally: Oakley 1990 and Wallbank 1995.

who are unfamiliar with the family justice system and exposes the potentially damaging consequences this may have for relationships between judges and LIPs.

Turning first to the matter of bundles, eight LIPs highlighted problems relating to effective communication with judges. Research has already indicated that positive experiences with judges tend to centre around respectful and proactive communication from judges (MacFarlane et al. 2013: 105–06; McKeever 2021). However, proactive communication was frequently hindered by limited capacity and time that judges have in the family court process. These LIPs reported that their judges were often unable to read entire court bundles in advance of each hearing, and instead relied upon parties to summarise case progress in oral submissions. This not only took LIPs by surprise, but also caused specific problems for those who struggled with advocacy and verbal forms of communication.

> When I first went, I was really impressed because I was like, 'wow, they read files that big?'. But now I understand they don't read them. They read the position statement and maybe the reference point referred to in the position statement but that's it. I presumed they'd be there every night reading the whole thing, because why would you not? You're deciding people's lives. If you're not going to do it properly, why do it? Go off and be a gardener. You're in a privileged position, you should understand that and read what you're meant to read, because not everyone can do it all for you in the courtroom.
>
> **Ama**

> We got clever with it by the end of it – we were concerned because we were seeing so many different judges and there was no continuity – we needed to get my point across, so the best way to do that was to write a personal statement before each hearing, and we'd give it to the usher to give to the judge. The thing is, you're supposed to give a copy to the other side too, but we didn't do that until we were all in the courtroom. We realised that the judges only had time to read a certain amount of information, so we wanted to make sure that our statement would be on the top, right? We got away with it most times, I think it was just one time that a judge had a go at us for not submitting papers properly.
>
> **Grace**

Throughout interviews, LIPs explained that judges were often strictly constrained by time, which resulted in frequent inconsistencies for LIPs either in terms of being assigned to various different judges. For these eight LIPs, an additional consequence of this was the fact that their judges often either had little or no opportunity to read these files at all before proceedings took place. For instance, Ama and Grace, who both attended several hearings over the course of their cases, explained that it was normal for them to attend hearings where judges had only been able to read the first few pages of the bundle in advance. This aligns with existing research, which has identified the greater amount of time that it takes judges to prepare for hearings if there are gaps in the bundles or they are not clearly organised (Trinder et al. 2014: 57–58, 69). However, this caused specific problems for LIPs who had difficulties presenting their cases verbally, because they were unable to rely on the court bundle as a means of conveying important information to judges.

In chapter five, I used ANT to explore how the court bundle plays a pivotal role in proceedings for those LIPs who struggle to present their points verbally during the court process. I argued that the court bundle was a material means of making a good impression on judges and establishing a good starting point for their hearing. Here, it is possible to build further upon this understanding by considering what happens when the court bundle is effectively removed from this equation. For instance, under a full-representation model, the burden is on legal representatives to arrive at hearings fully prepared and ready to brief the judge with relevant information if required. The court bundle, in this dynamic, becomes a material aid that can be referred to as necessary during the hearing, as well as a physical record of the events and information that preceded the hearing. When hearings involve LIPs, however, the court bundle plays a potentially far more significant role – not a supplementary aid for the hearing, but a vital means of communication. The time constraints and traditional practices that underpin the normal routines of judges therefore have specific consequences for the working relationships they may have with LIPs, because it is far more difficult for them to gain an accurate summary of the information contained in the bundle, and this potentially closes off an important means through which LIPs can actively contribute to their hearings.

While ANT is a useful analytical tool for tracing the way that this disrupts the courtroom dynamic, Bourdieusian theory can help us go further in terms of understanding the ways in which individuals may interpret and respond to their own experiences of disadvantage. As Bourdieu argues, fields are continually shaped by the actions of individuals within them. In other words, experiences of disadvantage are not passive – rather, individuals actively respond to their circumstances by drawing upon a range of different capitals in order to compete for value within a given context. For example, an interesting way in which Grace and her mother attempted to circumvent this problem, was to effectively disrupt the official process through which paperwork is submitted to judges, in order to ensure that she *was* able to convey some of her points in written format. This also raised an interesting difference between Grace and Ama's interpretation, which relates specifically to class. While Grace framed this as an obstacle of disadvantage that she sought to overcome even through illegitimate means, Ama blamed judges for placing her in this position of disadvantage. Ama was the only LIP interviewed who interpreted this as a matter of injustice, and perceived judges as unprofessional for not reading the court bundles. In doing so, she placed great emphasis on the relationship of responsibility that she felt judges held towards her within these hearings.

In terms of their backgrounds, Grace and Ama had quite different experiences of the family justice process. In her words, Ama had previously lived 'relatively comfortably' during her marriage but was rendered financially precarious due to her divorce and the financial abuse of her ex-husband. In contrast, Grace had spent her life so far living in precarious housing and work arrangements – which she partially attributed to her learning difficulties and caring responsibilities for her young child – and this was only exacerbated by the abusive behaviours of her ex-partner. There has been a great deal of sociological research on the ways in which experiences of class can mean that some individuals feel entitled to assistance and help throughout their interactions with society, and others do not expect this support. Skeggs (2004: 177), for example, uses Bourdieusian theory to explain that:

> '… the entitlement and access to the resources for making a self with value are central to how the middle-class is formed … but this is also about exclusion from the ability to [propertise] cultural resources; from access to the very resources for making the 'subject with value'.'

Here, Skeggs explains that a sense of entitlement to use particular resources in order to gain recognition and value within a context like the legal system, is often unique to those who have more privileged experiences of society. Further, she explains that this distinction is inherently underpinned by issues of access to those resources – in other words, the ability to 'propertise' these resources and feel entitled to use them, is well beyond the reach of those who are unable to access these resources in the first place. In terms of the different ways in which Ama and Grace interpreted their similar experiences of disadvantage, it is possible that Ama's sense of injustice at judges not reading bundles may be related to her previous experiences of being able to access and use the resources she is formally entitled to. While Grace also had these formal entitlements, these different interpretations may suggest that LIPs from disadvantaged socio-economic backgrounds do not feel entitled or able to expect particular standards of the family justice system or conceive their relationships with judges as ones characterised by duty and responsibility.

Taking all of this together, the experiences of these eight LIPs suggest that the ways court bundles are managed can have significant consequences for the potential relationship between judges and LIPs. In a practical sense, judges being unable to read court bundles has the potential effect of closing off a vital means of communication for those LIPs who may already be trying to work around family court procedure. More broadly, the commonly accepted practice of asking parties to summarise information already in the court bundle may also risk perceptions of mistrust, disrespect, or even unprofessionalism among those LIPs who are unfamiliar with the legal context. Although these are just two possible interpretations, this indicates that clear communication is a centrally important foundation of productive and positive relationships between judges and LIPs. It also provides an insight into the potential fragility of these relationships when perceptions of judges are rooted so firmly in the kind of impression that they make on LIPs during their hearings.

The importance of these impressions was also an important dimension of the second challenge to productive and positive relationships between judges and LIPs. Rather than anything in particular that happened between judges and LIPs, this challenge instead related to the ways that judges interacted with others in the courtroom. Ten LIPs described experiences where they had watched their judge greet or chat to their opposing lawyer in a friendly or social way, and this almost always led LIPs to feel suspicious of judges and their supposed impartiality within proceedings. All ten reported that witnessing these informal interactions made them worry that their judges would demonstrate loyalty to lawyers as a result of their social and collegial relationships.

> So the barrister that my ex has is apparently known as the best-looking lawyer on the circuit. I know, it's bonkers – anyway, we were in one of the hearings and I could tell there was flirting going on between him and the female judge. It was subtle, but the way she was talking to him and smiling, it was flirty. And for me, it was like being at a party when the other people are talking, and you're trying to elbow in.
>
> **Ama**

> A part of it sticks, and makes me think, what if that is what happens? What if they do have some sort of loyalty to their own? Because you can see it – I work for the [National Health Service (NHS)] and if a staff member comes in, you X-Ray them first, because you want them to get back to their job. What if there's something similar in the law world, where, 'OK, he's one of us – let's look after him'?
>
> **Ikraa**

As explored throughout the previous two chapters, there are several problems that arise when a LIP self-represents against an opposing lawyer, because LIPs are often extremely conscious of the inequality of legal, procedural, or cultural knowledge that exists between them. In these semi-represented hearings, judges play a particularly important role in not only substantively addressing these disparities by making accommodations or adjustments to ensure LIPs are able to play a meaningful role, but also in *being seen to* address these disparities, so as to go some way towards allaying perceptions of unfairness, which can further alienate LIPs within the process.

For these LIPs, the social and professional relationships they perceived to exist between lawyers and judges was a major factor in how they perceived their own relationship with judges, and by extension, their ability to play an active role in their proceedings. For example, Ama expressed her concern that the social familiarity between her judge and the opposing lawyer in practice created yet another barrier for her to overcome during their hearings. LIPs were frequently concerned that lawyers might be able to gain even further advantages by capitalising upon their social connections with judges. This aligns with existing research which has already drawn attention to the ways that LIPs are sometimes suspicious of the independence of judges and lawyers and tend to interpret familiarity between professionals as an absence of impartiality and objectivity (Dewar et al. 2000: 51–59).

Bourdieusian theory has so far been used to explore the ways that LIPs may be excluded from participating in hearings due to their limited access to legal forms of cultural capital or the unequal distribution of symbolic capital within society. However, it is also useful for appreciating the role and significance of social forms of capital within the courtroom environment. Bourdieu's notion of social capital indicates that the social connections we have with others are dependent on the contexts in which we become socialised, and therefore the ability to draw on these social connections as resources is linked to the ways in which individuals are able to interact with each other in the legal context (2005: 211). As Ama and Ikraa both recognised, judges and lawyers often work in the same circuits, and the frequency with which judges and lawyers encounter each other means that some degree of professional familiarity or even friendship is likely to be inevitable. However, from their perspectives, this social familiarity was something that their opposing lawyers might be able to draw upon and use to their advantage during hearings. Most importantly, these social and professional connections are resources they were unable to access. For Ama, the effect of this informal, 'flirty' relationship was that participating in her hearing was akin to 'elbowing in' at a party. While it is not my intention here to suggest that lawyers and judges do not conduct themselves professionally within their working relationships, this does suggest that displays of informality or friendliness between judges and opposing lawyers may be interpreted by LIPs as another component of an already exclusionary environment. The consequences of this are likely to vary depending on the individual LIP and the journey they have taken through the court process, but there is a tangible risk that overt displays of social familiarity may contribute to a loss of confidence in both judge and the legal process for some LIPs.

In addition to the exclusionary effects of social relationships, these experiences also demonstrate concern that the professional status of lawyers would attract loyalty within the courtroom. For example, Ikraa's ex-husband was a practicing barrister, but he was appearing as a LIP in their child arrangements proceedings. In this context, Ikraa expressed a specific anxiety that judges would favour him during hearings as a result of his professional status. The collegial nature of workplace relationships is by no means unique to law – as Ikraa explains, she also held a sense of loyalty to her colleagues, even if she did not know them personally. However, her concern that these relationships were also present within law is attributable to the way in which this can have different consequences in different contexts. The ability to draw upon and gain advantages through social capital within the NHS, for example, is that nurses and doctors are given priority and members of the public may have to wait longer to be seen. However, this cultural practice would have a very different effect in the courtroom – if lawyers were indeed treated more favourably by judges, Ikraa would be directly disadvantaged in attempting to demonstrate that her proposed arrangements were more appropriate than her ex-husband's.

Social capital is not only a resource that can be exchanged for advantages within a familiar context. It is also a device through which particular individuals can exercise symbolic capital. For instance, through Bourdieusian theory, it is possible to appreciate that the interests, motivations and inclinations of individuals are often aligned with the other people, groups and institutions with whom they interact, and that this is why the powerful are able to 'omnivorously' accumulate different forms of capital and move between different fields with ease. In this sense, it is possible to understand that there are stark differences in the ways in which the justice system is experienced by those who are already attuned to working within other parts of the legal system or similar professional contexts.

From these ten LIPs it appears that a significant aspect of this is not just the unfamiliarity of the legal system, but the fact that they felt isolated as the only ones who experience court in this way. The distinction between the experiences of those who are familiar with court and those who are not, is widely discussed in previous research. In Rock's (1993) court ethnography, for instance, he distinguished between 'insiders' and 'outsiders' in order to demonstrate the very different ways in which those who frequently participate in the court environment experience the court process, in contrast to lay individuals, such as defendants, who only engage with the court process on single occasions. Similarly, returning to Galanter's (1974: 101, 110) analysis, we can appreciate that 'one-shotters' have a far more ad-hoc experience of law, and despite spending less time in the court process, have more at stake and therefore occupy a more precarious position within the court system. In drawing this distinction between herself and her ex-husband, Ikraa compared this to the way in which she would extend privileges to her colleagues at work, not due to their social familiarity, but because of the importance she attributed to their professional status. In this sense, in addition to the legal knowledge and experience that her ex-husband was able to use in the courtroom, Ikraa felt that as a result of his professional status, he would also be able to draw upon his professional status as a resource in order to convince the judge in their hearing. Without access to these social and symbolic resources, Ikraa perceived herself as alienated within the context of what she perceived to be relationships of loyalty and familiarity.

Importantly, judges are themselves implicated in both of the challenges that underpin their working relationship with LIPs. The inability to read bundles ahead of time can invariably be attributed to the usual working practices of the court system, combined with the increased constraints on court schedules, especially after LASPO. From the perspective of a LIP, however, it is the judges themselves who are arriving at court hearings without a full and detailed understanding of their case. Similarly, pre-existing relationships with professionals are an inevitable part of working in the family justice system, but for LIPs observing these interactions, this may be experienced as a form of social or professional alienation. These perceptions and dynamics therefore have potentially significant implications for the kinds of relationships that LIPs are able to develop with their judges. In practice, these are extremely fragile relationships, and as explored here, the full-representation assumptions that underpin the court process can operate to threaten and constrain the ways that judges and LIPs may build the trust, understanding and communication that is necessary to sustain this important relationship and ensure that LIPs are supported to have a meaningful role within proceedings.

II. Relationships with Opposing Lawyers

As explored so far in this book, LIPs frequently occupy a disjointed role in proceedings because they are expected to simultaneously play the roles of both client and lawyer. This becomes particularly apparent in semi-represented hearings, where LIPs are tasked with presenting their case in opposition to a lawyer who is professionally trained and familiar with the legal, procedural, social, and cultural rules that govern the family court process. The relationship between LIPs and opposing lawyers can have a significant impact on the role that they can play within semi-represented proceedings. On one hand, positive working relationships can be a major source of support for LIPs, because lawyers are already very experienced at offering guidance and explanations for lay participants by the nature of the work that they do for their own clients. On the other hand, the inequality of knowledge and familiarity that exists between LIPs and lawyers can be detrimental to these relationships. The advantages that lawyers have in this context, combined with the fact that they are acting for the other side, can mean that LIPs regard them with suspicion and mistrust (Leader 2017). In turn, the vast amount of additional work, disruption and difficulties associated with LIPs can lead to resentment among lawyers who are trying to maintain their obligations to both their clients and the broader justice system (Bevan 2013).

Working relationships between LIPs and lawyers are therefore just as fragile as those between LIPs and judges. However, the LIP lawyer relationship is characterised by distinct obstacles and challenges. This is because, under a full-representation model, lawyers are naturally positioned as LIPs' adversaries, rather than as potential sources of support or fellow collaborators to the court process. As such, during interviews, all 17 of the LIPs who had participated in semi-represented hearings described situations where they felt that their opposing lawyer had tried to take advantage of them in some way. The two most common experiences related, first, to lawyers using their knowledge and experience to find ways of minimising LIPs' opportunities to actively participate in hearings, and second, to the ways that lawyers were actually permitted and aided to exclude LIPs by judges.

In chapter four, I explored some of the ways that legal and procedural norms can operate as exclusionary forces within the court process, due to the way that LIPs are typically unfamiliar with the rules that govern both decisions in cases, as well as the process by which such decisions are reached. While that discussion was focused on the ways that LIPs may be disadvantaged by their lack of familiarity with the justice system, this issue also arose in relation to how lawyers may exploit the advantages that stem from this familiarity. For instance, nine LIPs felt that their opposing lawyers would actively use their legal knowledge and their understanding of court customs to try and deny LIPs opportunities to participate in their hearings.

This often began in court waiting rooms. Four LIPs reported that opposing lawyers approached them before hearings in order to try and pressure them into agreements before proceedings.

> The solicitor came back into the waiting area and tried to intimidate me. He had an order written up, and tried to force me to sign it, saying it was normal to do that. I found out later that it is normal for them to come and speak to you, but he was really quite nasty though, saying things like, 'you're not going to win this' and 'you're clearly not suitable to raise your son'. And I don't know what came over me, so I stood up and quite frankly told him where he could shove it!
>
> **Caroline**

> His barrister said we had to agree outside the room, and that if we agreed, the judge would help me better, so obviously I wanted that. But then when we got into the courtroom, the barrister changed completely – he told the judge – 'she agreed outside, we don't need to discuss this bit'.
>
> **Kate**

Of course, the family court process has always been strongly underpinned by a strong commitment to promoting compromise and agreement between parties as far as possible.[2] As part of this, where both parties are represented, it is common for the lawyers representing each side to approach each other in the waiting area before hearings to determine whether there are any elements of the hearing that can be negotiated or agreed upon in advance of going into the courtroom. In the absence of another legal representative, lawyers may instead approach LIPs in order to try and initiate these negotiations, which can be extremely helpful for helping to narrow down the issues to be discussed in the hearing. For example, in their observations, Trinder et al. (2014: 62–66) found that when opposing lawyers were able to communicate effectively with LIPs, this had a positive impact on their relationship throughout the process as well as on the conduct of the hearing itself, because they were able to establish a settlement-oriented environment from the beginning. As a result, a major benefit for most of the LIPs they observed was that they were not only enabled to participate in this informal component of the court process, but also enabled to participate more fully in the hearing that followed.

However, the consensus of existing literature is that this is often not possible. For instance, research has emphasised that LIPs tend to struggle to participate in pre-hearing negotiations, in that they will rarely initiate negotiations themselves, and often rebuff approaches from opposing representatives or refuse to engage in negotiations (Moorhead and Sefton 2005: 173; Trinder et al. 2014: 45, 64). This attitude often stems from a perception that opposing lawyers may be trying to take advantage of them, and they do not want to be forced into agreements (Lee and Tkacukova 2018). As Trinder et al. (2014: 49) explain, 'trust was … the crucial issue in the waiting room negotiation process'. This is also underpinned by evidence that

[2] Further enshrined in PD12B.

suggests many LIPs are unaware of the role that negotiation plays within disputes, nor of the cultural practice for lawyers to try and narrow issues down outside the courtroom (Moorhead and Sefton 2005: 173).

This second scenario appeared to be the case for these four LIPs. While it is not possible to determine the intention of the lawyers that Caroline and Kate described, their interpretations of these interactions suggest that whether LIPs dismiss lawyers may actually depend on the way in which they are approached. For instance, while both explained ways in which the lawyers told them that it was normal or helpful to discuss the issues of the case with them before they went into the courtroom, neither viewed this as an attempt to support their participation in the court process. Rather, they viewed these approaches as attempts to intimidate them and take advantage of their limited experience and familiarity with the court process.

As discussed so far, through a Bourdieusian lens, it is possible to understand that LIPs are continually disadvantaged as a result of their structural exclusion from specialist forms of juridical capital. The cultural practice of engaging in negotiations in the waiting area is therefore another way in which LIPs may be excluded from the benefits of this process, because they are unaware that this is a normal albeit unwritten part of court procedure. Further, it is important to appreciate the ways in which approaches by lawyers may be interpreted when LIPs are not aware of this stage of the process. For instance, in chapter five, I discussed the ways in which, due to an unawareness of the settlement ethos of family law, some LIPs may interpret advocacy as an adversarial process in which they need to assert their own cases and defend themselves against the words of the other party. Similarly, a consequence of lawyers attempting to negotiate may therefore be that pre-hearing negotiations can also perpetuate adversarial attitudes, and exacerbate the difficulties that LIPs experience at other stages of the process because they are unable to narrow down issues in a way that would assist their progress.

Bourdieu's habitus is additionally helpful for understanding the subjective ways in which individuals continually interpret their own position and the opportunities available to them when they are faced with a situation like this. For instance, Caroline strongly resisted her opposing lawyer's advances but explained that she did so because he was 'really quite nasty', in implying that she would not be successful in the forthcoming hearing. In contrast, Kate did not resist the possibility of agreement, due to being convinced that this would help her during the hearing. Without access to legal forms of knowledge, experience of the court process, or relevant legal advice, she was grateful for any assistance before going into the courtroom. Instead, however, the barrister used the fact that she had made some agreements as a means to shut down and minimise those discussions during proceedings. Both therefore had calculated responses to these interactions, but in different ways felt that lawyers had unfairly taken advantage of the inequality of knowledge and experience that existed between them in order to benefit the other party. Taken together, therefore, it is possible to understand how LIPs may not only be excluded from the knowledge and understanding required to participate in pre-hearing negotiations, but also may actively interpret the advances of lawyers as attempts to intimidate or sabotage their cases.

This has significant implications for considering how the family court process may need to adapt in the future. For instance, in guidance for lawyers facing LIPs lawyers are advised to take extra care in terms of communicating clearly and avoiding 'inflammatory words or phrases', which may cause LIPs to feel 'further intimidated and antagonised' (The Bar Council, CILEx and the Law Society 2015: 6). While this guidance is useful, it does not make clear that the participation of LIPs may in practice entirely depend upon the sensitivity and tact of lawyers attempting to initiate negotiations. The way in which the court process continues to rely on lawyers to extend this assistance is additionally problematic, because it does not consider the ways in which LIPs may no longer have access to legal advice or guidance, especially after LASPO. In the absence of this support, many LIPs may draw upon other sources of help like social media and professional McKenzie Friends. As a result, many may already be predisposed to holding adversarial attitudes or suspicion of legal professionals as a result of the advice they receive from these sources. However, this should not be taken to mean that LIPs are not interested in settling or narrowing down aspects of the case. For instance, more than half (55 per cent) of the LIPs who responded to Lee and Tkacukova's (2018) survey stated that they would have preferred to settle outside of court if possible, but at the same time, the majority of respondents were suspicious of legal representatives who were representing the other party. Additionally, when LIPs respond in this way, it is likely to inhibit their ability to settle within court proceedings, because as McKeever et al. (2018: 119–20) note, these reactions cause lawyers to be less willing to try and engage with them before hearings in the first place.

These challenges were not restricted to the waiting room. Rather, seven LIPs described experiences where they felt that the opposing lawyer unfairly used legal forms of knowledge, such as case law and statutes, in order to take advantage of them during hearings.

> His barrister referred to a case – but he hadn't explained anything about it in his position statement, so the judge told him off, and [the barrister] went to print a copy of the case off for me and asked the judge to call a 20-minute break so I could get up to speed. But I'd never read a case before, how was I supposed to 'get up to speed' in 20 minutes? He completely took advantage of me and that was that for that hearing.
>
> **Ama**

As discussed in chapter four, it was common for LIPs to feel excluded from 'legal' conversations in which judges and lawyers used specialist terminology or negotiated aspects of relevant statute or case law. However, this exclusion was also experienced as a result of the ways that lawyers were able to frame hearings using their legal knowledge and professional skills. For instance, LIPs frequently felt that by keeping conversations focused on points of law, lawyers were able to minimise the opportunities for LIPs to speak, and thus exclude them from participating in important negotiations. From Ama's perspective, her opposing lawyer actively used his specialist knowledge in order to create an opportunity to take advantage of Ama's lack of experience with case law and legal principles. Without the support of a lawyer, Ama was not only unable to make use of this text but was also excluded from the discussions which subsequently took place.

Bourdieusian theory can also be used to appreciate how lawyers may be able to capitalise upon their specialist capitals to gain greater advantages within the legal context. Specifically, the ability to navigate a case report and understand a written judgment is dependent upon both specialist and symbolic skills, including the legal reasoning that is mastered through professional legal education, as well as wider privileges that enable individuals to engage confidently with complex, formal texts. As anyone who has ever taught a class of first-time law students can attest, it often takes a great deal of practice before one is able to confidently read a judgment, understand the reasoning, and extract relevant principles. Judgments themselves are a form of 'story-telling, [which] is made to function as argument' (Rackley 2010: 46). They contain a range of different 'rhetorical and literary techniques' that demonstrate the reasoning process through which a particular decision is reached. Rackley explains that while some well-written judgments include 'short sentences, plain language and clear reasoning to communicate [their] outcome', many badly written judgments are 'long, rambling, impenetrable and obfuscatory texts' (2010: 47). Further, the task of decoding a judgment – whether written well or badly – hinges not only on the ability to comprehend the style and forms of language used, but also to track backwards through these narratives in order to identify particular aspects of the judgment which are binding and relevant to their case. Even from the perspective of lawyers, therefore, judgments can vary in terms of their accessibility.

While Bourdieusian theory is useful for tracing how inequality may manifest in the courtroom, this can be reinforced by using ANT to more closely examine what this means for relationships between LIPs and lawyers. In other words, by looking at the way in which individuals behave during court hearings, it is possible to see that in addition to some actors having greater advantages than others, those advantages may also enable actors to manipulate others in order to further their position within this unequal network. For example, In Ama's case, rather than translating the principle of the case into lay terms for Ama as he was expected to by the judge, the lawyer instead suggested to the court that it would be enough to give her the opportunity to read the case, which led the other actors in the hearing to continue without due consideration to the difficulties she would encounter in doing so. In terms of how this interaction was interpreted, therefore, Ama did not attribute this exclusion to the organisation of the process, but rather to the lawyer's ability to make use of his advantages as a means of effectively preventing Ama from participating in the hearing. This highlights a specific way in which these interviewees experienced disadvantage and vulnerability within hearings – not simply as a case of lawyers having *more advantages* within hearings, but as a process through which they felt actively *dis*advantaged by the unfair ways in which legal professionals used their training and experience against LIPs.

The inequality that is inherent in the LIP-lawyer relationship is something that judges work hard to mitigate. As explored earlier in this chapter, judges can play a crucial role in ensuring that LIPs feel able to play an active role by making accommodations and adjustments, and taking the time to make sure that everyone is on the same page at all times during hearings. However, these efforts do not always prove effective. Even putting aside the fact that judges do not typically have the time or capacity to take an inquisitorial approach in every case involving LIPs, LIPs are not a homogenous group with consistent support needs. As such, while judges may have some tried and tested methods of helping LIPs to participate in hearings, this is unlikely to work in every case. For example, when discussing the issues that they had with opposing lawyers, ten LIPs explained that their judges' actions had actually helped lawyers to take advantage of them in the ways described so far.

Traditionally, when both parties are represented, the applicant to proceedings is expected to give their submissions first. This provides a vital starting point for the hearing, because the applicant's lawyer will use this time to outline the key details of the application to be addressed. Following this, the respondent's lawyer is permitted to make their 'response' to these points. However, in cases where applicants are unrepresented, it is common for judges to take the initiative of reversing this order so that the lawyer representing the respondent speaks first. In doing so, the lawyer is able to summarise the case and provide vital structure to proceedings, and the LIP is better placed to respond to points rather than being expected to identify these issues for themselves (Moorhead and Sefton 2005: 181; McKeever et al. 2018: 117). However, while this practice is clearly well-intentioned, it may run the risk of further fracturing the relationship between LIPs and opposing lawyers.

> Normally, being a LIP, the judge explained to me that they start off by talking to the lawyer, so you can follow what they say and do, and I understand why that makes sense. I must admit though, that let them control the room. They take the conversation into a particular direction, then you find yourself defending what they've said, and you can't get all your points across, because they control the way the hearing goes.
>
> **John**

> His barrister always took over everything and stood up to talk about case law, and I know that's just what they do and I don't know anything about that – I'm very quiet anyway and don't like public speaking, but I suppose because I was self-representing he just stood up and made it all about that.
>
> **Beth**

In Moorhead and Sefton's (2005: 181) study, judges reported that commonly they 'relied on opponent lawyers to make the running in cases', as it was 'easier, and better just to ask the lawyer to summarise the situation'. This was also raised in Trinder et al.'s (2014: 62) findings, where in 'umbrella' semi-represented cases, hearings would progress more smoothly when opposing lawyers picked up more of the work for LIPs, and this prevented judges from having to alter their role within proceedings. Though the judges in Moorhead and Sefton's study did not view this as problematic, the researchers did express their own concern that this 'might give the impression to an unrepresented litigant that the hearing is an agenda set largely by the judge and the lawyer, even where the litigant is the person making the application'. Further, this may also lead to feelings that LIPs have not been able to say everything they wanted to say during the hearing, which can influence the perceived fairness of hearings (2005: 190).

The perspectives of these ten LIPs appears to support this concern. Although John appreciated that the lawyer going first provided structure to the hearing and made organisational sense, he felt that this approach allowed the lawyer to dictate the content of conversations that took place during proceedings. Further, as Beth's experience demonstrates, this enabled lawyers to ensure that this content was focused on law, but also had the effect of further silencing her important contributions within her hearing. As discussed earlier, the exclusion that LIPs may feel within court hearings becomes even more apparent when the dynamic is no longer two distinct sets of conversations – 'legal' and 'non-legal' – but rather one conversation where lawyers are using their resources to dictate the issues to be discussed, and LIPs are expected to respond to these issues whilst being limited in the specialist knowledge and vocabulary they can use to do so.

As noted in chapter three, Bourdieusian theory is useful for understanding how particular attributes become privileged within fields – namely, by the ability of the powerful to continually reiterate their own interests within those contexts. Success within the legal context, for example, relies upon the ability to use exclusive forms of communication which are often inaccessible to those without professional legal training. An important difference between these two experiences, however, was that while John wanted to steer the conversations in his hearings in such a way that he could convince the judge of his position, Beth was crucially hindered in her ability to focus discussions on the implications of her ex-partner's abuse. The issue is not only that LIPs may misunderstand the intentions behind this practice, but also that this practice may facilitate specific disadvantages for victims who are navigating intersecting experiences of class and gender based inequality. Without access to knowledge about the case law that her opposing barrister was using, or the ability to draw on similarly valued forms of knowledge, victims may feel unable to shift these discussions on to important safety concerns.

While it cannot be determined whether lawyers intended to have this impact on LIPs, the way in which LIPs perceived these interactions as attempts to take advantage of them before and during hearings is indicative of the difficulties they experienced in terms of participating in those proceedings. In addition to the ways in which this may affect perceptions of the family justice system and the legal profession, the failure of these working relationships exacerbates the difficulties that LIPs already face throughout the process. Opposing lawyers can – and in many cases, do – provide a vital source of support for LIPs. From taking on additional burdens relating to court paperwork and administration, to guiding LIPs through legal obstacles that may arise during the case, to working with LIPs to narrow down issues before a hearing, lawyers can often be a determining factor in ensuring that LIPs have a positive experience of the court process. However, this working relationship is also complex and extremely delicate. The lack of a clear role for LIPs means that there is a great deal of scope for misunderstandings, mistrust, and suspicion within these relationships. As demonstrated here, unproductive interactions with lawyers both in the waiting area and in the courtroom itself may pose significant detriments to LIPs' ability to play a role in the court process. Further, judges themselves may end up being implicated in these exchanges, which can have significant consequences for the relationships that LIPs have with both.

Deficiencies in either of these relationships poses organisational and practical problems for the court process and those working within it. Delays, additional work, and challenges to effective case management are all commonly cited consequences of LIPs failing to appreciate the ways that the family court works.[3] It is understandably tempting to attribute these problems to LIPs and their lack of understanding. However, it is important to note that LIPs are the ones who suffer the consequences when these working relationships fail. When LIPs perceive lawyers and judges as working against their interests, they are cut off from various forms of support and are further alienated within the process. This is indicative of a system that is ill-equipped to respond to the needs of its users, and a need for greater understanding about how these relationships can be cultivated so as to ensure that LIPs are able to play an active and meaningful role.

III. Relationships with Other LIPs

While the subject of lawyers frequently dominated conversations with most LIPs, the story was quite different for six LIPs who had only ever self-represented alongside another LIP in unrepresented hearings. As noted earlier, large-scale LIP studies have typically categorised unrepresented hearings as the most chaotic (Trinder et al. 2014: 64–66). This is unsurprising, given that in these hearings neither party has had the benefit of support to help to manage their expectations or narrow down issues, and there is no legal professional to offer guidance and structure within hearings themselves. In fact, many unrepresented cases may never reach resolutions without the support of at least one lawyer to sustain contact and communication between the parties and the court process (Trinder et al. 2014: 62).

Although there were only six LIPs who could share personal experience of unrepresented hearings, my conversations with them nevertheless indicated that the absence of an opposing lawyer may also make a difference to the kind of role that LIPs play. Such absence, for instance, meant that there was a great deal more emphasis on the relationships that LIPs had with their judges. In practice, judges were effectively forced to shoulder the burden of ensuring that a case did not fall

[3] See further discussion in ch 2.

apart. Without a lawyer to rely upon, judges tended to take a much more active role in proceedings, which frequently involved providing clear guidance, asking questions, and directly engaging with LIPs throughout the hearing. While clearly unsustainable within the current court process, this dynamic precluded many of the concerns about lawyers and their ability to take advantage of LIPs. Instead, unrepresented hearings came with their own unique dynamic, in which LIPs appeared to position themselves in competition with each other to gain the judge's favour or approval.

As the experiences and perceptions explored so far in this book have already demonstrated, it is short-sighted to assume that LIPs are usually passive within the court process. Rather, LIPs frequently anticipate barriers and disadvantage they may face at different stages, and often take action to try and mitigate this and secure the best position they can. However, these efforts often end up being inhibited by the constraints of the court process. The fact that unrepresented hearings tended to be less structured than semi-represented hearings therefore appeared to allow more scope for LIPs to gain concessions and flexibility which aided their participation. Across all six interviews, LIPs gave examples of interactions where they had managed to convince their judge to give them greater opportunities to participate.

> I found out what judge I was going to be in front of as well, so then I researched the judge, and I discovered about him – the first one, that he was all about his paperwork. He's published a paper about trial bundles and how to put them together, so I followed that, and the judge noticed and was impressed. Because I did it the way he liked, he was really good and didn't kick off when I added more pages to each bit, even when I brought them to court with me.
>
> **Sarah**

> I think I got away with saying quite a lot because we were so polite – I think that made the judges more patient with us. I was extremely respectful and polite, and I didn't go in there shouting my mouth off like most of the people you've probably spoken to. We always looked the part; we always shook hands with them when we went in and when we left. But that's the people we are. We're middle class. That stood me in good stead.
>
> **Grace**

Here, Sarah and Grace both explain how they gained extra opportunities to contribute to their hearings, such as being permitted to submit extra papers or say more during advocacy, and how they attributed this to the good impressions that they made on their judges. This approach has also been identified by other research, such as Leader's study (2017: 169), which also found evidence that LIPs may try to make good impressions on judges but argued that the effectiveness of this depends upon the approach taken by the judge in question and how they interpreted this behaviour.

By drawing on the experiences of these LIPs, it is possible to deepen this understanding by considering how these good impressions are inextricably related to broader structures of class. For instance, one of the fundamental propositions of Bourdieu's concept of field is that fields are made up of individuals who are constantly competing for recognition and value within that context. In terms of this competition, individuals are only able to draw upon and use capitals which they have access to – and therefore, those with access to valued capitals – such as the specifically legal capitals which are privileged within the court context – are among those with the most power to shape that field according to their own needs and attributes. While LIPs like Sarah and Grace were unable to draw on and make use of specialist juridical capitals that were typically employed by lawyers in semi-represented hearings, they were nevertheless attuned to the ways in which other capitals and attributes besides these were also symbolically privileged within the court context. For instance, the legal professionals who typically occupy these spaces have also undergone a significant amount of education and professional training. As such, attributes relating to those experiences, such as discipline, organisation, and respect for authority, are all also prominent features of the way that judges prefer people to behave in the court context.

Although LIPs may not have access to the capitals that arise from professional training, these qualities and attributes are capitals which may be relatable for some LIPs. Sarah, for example, was able to research the individual preferences of the judge she was due to face. By making sure that the judge noticed that she was organised and professional, Sarah was able to obtain a degree of advantage during her hearing, with her judge not only reading her bundle but also not penalising her for submitting extra paperwork at the last minute. As with several other LIPs, Sarah felt more able to present herself and her position on paper, so by gaining this concession she was able to effectively circumvent the disadvantage that many other LIPs experienced when their judges expected them to summarise their bundles verbally. Similarly, Grace drew on her own ideas about 'middle-class' behaviour and found that demonstrating attributes such as politeness and respectfulness allowed her greater opportunities to contribute to her hearing, because judges were more patient with her and allowed her further opportunities to speak out of turn. These concessions were a significant advantage for Grace because this enabled her – at least in part – to mitigate the specific challenges she experienced during advocacy because of her learning difficulties. As discussed earlier in this book, although Grace had assistance from her mother with other aspects of the process, the task of speaking in court was particularly difficult for her because of the additional time she required to digest information and formulate responses. The ability to present arguments verbally in more than one instance of speaking was therefore a major aid to her ability to consider things that she wanted to say and respond to things at later points in the hearing. Rather than being unable to communicate everything in one go, this adaptation was an important way in which she was enabled by some judges to contribute to her hearings and fully present her position.

These are just two examples of ways that LIPs attempted to portray themselves well during hearings, but by thinking about this through a Bourdieusian lens, it is possible to appreciate that there may in fact be a diverse range of other non-legal resources that LIPs may try to use to convince judges to give them extra help within their hearings. Further, these efforts may have greater efficacy in unrepresented hearings, where proceedings are generally less rigidly organised than those experienced by other LIPs and judges were forced to work much more closely with LIPs if cases are to progress. However, it is also important to consider the classed ways in which these non-legal resources are put to use, and the impact of this experience on the ways in which LIPs conceived their own positions within the court process. Namely, it was clear that LIPs' attempts to make good impressions on their judges were not simply a case of drawing on non-legal forms of capital, but often involved actively using these resources to distinguish themselves from other LIPs.

In addition to explaining that she demonstrated polite and respectful forms of behaviour, Grace also explained that she did *not* go into the courtroom 'shouting her mouth off'. Similarly, all six of the LIPs who took part in unrepresented hearings emphasised ways in which they attempted to stand out from other LIPs through their behaviour, appearance, or demeanour. For example, these LIPs would criticise other LIPs they had seen in the waiting room or faced in the courtroom by talking about the way they were dressed or the way they spoke to court staff. Through a Bourdieusian conception of class, it is possible to appreciate the ways in which individuals are always in a constant state of competition for value. In addition to the ways in which value is accrued through using certain privileged capitals, it is also possible to be *devalued* through the use of others. In addition to the challenges faced by LIPs when they could not use legal forms of knowledge which carry the most value within the justice system, LIPs therefore also seemed to face barriers when it came to *avoiding* particular capitals which would further disadvantage them in this context.

In this sense, it is useful to look at the ways in which LIPs are represented in the range of online resources and literature which has been created by the government, the justice system, and legal professionals. Many guides make practical suggestions as to how LIPs may behave respectfully and appropriately in hearings, such as to raise their hand when they wish to speak, rather than interrupt, to address judges politely by using formal titles, and to 'get organised!' or 'dress for success' (Bar Council 2013; AdviceNow 2020). This practical guidance is invaluable and essential for many LIPs, but it is also possible that LIPs may perceive judges to have certain ideas about who LIPs are, which are associated with working-class tropes, such as being loud, impolite, lazy, or informal. In his popular book, Jones (2012) discusses the ways in which caricatures of the working-class are commonly represented in modern British culture, and how these demeaning representations have perpetuated stereotypes about the working-class, as a collective who are characterised by attributes such as being lazy, violent, and uncivilised. The divisive impact of these stereotypes is explored differently in many contemporary analyses of class – for example, Wilkinson and Pickett (2010) explain that one of the key implications of stereotypes is to both create and entrench feelings of inferiority and superiority within society.

The family justice system itself is by no means immune to these conceptions of LIPs, although the judiciary is keen to minimise the impact of this. In the

Equal Treatment Bench Book (Judicial College 2021: 7), judges are warned that 'a thoughtless comment, throw away remark, unwise joke or even facial expression may confirm or create an impression of prejudice …'. Nevertheless, it is perhaps unsurprising that these LIPs perceived distinguishing themselves from these ideas as an important prerequisite to portraying themselves well in front of their judges.

Five of these six LIPs were mothers, and there appeared to be a particularly gendered dimension to their experiences of trying to gain concessions during hearings. For instance, they not only compared themselves to their self-representing ex-partners, but also to various new partners and girlfriends that accompanied the other party to hearings.

> I think there are other factors as well, like showing them you're serious. I think when you're going to court you have to remember you're going to a court. Smart black trousers, a grey jumper – they like quite dull colours. Normally I'd spike my hair as it's short, but I made sure I blew dry it flat and just sort of tucked it behind my ears. No jewellery, just little earrings. His new girlfriend, she's a big girl, in a skin-tight dress with a stone down the front of it, and she's got a very big bust, so you could sort of see cleavage and everything. I mean, as soon as she walked in, the judge looked very like, 'oh God', sort of thing! I do believe it does help, because you look sort of respectable, if you like.
>
> **Jacky**

Jacky, for example, placed great emphasis on the importance of demonstrating to her judge that she took her case seriously, and demonstrated this by drawing direct distinctions between herself and her ex-partner's new girlfriend. Despite his girlfriend not being a party to proceedings, Jacky believed that the way his girlfriend had presented herself would contribute to a bad impression of her ex-partner. Importantly, by *not* dressing in this way, Jacky felt that the difference between them reflected well on her. Ideas about what judges expect from LIPs, therefore, were inextricably bound up in notions of class, but also clearly intersected with ideas surrounding gender and professionalism.

In chapter three, I drew upon Sommerlad and Sanderson's (1998: 28–29, 37–38) use of Bourdieusian capital to explore the ways that women can be ascribed certain characteristics based on their gender which are then devalued within the juridical field. In their work, capitals associated with femininity or motherhood were ascribed to women by others in the field, and these were then undermined, misrecognised, and devalued in ways that those held by men were not. Within the context of the courtroom, therefore, it is possible that female-presenting LIPs are not only subject to gendered and cultural expectations of motherhood, but also specific and harmful standards of femininity. Most importantly, this may be central to the ways in which LIPs perceive their own position within proceedings and assess the opportunities available to them within the legal system. For example, when Jacky distinguished herself from her ex-partner's girlfriend, she drew on capitals and resources which related specifically to her performance of femininity – not just presenting herself physically in a way which she felt would make her look professional, but in a way that would make her seem more respectable than the other women in the room.

The notion of 'respectability' is most notably explored by Skeggs (1997), who emphasises the ways in which women's experiences of class cannot be detached from their experiences of gender. This suggests that in addition to competing for recognition with regard to symbolically privileged capitals such as politeness, organisation, and being smartly dressed, female-presenting LIPs have a unique experience of attempting to make positive impressions in the courtroom. This is because they are also always competing for value in terms of how judges perceive their physical appearance, and perceive judges to award concessions on the basis of their gendered respectability as well as their ability to emulate particular classed capitals. In practice, this means that even within unrepresented hearings, female-presenting LIPs may face greater obstacles to gaining concessions during hearings due to the ways they feel required to distinguish themselves from negative tropes of both working-class status and their femininity. Importantly, Jacky achieved this by changing aspects of her presentation, such as her ordinarily spiked hair or more colourful clothes, in order to avoid negative connotations she perceived to be attached to these characteristics. In addition to the ways in which particular behaviours or attributes may make good impressions, Jacky's experience highlights the important way in which this in practice rests upon the ways in which the majority of LIPs are already vulnerable to making *bad* impressions – especially if they are women.

The contradictory insights provided by these LIPs suggest that whether lawyers are present or absent makes an enormous difference to how cases are able to proceed. While at least one lawyer remains, the court process can, to varying degrees, maintain a broad resemblance to the full-representation model. Without any lawyers at all, it is far more difficult for judges alone to manage hearings in a way that is explicitly focused on the relevant law, procedure and customs that typically structure proceedings. In some ways, this inadvertently created more positive experiences for some LIPs, involving a stronger and clearer line of communication with judges who were left with no other option but to take an active role in managing hearings. However, in other ways, this unstructured dynamic can make the processes of the family court even more mysterious and impenetrable to LIPs. Although perceptions of the court process were far less defined by the aforementioned imbalances of knowledge and experience between LIPs and legal professionals, the process was nevertheless perceived as a competitive environment in which LIPs pitched themselves against one another and tried to set themselves apart in the eyes of their judge. In other words, the rules of the game in unrepresented hearings are less clear, and this can have significant implications for the kind of role that LIPs try to forge for themselves within proceedings.

IV. Finding a Role

At the beginning of this chapter, I emphasised that many of the problems that LIPs face within the family justice system stem from the fact that they lack a clearly defined role within proceedings. Instead, LIPs have typically had to make do with occupying the margins and the gaps within the justice system, sometimes treated as lay participants akin to witnesses or represented clients, and at other times, expected to straddle the simultaneous positions of both lawyer and client. The way that this role plays out in practice depends upon several factors including the circumstances, resources, and specific characteristics of the person who finds themselves in court as a LIP, as well as the scope for flexibility that exists with their hearings. Some LIPs may draw upon available support from their judges or opposing lawyers in an effort to anticipate and comply with the traditional rules and customs of the court process. Others may eschew this support and try to forge their own role by using other methods to gain concessions or additional opportunities within hearings. The task of finding a role within proceedings, therefore, crucially hinges upon the kinds of relationships that LIPs can establish with the judges, lawyers, and other LIPs that they encounter within their proceedings.

However, unravelling the specific dynamics that inform these relationships is far from simple. As explored throughout this chapter, each of these relationships comes with a unique set of expectations and perceptions. While both judges and lawyers hold obligations to the court process and can offer potentially vital forms of support to LIPs, it is rare for them to both be regarded in this way. Although judges may be conceptualised as a potential source of help and support, lawyers are often associated with mistrust. At the same time, both are vulnerable to perceptions of unprofessionalism or elitism. The ways that these relationships manifest within the courtroom can also be determined by the ways that LIPs relate to other LIPs, especially within unrepresented hearings where there are no lawyers at all to provide structure and focus to hearings, and proceedings may descend into a direct competition for judges' favour. Further, the precise format and nature of each of these relationships is likely to be even more complicated after LASPO, given the ever more diverse range of circumstances in which people are forced to rely on the safety net provided by the family court.

What can be clearly understood, however, is that these different relationships, whatever format they take, are the conduits through which LIPs may meaningfully participate in their own proceedings. The significance of meaningful participation has already been explored by others. For instance, McKeever (2021) has previously plotted LIPs' experiences of court hearings in Northern Ireland on a spectrum ranging from non-participatory experiences at one end, to tokenistic participation, to fully participative experiences at the other end. Non-participatory experiences may be situations where LIPs feel excluded, are expected to occupy a secondary status within hearings, and as such become unable or unwilling to engage with legal proceedings at all. Tokenistic experiences are those where support is provided, but is frequently partial, incomplete, or characterised by barriers. In contrast, fully participative experiences encompass meaningful engagement with others in the process, which involves support and encouragement to communicate, collaborate, and engage in the process as equals with an element of self-determination, within recognised limits.

While McKeever's spectrum provides an important way of distinguishing between positive and negative experiences of participation, it is also vital to acknowledge the complicated ways that each of these potential experiences are underpinned by the relationships that LIPs have with others in the court process, and the extent to which these dynamics operate to support or inhibit LIPs within proceedings. These relationships are informed and established through a complex web of misunderstandings, suspicion, and stereotypes. In other words, without a clearly defined role in the court process, LIPs are forced to negotiate their own functions within the court process, which may either accord with or subvert the expectations of other court users. In turn, this may position them as disruptive, litigious, or unreasonable, which can have a cyclical impact on their ability to foster positive working relationships and play a meaningful role in the court process.

7

Perceptions of Family Justice

LIPs' journeys through the family justice system are rarely consistent. As explored throughout this book, these journeys are unpredictably shaped by the various experiences that LIPs have of navigating the rules and norms that govern the family court process, of using different mechanisms to communicate and contribute to hearings, and of interacting with other court users during different stages of the process. In turn, each of these specific experiences and interactions has a cumulative effect on how LIPs perceive the family justice system as a whole. Of course, given the personal and emotional nature of family disputes, it is inevitable that individual perceptions of the system are likely to be heavily influenced by whether LIPs agree with the outcomes reached. However, this alone vastly oversimplifies how much there is to learn from LIPs' perceptions. Drawing together the different ways that LIPs view the family court process is a valuable opportunity to untangle the level of trust that LIPs feel they can place in the family justice system, and the extent to which LIPs recognise the family court as a legitimate means of obtaining resolutions to family problems.

The purpose of this chapter is to step back from the detail of LIPs' experiences and to consider more broadly how LIPs' journeys inform perceptions of family justice. It begins by examining the extent to which the process aligns with LIPs' expectations of the family court. It identifies and explores a common disconnect between LIPs' ideas about what the court process will be like and how it is experienced in practice, reflecting on how this operates to shape perceptions of the family justice system. The chapter then moves to explore some of the ways that LIPs understand the decisions which are reached through the court process. Here, it emphasises that although LIPs may have contradictory understandings of how judges come to their decisions, their perceptions of outcomes nevertheless stem from a deep-rooted sense of exclusion that underpins their time in the process. Finally, the chapter considers the broader implications of LIPs' perceptions by highlighting how individual negative perceptions and experiences of the court process may be circulated among others engaging with the family justice system, with potentially devastating consequences for public faith and the future efficacy of the family justice system.

I. The Expectation-Experience Disconnect

Although law is, in reality, an ever-present force that frames almost all of our day-to-day interactions, the power and mystery of the legal system lies in the way that it constructs and maintains specialist forms of knowledge and behaviour to govern formal interactions with law, such as court hearings (Ewick and Sibley 1998). As such, unless they have personal prior experience of the legal system, most lay individuals have very little to refer to when it comes to knowing what to expect when they go to the family court. Rather, ideas about what court hearings entail may be based on how the justice system has been represented in the media or in the experiences of others, which may in turn be drawn from different jurisdictions or different areas of law that each have their own cultural, procedural, and legal norms. This is further complicated, of course, by the fact that the family court process comprises several different types of hearings. From relatively short and informal directions hearings where judges review information and decide upon next steps, to more substantive FFHs and Final Hearings at which LIPs may be expected to give evidence or cross-examine other parties and witnesses, there are many different kinds of experiences that LIPs may not anticipate without prior experience or sufficient guidance. An important part of supporting LIPs to meaningfully engage in these hearings, therefore, is to ensure that they are equipped with an idea of what to expect each time that they come to court. This is especially important in the post-LASPO context, where it is increasingly likely that LIPs have had limited access to legal advice in advance of their hearings.

During interviews, there appeared to be a major disconnect between LIPs' expectations of what the family court would be like and how it was experienced in practice. For instance, 15 LIPs explained that on at least one occasion, they had arrived at court to find that the subject or format of their hearing was not that which they had prepared for.

> There's no organisation, not just from me but the courts themselves. There's missing paperwork, they don't make you aware of everything, there's delays. Sometimes you can turn up to a hearing and the judge wants to discuss something completely different to what you thought the hearing was meant to be.
>
> **Joan**

Studies have repeatedly identified that LIPs often arrive into the process without an understanding of what is required of them, and some in particular LIPs disproportionately struggle to complete tasks or participate effectively during hearings at every stage. These LIPs are sometimes categorised as 'vanquished' or 'out of their depth' (Hunter et al. 2002; Trinder et al. 2014: 65). However, this is even further complicated when the court process itself does not go to plan. Six of these 15 interviewees explained that the reason they experienced confusion in terms of their hearings was because they had simply never received crucial court documents in advance. Joan's hearings, for example, were frequently characterised by disorder and confusion because there was no one in the court process to check that she had all of the correct paperwork for the right type of hearing, and this led to delays and problems upon arrival at court on more than one occasion.

While a Bourdieusian lens has so far been useful for understanding the ways in which legal knowledge and professional training are important requirements for individual aspects of the court process, it can also be used to reflect upon the security that juridical capital provides during the broader court process. For example, experience of how the system works and familiarity with different hearing types means that lawyers instinctively know what to expect between hearings. Traditionally, represented individuals would therefore have the benefit of protection from court errors, because their lawyers would be able to draw upon this knowledge and experience in order to identify any abnormalities or problems that arose with regard to paperwork before they got to their court hearings. However, without this, LIPs are unlikely to be able to recognise when errors occur or when other parties are not following the normal conduct of proceedings. This aligns with evidence from other studies, such as Trinder et al. (2014: 31), where researchers found that some LIPs simply did not receive notices of their hearings because these were sent to the wrong address.

As discussed earlier, it has already been acknowledged that 'insiders' and 'outsiders' experience the court process differently as a result of their familiarity with the legal context. Ethnographic accounts have specifically explored the different ways in which legal professionals and defendants experience temporality within the crown court environment (Rock 1993). Insiders – professionals working within the system – experience their time in court in a cyclical manner, according to regular rhythms of hearings which begin and end with regularity. In contrast, outsiders – users of the system – experience their time in court in a linear sense, with a definitive beginning and ending. A consequence of this is that insiders are able to derive a sense of security and certainty from their experience of the court process due to the frequency with which they follow cases through the system, and the familiarity they have with each stage of the process as it is repeated in this cyclical manner. Outsiders, however, have experiences of court which are characterised by uncertainty, and face specific challenges when it comes to conceiving or envisaging forthcoming stages or the broader direction of cases beyond individual hearings (1993: 262). These different experiences reveal an inequality of access that insiders and outsiders have to the internal practices and routines of the family court process. As LIPs are going through the court process for the first time, and do not have the benefit of an 'insider' to identify any irregularities, it is inconceivable that LIPs will be able to recognise that papers have gone missing until they come face to face with the consequences of that error and arrive at court unprepared for the hearing.

As Trinder et al. (2014: 31) note, there is a tendency to assume that LIPs are being uncooperative, when they may simply not understand or even be aware of what is being required of them. While many of the delays and disruptions associated with semi-represented or unrepresented hearings are typically attributed to LIPs' misunderstanding of procedural requirements, it is important to also emphasise that these problems may also stem from mistakes made within the court process itself when it fails to equip LIPs with the guidance or support to pre-empt and prevent these errors. The court process continues to operate under the assumption that lawyers will be there to anticipate and resolve any errors. However, this is both inappropriate and ineffective in a post-LASPO context where the majority of cases now involve LIPs, who rarely come to court with clear expectations for how hearings should proceed.

The disconnect between expectation and experience was not only evident in situations where procedural errors occurred. Even when court hearings went entirely to plan, all 15 LIPs explained that they nevertheless struggled to predict either the type of hearing they were due to attend or the format that their hearing would take.

> Loads of times I got there, and you think you are all there to discuss one thing, but then you find that the judge is making a decision about something else you haven't thought about yet, and you're full-on expected to give evidence. So, you have to do it off the top of your head.
>
> **John**

> She said to us that we were breaking for lunch, and when we came back, she wanted our proposals [for a final hearing]. So, we went, and we only had an hour and 15 minutes to work out a proposal for permanent contact, and we had only expected it to be a directions hearing.
>
> **Grace**

Both Grace and John described occasions on which they had turned up to hearings expecting a standard directions hearing, but found themselves in a FFH and Final Hearing, respectively. Most studies have to date focused on emphasising how difficult it can be for LIPs to effectively prepare for court hearings, due to the complex and technical nature of legal paperwork or challenges surrounding court bundles. However, these challenges may be even further compounded by the fact that LIPs also frequently prepare for the *wrong type* of hearing. All 15 LIPs described situations where they had returned to court to find that the hearing was not what they had expected, with judges aiming to discuss matters that LIPs had not prepared for.

This suggests that unfamiliarity with the court process means that LIPs may not only struggle to identify errors within the usual process of the family court, but may also struggle to keep up with their case even as it moves linearly between the different stages of this process. Successfully navigating the process, therefore, even as an 'outsider' to the family justice system, requires LIPs to prepare for various kinds of hearing and to anticipate the different things that they will need to do at every stage. This, however, hinges entirely on LIPs having an understanding of the content and purpose of each hearing type, as well as the ways in which these hearings work together to progress cases through the family court process. Without this familiarity, LIPs frequently had to adjust their expectations on the spot and try their best to engage with hearings despite being unprepared. As John notes, the evidence he had to give during his FFH was 'off the top of his head', because he did not expect to engage in cross-examination that day.

So far, ANT has been useful for deconstructing stages of court hearings in order to reflect upon the specific requirements of each task and the unique barriers that may subsequently be faced by LIPs. With the same approach, it is also possible to deconstruct the family court process and consider the different court hearings that make up this process. Rather than a seamless journey through the family court, the family court process is a series of hearings which are deployed in a typically regular pattern. This process is adapted to the needs of different cases – for instance, where there is a particularly complex background to the case or there are significant difficulties drawing together this context, some parties will be asked to attend more directions hearings so that judges can ascertain more relevant information about their circumstances. During the earlier stages of the court process, judges may also order parties to attend a FFH in order to determine the truth of abuse accusations for the purposes of consideration in later hearings. Although not all cases do, some will also conclude in a final hearing, where agreement or compromise has not been possible earlier in the process.

Although the process is relatively adaptable to the case concerned, the different kinds of hearings are designed to contend with individual obstacles such as a need for further information or proof, or a failure to agree. Taken together, these different hearings are designed to contribute to the general trajectory of the family court process, which as a whole, is geared towards reaching resolutions. Although he did not appreciate it until after his case had concluded, the fact that John did not understand the role that his FFH had within the broader context of his journey through the family court process was therefore a significant barrier to his participation in his case as a whole. The outcomes of FFHs are crucial to the direction in which cases subsequently progress because they have a significant bearing on the kinds of issues and arguments used in later hearings and on the final form that any child arrangements may take. Yet, John explained that the evidence he was expected to provide and the significance that this evidence would have for the later stages of his case was something he had yet not thought about at the point of arriving for this hearing. As Trinder et al. (2014: 36) explain, the value of receiving legal advice specifically at an early stage in the court process is to at least make LIPs aware of the 'possible range of feasible outcomes'. However, this also suggests that in addition to specific difficulties that LIPs encounter in terms of the format of hearings, they may also be intellectually and practically excluded from the ways in which these hearings *fit together* to produce outcomes.

Grace's experience of being taken aback by a final hearing was slightly different, in that while the outcome of this hearing would not affect her subsequent experiences in the family court process, it would render all of her previous work and efforts redundant. The purpose of a Final Hearing is to end the court process and provide an ultimate outcome to the case through an adjudicated decision. Research consistently indicates that these hearings are much more common in cases where parties are unrepresented (Moorhead and Sefton 2005: 227; Trinder et al. 2014: 59). At this stage, there was a great deal of pressure on Grace, because without the ability to spend weeks prior to their court date preparing for a final hearing and attempting to reinforce her final proposals against what the other side might say, she was forced to write up her proposals in the court cafeteria. This further compounded the existing difficulties she experienced elsewhere in the process, because of the additional time she needed to process and respond to information. As discussed earlier, Grace managed to overcome some of the barriers she faced by relying upon her mother's support and investing a great deal of energy into her written preparations. Requiring LIPs in these circumstances to prepare arguments at short notice, especially in a stressful and emotionally charged environment, significantly exacerbates experiences of vulnerability that are not currently accounted for within the court process. Importantly, this also demonstrates the way in which the court process itself may fall short in terms of ensuring that individual LIPs are fully supported and enabled to participate in different kinds of hearings, especially in light of the diverse needs and circumstances which are likely to be even more common among those self-representing after LASPO.

These experiences also highlight the ways in which LIPs may not always experience their time in court in the linear manner that Rock (1993) argues is typical for 'outsiders' to the court process. In addition to the difficulties discussed so far in this book, the strained nature of the family justice system after LASPO may mean that LIPs themselves are more likely to experience isolation and confusion within the process without consistent and appropriate guidance. As a result, interviews with these 15 LIPs revealed that hearings were often experienced as unpredictable and erratic.

> It's like there are these rules and regulations that you have to follow whether you like it or not, and you have to bite the bullet and say, 'yes, sir; no, sir; three bags full, sir' for a bit. It's quite annoying and tiring – the women at the group I go to, we always use the term 'jumping through hoops'.
>
> **Sal**

> Family courts, when you've got no experience, are like a series of roundabouts. You go to your first roundabout and it's round in circles, and you go to your next roundabout if you're lucky, and then it's round and round again, and usually you end up back to the first roundabout.
>
> **Chris**

In particular, these 15 LIPs often struggled to comprehend the ways in which hearings were supposed to link to each other in terms of reaching a conclusion to their case. For example, although it was not a question specifically asked during interviews, both Sal and Chris' descriptions of the family court as a series of obstacles are revelatory of the non-linear ways in which some LIPs may experience the family court process without the guidance of a legal representative. Both Sal and Chris were contending with depression and dyslexia, which meant that they disproportionately experienced problems understanding court paperwork and preparing for each hearing. However, this was further compounded by the challenge of trying to understand the purpose of each court hearing or the relevance of these hearings to the final outcome they received. Instead, they described experiences of turning up at court without any expectation as to the content of their hearings.

This suggests that individuals who struggle with learning difficulties and mental health issues may be at disproportionate risk of perceiving the court process as something which happens *to* them, rather than something they are able to participate in. This view of the court process is, however, unlikely to be limited to LIPs with these characteristics and circumstances. One of the main challenges of undertaking interviews with LIPs was that in describing their experiences of the family court almost all had trouble telling their story from beginning to end. Rather, interviews would almost always focus on issues, rather than individual court hearings. While this posed challenges during interviews, it did also provide me with an insight into the confusing and senseless ways in which LIPs perceived their hearings to link together, and the ways in which they may often be intellectually excluded from the routines and patterns inherent in the experiences of those who are more familiar with the aims and format of proceedings.

Outside of the family justice system, ANT has been used in order to explain the ways in which legal contexts comprise non-human technicalities, such as legal texts (Riles 2000; Jacob 2017). Although these works reveal myriad objects and technicalities which combine to produce a legal context, one very significant technicality which frames the experiences that people have of law, is time (Grabham 2016: 386). Considering the family court process through a temporal lens is also useful in order to understand the consequences of LIPs experiencing their hearings in this fragmentary way. By approaching each hearing as a hoop to jump through, or a roundabout to navigate, Grace and Chris both conceived the process as something where they could only envisage the stage which was immediately next. Rather than viewing their current hearing as a stepping-stone towards subsequent hearings or a final outcome, their efforts and focus appeared to be restricted to getting through the challenge of the current hearing. Further, the conception of these stages as obstacles, rather than increments towards an ultimate outcome, further reiterates the perception that they are not active participants in this process – rather, someone or something else is setting down these obstacles. As Sal explains, to get through the process, she had to 'bite the bullet', and follow the rules and procedures laid down by the judges she perceived to be in control of her court experience.

The distance that Sal and Chris drew between themselves and the authority to influence the direction in which cases progress after each hearing, may therefore be indicative of the difficulties they had in making sense of their place in relation to the family court process. It also provides yet another illustration of the important disconnect that often exists between the expectations that LIPs have of the process and the reality that they experience when they arrive at court. Expectations often vary – some of the LIPs interviewed in MacFarlane et al.'s (2013: 8) study began court proceedings with a reasonable degree of confidence, whilst others began with trepidation. However, within a short time all became 'disillusioned, frustrated, and in some cases overwhelmed by the complexity of their case'. In contrast, Trinder et al. (2014: 79–80) found that in practice, many LIPs did not know what to expect or could not provide much detail about their prior expectations. To this end, the researchers suggested that LIPs may feel out of their depth before proceedings even begin. It is imperative, therefore, to retain critical attention on the various ways that the design and practices of the court process itself may play a significant role in compounding and exacerbating this disconnect between expectation and experience for LIPs in the family justice system.

II. Understanding Decisions and Outcomes

Given the barriers to effective communication and participation that LIPs face during their time in the family justice system, many of the professional apprehensions surrounding LIPs stem from concerns that a lack of legal representation may impede the capacity of the family court to reach appropriate decisions and outcomes. This is an important concern which cannot be understated. As explored throughout this book, the ability to ascertain all relevant information and determine suitable solutions is frequently dependent on judges and lawyers *adapting* the traditional processes of the family court. Without such adjustments, it would be extremely difficult for LIPs to contribute to the decision-making processes and, in turn, almost impossible for judges to have a full view of the facts and circumstances on which these decisions hinge so crucially.

This ad-hoc support and flexibility in response to LIPs clearly goes some way towards ensuring appropriateness of outcomes. Nevertheless, the fact that LIPs themselves do not have an explicitly defined role within these decision-making processes has a significant influence on how they come to understand those outcomes. Of course, regardless of representation status, any litigant's view of the family court is likely to be influenced by whether the decision reached aligns with their idea of what a good outcome might be. However, for LIPs, these views are bound up in several other factors, such as whether they feel that they have had adequate opportunities to get their points across during hearings, and whether they perceive others in the process to have been receptive and responsive to their contributions. Even in the most sensitively managed hearings, the very fact that their participation is dependent on others working to create space for them within proceedings may affect how decisions and outcomes are perceived. This is only likely to be compounded by the challenges discussed so far in this chapter, where LIPs may actually be taken aback by final hearings and feel that an outcome has suddenly been imposed unexpectedly.

During interviews, LIPs appeared to have contradictory understandings of how judges came to decisions depending on whether these decisions appeared to go in their favour. However, regardless of whether LIPs agreed with outcomes, perceptions appeared to be strongly shaped by earlier experiences of exclusion within the court process. For instance, nine LIPs described experiences of hearings where decisions appeared to go in their favour. Yet, this was frequently attributed to a matter of luck or chance rather than something they had been able to influence.

> When I accidentally said something good, the judge would nod and agree, and I'd think, 'you've saved yourself there' – and I would've done, by the scruff of my neck. It's like a game.

> In fact, no, it's like a game of chess, because no one normal understands how to play chess.
>
> **Gary**
>
> It's difficult because you trust the system, it's supposed to help you, so you trust it. And it isn't working. So, when you go to court, at the end of the day it's luck of the draw. It's a bit like a lottery, in fact, it's literally a lottery – of which judge you get, and if you say the right thing at the right time.
>
> **Grace**

Given the specialist nature of legal knowledge and the unfamiliarity of the legal process, it is unsurprising that LIPs may struggle to understand how and why decisions are made. Research has already extensively highlighted the ways that LIPs may have difficulty understanding what is happening during hearings and how outcomes are reached (Leader 2017: 145). For example, although Gary described instances in which he would contribute to the decision-making process, he attributed this success to accident.

Through the lens of ANT, court decisions may be understood as phenomena that arise from complex networks of human and non-human actors. For instance, when hearings proceed according to the traditional format of a full-representation model, decisions are reached through a clear linear process involving active contributions from representatives on both sides. This process begins with the presentation of arguments and evidence by each side, before both sets of submissions are considered by the judge, who makes a decision as to which side's arguments are most clearly aligned with governing legal principles. Under the core tenet of ANT, everything can simultaneously be understood as both an actor within a network, as well as a network in and of itself. Therefore, this linear process can be broken down and analysed at an even more granular scale. Doing so reveals that the efficacy of a representative's submissions in fact hinge upon their ability to successfully recruit and operationalise smaller, constituent elements which are helpful for influencing the ultimate outcome. These component parts include things like producing comprehensive and concise paperwork, effective oral advocacy, and formulating an argument that includes explicit references to governing legal principles. When successfully employed together, these components produce a convincing case which draws the judge towards a particular outcome.

When hearings involve LIPs, LIPs may also try to recruit these component parts to produce a convincing case. In fact, the court process dictates their participation in paperwork, advocacy and – if necessary – cross-examination. Further, when legal professionals work to include LIPs in hearings, this often involves helping and encouraging LIPs to use these components, as well as creating additional opportunities to use them. However, without corresponding understandings of *how* to use these components to influence outcomes, these efforts might be described as rather hollow in practice. In other words, the specialist nature of legal knowledge and governing principles means that LIPs are intellectually excluded from the basis on which the convincingness of their case is judged, which can in turn inhibit any efforts to meaningfully include them in decision-making processes.

For example, despite being required and encouraged to participate in all these aspects of the court process, Grace compared the decision-making process to a lottery – as something dictated entirely by luck or chance, rather than something that can be controlled or influenced through these mechanisms. Although similar, Gary's interpretation of this process was slightly different. Rather than viewing judges' decisions as purely random, he recognised that the decision-making process had defined rules, but that those rules were specifically inaccessible to him, as well as most others in his position.

These perceptions provide an important point of contrast between how LIPs may perceive their ability to contribute to court hearings and how they may perceive their ability to influence the *outcomes* of those hearings. As explored earlier, several LIPs employed a variety of different strategies, such as politeness, organisation, and physical presentation to try to maximise their opportunities to contribute to hearings. Through these strategies, LIPs were often able to submit additional written submissions, were permitted to speak for longer, or even more than once. However, without access to the legal principles which govern judges' decisions, these opportunities were restricted to increasing the quantity of what they could say during hearings, rather than being able to influence decisions specifically and purposefully. This meant that their chances of influencing decisions were resigned to the possibility that they might 'accidentally' do or say something convincing that judges would take note of during hearings. Among these nine LIPs, there was therefore a general acceptance that although a good impression would serve them well in terms of having the opportunity to have their voices heard during hearings, this is rarely enough to actually influence the decisions made by judges. Rather, when judges made decisions which went in LIPs' favour, this was because they had managed to strike lucky in saying something valuable during their contributions.

This understanding of decisions also manifested in the ways that LIPs behaved during hearings when they were perceived to be going well. Seven of these LIPs were reluctant to dispute points in hearings when they had already perceived themselves to have gained some advantage through luck or chance.

> I didn't get as much [contact] as I hoped for, because to be honest, I was so nervous. I just felt so nervous I didn't want to ask for any more because I was frightened that they might go, 'you're not having any of it'. If I had a solicitor, obviously I wouldn't have had that fear.
>
> **Jacky**

Three of these seven LIPs explained that often, they did not dispute points or argue further for fear of losing the position they had already managed to gain through the court process. For example, Jacky explained that during hearings, she feared that she would lose the amount of contact that the judge had already accepted she should have with her child. Where LIPs perceived decisions as based on luck, therefore, a consequence was the extent to which they were reluctant to push this luck. Without access to the logic of the decision-making process, or the ability to root her arguments in legal principles, Jacky and these other LIPs perceived any success in their hearings as ultimately insecure and fragile.

This highlights an important way in which exclusion from the decision-making process can manifest in experiences of vulnerability within the courtroom. Jacky specifically explained that a lawyer would have allayed this fear of losing what she had already gained. From her perspective, a lawyer would have been more secure in their attempts to negotiate a higher proportion of contact within a child arrangements order, because as a result of their legal training, they are able to use and develop the rationale on which that original level of contact has been granted. In addition to the ways in which legal representatives are able to draw upon training and experience in order to navigate processes like advocacy or cross-examination, therefore, they also provide an important resource through which lay individuals are able to influence the decisions made during hearings. Without an understanding of the rationale through which her judge would accept greater levels of contact, Jacky did not attempt to make additional requests in her hearing, because to do so without this support would have been to gamble the progress she had already made. As Leader (2017: 218) explains, an important consequence of being excluded from the logic of this decision-making process is that if LIPs do not understand why they have not achieved the outcomes they were expecting, they will inevitably respond with conspiracy, negative perceptions, or mistrust of the system. For LIPs who interpret decisions as a matter of luck or chance, therefore, it is possible that they will also be inhibited in subsequent hearings and conversations, because they are unable to repeat things that went well and may consider them arbitrary if they do not go the same way again.

This understanding of decisions may also have specifically gendered implications for victims of domestic abuse. Although these LIPs rarely perceived decisions as going in their favour, they were explicitly aware of how much worse their outcomes might have been, especially when they had been involuntarily drawn into the process by their ex-partner. During interviews, two LIPs referred to these ideas of luck and chance in weighing up their decision not to pursue allegations or raise important safety concerns during hearings brought against them by their ex-partner.

> When they were talking about my allegations of rape and [domestic violence], and they didn't believe my allegations, the judge made a really offensive off-hand comment, but I was so shocked at the time I didn't complain because I didn't want to rock the boat and risk getting an even worse outcome for my children or lose them completely.
>
> **Erica**

Here, Erica felt that losing favour with her judge might place her at risk of losing the established contact she already had with her children, despite the clear importance of the safeguarding issues she needed to raise. An important difference between Erica and Jacky, therefore, was that Erica's reluctance to push her luck during hearings was based on fears that doing so would result in unsafe arrangements for her children.

Importantly, this highlights a specific consequence that the exclusionary effects of the family court process may have for victims – that the family court process may not be viewed as a means of achieving appropriate outcomes, but rather a process through which protection is obtained on the basis of luck or chance. Existing literature already indicates that because of the damaging ways in which domestic abuse is constructed within the family court, women frequently feel pressured not to raise allegations of domestic abuse, because these allegations are often minimised as either personal hostility or simply as high conflict relationships (Birchall and Choudhry 2018). However, when this is coupled with a broader perception that the decision-making processes of hearings are already predicated upon luck or chance, this may mean that victims are even less likely to raise these issues. For instance, Erica felt unable to assert the important relevance of her abuse to the outcome which was eventually reached. Instead, her main objective in her hearing was simply to *not make things worse*. There is therefore a risk that when survivors in particular view the decision-making process as based on luck or chance, they may not wish to gamble their existing contact arrangements by raising important issues which are in fact crucially relevant to the legal principles which underpin the decision-making process.

Taken together, what this suggests is that even when hearings appeared to be going in their favour, or at least not as badly as they feared, some LIPs consciously remained silent during their proceedings due to concern about what they had to lose. The perception that success (or at least, not disaster) is attributable to matters of luck and chance is concerning due to the ways that this may affect broader views about the efficacy of the family justice system, as well as the ways that it may influence future engagement with the legal system. Importantly, this indicates that the challenge of achieving appropriate outcomes in LIP hearings is markedly broader than simply giving LIPs ample opportunities to contribute. Rather, this needs to also incorporate an understanding of how and why LIPs may feel more or less able to make these contributions, and to consider how they may be empowered to dispute, correct, or question aspects of the decision-making process without being branded as disorderly, litigious disruptions to the court process.

While these nine LIPs drew upon experiences of hearings that appeared to go in their favour, the vast majority, 20, described hearings where the judge appeared to side with the other party. Within these hearings, there was a consensus that they were powerless to influence outcomes. Rather, LIPs described these decisions made by judges as pre-determined or inevitable.

> What the court want to see, is me kick off – so that I look like a nutter,[1] and they have a reason to side with [ex-partner]. Like, they've already made up their minds before they walk in, they're just looking for an excuse.
>
> **John**

Literature already indicates that LIPs struggle to comprehend the decision-making process of court hearings. Interviews with judges suggest that even when LIPs report that they understand court decisions, judges nevertheless suspect that these

[1] Informal British slang for a mad or eccentric person.

decisions are not fully understood (Moorhead and Sefton 2005: 166–67). However, the experiences of LIPs further elaborate this understanding by indicating that the difficulties that LIPs have understanding decisions often led them to 'fill in the gaps' for themselves. In other words, all 20 LIPs were convinced that judges had already made their decisions before entering the courtroom. Further, several speculated or assumed that these predetermined decisions had been made based on aspects of their personalities or backgrounds that judges had taken a disliking to.

This perception can be juxtaposed against the more positive experiences that some LIPs reported in terms of the benefits of making good impressions on judges. In contrast to those who were able to distinguish themselves from negative LIP tropes or stereotypes, some LIPs felt that judges decided against them because they were viewed in exactly this way. John was a father who had left the family home for several years and failed to support his children financially during his absence. He felt that, on paper, this background created an insurmountably negative impression of him which caused his judge to base their decision on their own personal opinions concerning his past behaviour, rather than his suitability as a parent, which he viewed as two distinct issues.[2] As a result, he perceived the decisions in his hearings to have been made before they had even taken place, and that any negative impressions he made in person would serve only to further justify those outcomes.

In the same way that some LIPs may draw upon privileged capitals to present themselves in a positive light to judges, this therefore suggests that some LIPs may recognise that they have qualities and characteristics which are actively devalued within the legal context. For example, as explored so far, a major aspect of LIPs being able to make a good impression on judges is to distinguish themselves from negative tropes that they believed to exist about LIPs – such as laziness, loudness, or being improperly dressed or ill-educated. John also appeared to draw on these ideas – for him, 'kicking off' and 'looking like a nutter' were examples of behaviour that would serve to justify the predetermined decisions of judges. Rather than simply being unable to gain advantages during hearings, therefore, John explained that from his perspective, a consequence of demonstrating capitals or characteristics which are actively devalued in the legal context, was to be excluded from the decision-making process entirely.

While personalities and personal impressions were frequently central to LIPs' perceptions of how judges made decisions, there was also a sense that decisions were pre-determined by the legal process itself.

> Each judge has a character just like everyone, we're all human. But I found that judges have a set pattern of how they are, so one will be black and white – 'I don't care what's happened, there's going to be this and this.' There will be judges who are empathetic but

[2] It should be noted that these are indeed often viewed as two distinct issues by legal professionals and judges when it comes to promoting contact with children, however John expected the opposite. See further: Barnett 2014.

> will still go with the decision they've already made, because they all decide before they walk into the courtroom.
>
> **Kate**

> It was a panel of magistrates, and they didn't listen to anything. It was like they were following a process and at the end of the process there was gonna be contact. They already had a decision in mind, they kind of listened but then made the decision they were gonna make anyway.
>
> **Fiona**

Kate and Fiona also interpreted the outcomes of their hearings as inevitable, but with a subtle difference – rather than judges making pre-emptive decisions about them based on their personalities or backgrounds, these decisions were pre-determined by the routines of the legal process itself. For instance, both Kate and Fiona referred to the idea of routine when describing the approaches taken by judges in making their decisions. In Kate's view, judges would disregard the context to the case and instead have a set order of considerations which they would repeat each time, and for Fiona, judges followed a process, through which there was a clear, predetermined outcome. Rather than personal impressions, therefore, for Kate and Fiona the process itself appeared to provide this justification for the decisions that had already been made by judges.

This is indicative of the ways that barriers faced within the court process can influence how outcomes are ultimately perceived. Importantly, this is more nuanced than litigants simply perceiving decisions as good or bad depending on whether they agree with the outcome. Rather, barriers to engaging fully with various routines within the court process can in turn mean that outcomes are also assumed to be determined by way of mystified routines and patterns. Both of these interpretations therefore suggest that an important consequence of the ways LIPs may struggle to participate is that it may lead them to perceive outcomes as detached from their contributions and their interests. In Tkacukova's (2016: 443) study, she explained that a common effect of LIPs not understanding the broader context of the legal system, was the perception that the court system was something that happened regardless of whether they contributed during hearings or not. Although Tkacukova's research concerns financial remedy proceedings, this perception of the court system also clearly permeated the experiences of these LIPs engaging in child arrangements disputes.

Most importantly, this perception paints a picture of a family justice system where LIPs' contributions are not relevant, necessary, or valued when it comes to making decisions, because those decisions are already determined by set patterns and routines. This raises serious implications for the effectiveness of the family court process for achieving resolutions in these cases. Tyler (1990: 154–60), for instance, has written extensively about the importance of procedural fairness to the perceived acceptability of decisions that are made within the legal system. It is not, he argues, simply a case of whether people believe that outcomes are fair, but whether the process by which those decisions have been made are perceived as fair.

Additionally, a key part of whether people perceive processes as fair, is whether they have been able to contribute to that decision-making process and whether the authority who makes those decisions is acting legitimately (Zimmerman and Tyler 2009). The judiciary have also expressed concern about the consequences of this perception – the Judicial College (2021: 7), for example, have called for judges to bear in mind that a general aim of court proceedings is to ensure that regardless of outcome, parties leave court 'with the sense that they have been listened to, and had a fair hearing'.

While it is inevitable that whether a LIP agrees with an outcome will always be a major factor in whether they leave the family justice system with a positive view of the process, the two contradictory interpretations of decisions explored here suggest that perceptions are also significantly shaped by the journey that they take through that process. Moreover, LIPs' exclusion from the logic and reasoning behind decision-making processes may lead them to assume or speculate alternative understandings of how judges come to decisions. Although LIPs may come to different conclusions about how decisions are made – some may believe decisions are random, others may assume there are covert procedures in place to determine outcomes – these perceptions are inextricably bound up in prior experiences of exclusion within the process. The potential implications of this are clear. Without the actual or perceived ability to meaningfully contribute to the decision-making process, case outcomes may range from unsatisfactory child arrangements which risk ending up as 'return' cases,[3] to risks of potentially unsafe arrangements in cases involving domestic abuse.[4] Concerningly, four LIPs who were left with unsafe ongoing arrangements explained that they would not return to court. Without appropriate support and intervention, the family justice system was no longer perceived by these LIPs as a realistic means of remedying arrangements due to the trauma they had experienced in attempting to use the court process. This raises crucial concerns about both the capacity of the court process to accommodate LIPs with various needs and circumstances, as well as the way in which barriers to participation may mean that the family justice system is no longer perceived as a means of obtaining support and assistance in relation to private family law problems.

III. A Cycle of Exclusion

So far, this chapter has demonstrated that LIPs' expectations and perceptions of the family court process, as well as the decisions reached, are heavily shaped by the ways that they experience exclusion and disadvantage throughout their journeys

[3] 'Return' cases are those in which families end up using the court process multiple times due to heavily entrenched conflict and complex circumstances. Approximately a quarter of family court cases are return cases. See: Cusworth 2021.

[4] Unsafe outcomes have commonly been identified in existing literature, see, eg: Birchall and Choudhry 2018; Lefevre and Damman 2019.

through the family justice system. The effects of these experiences are diverse and cumulative, with views and understandings of family justice likely to transform and fluctuate at various stages of the court process. Family justice professionals, academics, and policymakers all have a great deal more work to do to understand the specific and broader injustices that LIPs face during their time in the court process. However, it is also important to look beyond this process. In other words, when LIPs leave the family justice process, what are the implications of these perceptions and understandings? Whether satisfied with their outcomes or not, negative experiences of the court process along with assumptions about how this process works are not static or isolated to the individual. Rather, these may be circulated among others who may also be engaged with the family justice system, or among populations who are at risk of needing to rely on the court process. This, of course, has corresponding implications for how this system is perceived on a broader scale. This is particularly important given the frequency with which LIPs go on to help others going through the process, and the increasing prominence of informal online support.

Despite only 14 LIPs volunteering to be interviewed through social media, the vast majority, 20, reported that they relied upon social media as a source of information and support during their time in the process. For many LIPs, Facebook groups in particular provided an important source of community through which they could access continuous support from other people who understood what they were going through.

> Well I found my way onto a couple of websites – we call it the secret mummies group, but it's basically women in the same situation. And so, some advice I got from there. To be honest, I found the secret mummies group more helpful than the legal advice because it's ongoing.
>
> **Cheryl**

Within the fragmented context of advice and information that exists after LASPO, the task of accessing free legal advice is far from straightforward. While many advice services and law firms are doing their utmost to provide help to the huge numbers of LIPs who are ineligible for legal aid, this is often difficult to find and limited to isolated advice sessions rather than continuous support. The unique benefit of social media, therefore, is that it is a means of accessing support from other LIPs in a way that is often continuous and individualised. For example, even though Cheryl had been fortunate enough to access two free sessions of legal advice in her local area, she preferred to seek help from her Facebook group. This was because the 'mummies' in this group were present with Cheryl – albeit virtually – throughout her experience of the court process and provided ongoing support which extended beyond the provision of information and into the realms of emotional support, whereby Cheryl became integrated into a community of mothers contending with the same social, cultural and practical demands of being a young mother going through the family justice system.

An increased use of social media communities by LIPs may, in some ways, be incredibly positive considering the limited availability of advice. For instance, someone who has been through the process as a LIP before is likely to be able to demystify things like the administrative barriers of court forms, and LIPs in similar proceedings may be able to assist each other by sharing examples of how to set out court bundles or explaining some of the terminology that arises in court proceedings. However, given the difficulties that LIPs face when it comes to successfully navigating the legal, procedural and cultural rules of the process, a concern is that this reliance on the experiences of other LIPs may also perpetuate misunderstandings about the court process. If misunderstandings or inaccurate assumptions are disseminated within these communities, this may exacerbate the vulnerability, disadvantage, and exclusion that LIPs are already contending with.

In particular, this is likely to disproportionately affect those LIPs who are already facing significant barriers within the process. For instance, these Facebook communities were extremely important for LIPs who reported that they were representing themselves against an abusive ex-partner. These LIPs were often socially isolated and among those with the fewest resources. While private groups had the potential to facilitate safe spaces for victims, a particular concern that arose during interviews was the specific danger encountered by these LIPs while they sought assistance from others within larger, public support groups on Facebook.

> It's a space where women can feel safe, where they know they are always going to be believed. That's why I was so cautious about letting you into the group, because we all trust each other.
>
> **Erica**

> It's just control beyond belief, he's been monitoring my Facebook and the groups I use. He's looking not just at my posts but to see if I've commented on things as well. I know he is because there's no mutual friends, there's no reason for him to join these groups as he's represented and the resident parent, so it's just intrusive and harassing.
>
> **Edie**

Within public groups, Edie and three other LIPs explained that perpetrators were able to continue methods of intimidation. Women's Aid (2014) have already established the prevalence with which perpetrators are now able to use online tools such as social media in order to perpetuate ongoing abuse or stalk ex-partners even after those relationships have ended. However, the growing use of online communities potentially provides new opportunities for perpetrators to do this – through monitoring Edie's use of these support groups, her ex-partner was able to gain information about the arguments she was compiling for upcoming hearings, as well as gain insight into her general activity and routine offline. As part of this, she explained that he would occasionally send her threats or intimidating messages to suggest that he could use her online activity against her when they got to their court hearings. In terms of her ability to self-represent, this contributed to existing feelings of isolation and apprehension for upcoming hearings and reiterated the already inherent power imbalances she felt both within their relationship and within the court process as a whole.

In contrast, the group administered by Erica was private, in that mothers had to request to become members. Both this group and the secret Mummies group used by Cheryl were created and used with a definitively private intention – secure spaces free from perpetrators, in which victims could speak freely about their experiences and the emotional context to their case. In addition to preventing perpetrators' access to the private online groups, the sanctity of these spaces was also strongly maintained in response to other professionals and individuals who were involved with the family justice system. The privacy of these online groups was particularly important for two reasons. First, six LIPs explained that perpetrators had been able to use applications to draw them back into contact through the court process and felt that this was not effectively acknowledged by lawyers or those working within the family justice system. As discussed in chapter two, this is an enduring problem within the family court, and despite improvements to PD12J, has historically been insufficiently acknowledged by those working in the process (De Simone and Hunter 2009: 268; Birchall and Choudhry 2018: 42). Second, and relatedly, victims have also experienced continual difficulties establishing the relevance and significance of their experiences of abuse in their interactions with family law professionals, especially when this is constructed as oppositional to facilitating contact between their children and their fathers (Hunter and Barnett 2013; Barnett 2015). Reiterating this, all 12 victims who were interviewed for this research described conversations with either solicitors or CAFCASS where they felt that their allegations were not taken seriously.

Rather than simply a space to gain information, therefore, the use of social media may be a conscious response to the vulnerability that some LIPs experience within the court process itself. Importantly, as Cheryl explained, the kind of support that she perceived as most valuable was not the practical assistance she received but rather the emotional support from other mothers further on in the process. This indicates that LIPs may *choose* to rely on social media not only because it is easier to access, but rather because it is preferable and provides forms of support that are not available from official sources of help.

At this point, it is useful to trace the potential connections between negative experiences of the family court, perceptions of this process, and the kinds of ideas that may be circulated among these communities. As Tyler (1990: 20–39) argues, the reasons that people follow the law are not simply because they fear the consequences, but also because they are invested in the legitimacy and justness of the authority of law. In other words, negative experiences of the legal system can undermine the trust that people have within that system. Drawing this idea through, it is possible to appreciate two key implications of the relationship that currently exists between LIPs and the family justice system. First, there is a distinct possibility that victims in particular are likely to be drawn to these social media communities. Negative experiences with family justice professionals, combined with broader cultures of disbelief that frame how abuse is understood within society and the gendered experiences of navigating the legal system, are likely to position this group as one particularly disposed to relying on social media for support. For these LIPs in particular, social media may hold both essential benefits as well as concerning dangers. On one hand, social media communities may function as a refuge from perpetrators as well as professionals working within the justice system who have failed to respond appropriately to allegations and experiences of abuse. On the other hand, it may also function as yet another space in which victims are subject to continued methods of intimidation and control, which exacerbate the disadvantage they experience within the family court process.

Second, this suggests that social media is likely to be an increasingly significant, unregulated space through which LIPs may seek and circulate misunderstandings, assumptions, or negative experiences of the court process. The increasing prevalence of social media as a source of information is already emerging, with various research projects already established to consider the quality and efficacy of the assistance offered through Facebook groups, and this is only likely to be amplified by the COVID-19 pandemic (Tkacukova 2020; Smith 2019). In particular, studies have identified that social media and forums are spaces in which McKenzie Friends may advertise their free or fee-charging services to LIPs who are seeking help (Tkacukova 2020). A concern that characterises much of this literature is the unknowable extent to which McKenzie Friends may use these spaces to present themselves as professionals offering a legitimate service, thus potentially taking advantage of LIPs by charging for unqualified and potentially defective legal assistance. However, interviews with LIPs revealed that the relationship between social media and McKenzie Friends may in fact be more nuanced than simply being an arena in which individuals can advertise their services. For instance, as part of every interview, I concluded by asking LIPs what, if any, advice they would give to other people self-representing. Through this question, it became apparent that, after their case had concluded, four LIPs went on to act as McKenzie Friends for other mothers in their Facebook groups who were going through the court process. Far from being motivated by the possibility of collecting fees for their help, these LIPs were motivated solely by the idea of providing continuous, emotional support for others which extended beyond the confines of their online forum.

Literature has already indicated that a significant proportion of people go on to offer assistance as professional McKenzie Friends following their own negative experiences of the court process, and are genuinely motivated by a desire to help others, even if they do end up providing detrimental or inadequate support (Legal Services Consumer Panel 2014: 11–12; Smith et al. 2017: 19). The motivation for LIPs going on to offer help to other victims for free, however, appeared to hinge on specifically gendered experiences of the court process. Thinking about this through the theoretical framework, it is possible to appreciate that the desire to instruct a McKenzie Friend or even offer help to other LIPs in this capacity, may specifically relate to the gender-based disadvantage that mothers experience during the court process. In practice, this requires a degree of cultural familiarity, including an appreciation for the ways in which mothers and child contact are constructed within family proceedings, and how abuse is perceived and recognised by others within that process. The motivations for helping other LIPs through the process centred around a desire to emotionally prepare others for the reality that the court process operates differently for victims of abuse, and that victims are likely to face additional barriers within this environment.

What all of this suggests is that LIPs' journeys through the court process have wider significance beyond the individual litigants concerned. In reality, experiences of this process are likely to have significant ramifications for perceptions of family justice long after cases have concluded. The implications of these experiences are wide-ranging and multi-faceted. However, it is likely that social media communities and forums will play an increasingly central role in shaping the ways that LIPs come together to both understand their individual experiences as well as build a broader image of the family justice system. In many ways, online communities are likely to serve as a vital means of supporting others. However, these communities may also facilitate further exclusion and disadvantage for LIPs within the system if they are primed to arrive with adversarial, wary, or pessimistic attitudes about the process. Such attitudes may close off access to the potential mechanisms of support and flexibility that lawyers and judges are working to build into the current system. At worst, this may further reinforce existing stereotypes and tropes about LIPs as disruptive, litigious, uncooperative individuals, thus only bolstering the cycle of exclusion that underpins the journeys that LIPs take through this system.

IV. Family Justice Journeys

The complex journeys that LIPs take through the family court have a significant impact on how they come to view the family justice system. This chapter has stepped back from the specific ways in which LIPs may experience exclusion and disadvantage within the process in order to reflect more broadly upon the significance of these different journeys on broader perceptions about family justice. In doing so, I have emphasised that these perceptions extend far beyond the parameters of whether they agree with the outcomes reached. In reality, perceptions are varied and fluctuate during the process, but they are consistently underpinned by a perpetual sense that they are intruding into an otherwise ritualistic process. While the positive efforts of judges and lawyers to adjust and accommodate LIPs cannot be understated these efforts are, at all stages, impeded by the fact that LIPs do not automatically have an accepted role within hearings and are reliant on others to make space for them. This, in combination with their exclusion from specialist understandings about how the court process works or how different court hearings build towards the outcomes that are ultimately reached, fosters an environment in which LIPs are often left with little option but to be swept along with the court process.

It is imperative to recognise that although there are clear parallels between LIPs journeys there are no two journeys that are completely alike. For instance, this chapter has emphasised that many LIPs struggle to follow the nuances of the decision-making process and will often speculate or assume to fill in the gaps for themselves. The conclusions reached are likely to vary significantly and may be framed by a variety of factors including personal characteristics, individual circumstances, the interactions they have had with legal professionals, and the dynamics they have with the other party to their proceedings. While it is impossible to give a comprehensive view of what LIPs may think and feel about the court process, this chapter has argued that there is nevertheless important value in reflecting on what can be learned from these interpretations. This is because, at root, these perceptions are underpinned by the idea that LIPs are unable to influence decisions or meaningfully participate in the decision-making process.

This perception may, for many LIPs, be distinctly accurate – especially those who struggle to contribute to hearings or to work productively with the legal professions they face during their time in the process. However, regardless of accuracy, this perception is dangerous for family justice. It is dangerous because it is indicative of what I have termed a 'cycle of exclusion'. When perceived – and actual – exclusion from the motions of family justice is cyclical, this means that these negative encounters with the legal system will repeat time and time again and are no longer limited to the experiences of individual LIPs. Conceptualising barriers, problems, and disadvantage as isolated to individual injustices is short-sighted, especially given the increasing prominence of informal online support and the frequency with which LIPs go on to help others going through the process. The attitudes and understandings that LIPs have when they leave the family court process have never been more important for appreciating the ways that negative perceptions and experiences of the court process may be circulated among others engaging with the family justice system. In short, the sustainability of the system as a safety net for families may ultimately depend upon its ability to garner support from those that it has so far operated to systematically exclude.

8

Conclusion

This final chapter provides a reflection on the relationship between LIPs and the family justice system. Throughout this book, it has been possible to identify some of the common themes that characterise this relationship. At the same time, it has also been possible to expose and explore some of the conflicting ways that LIPs may understand their relationship with the legal system. In reality, this relationship is extremely complicated, with experiences and perceptions of family justice varying not only between LIPs and court professionals, but also between LIPs themselves, who are now coming to court in a vastly diverse range of circumstances. Here, I will attempt to draw together some of the defining features and challenges that are central to the relationship that LIPs currently have with the family justice system. I do this, not to provide a condemning account of the system that attempts to support LIPs, but with a view to highlighting the future possibilities for this relationship. While family justice may certainly be described as at breaking point, there are nevertheless opportunities to re-evaluate the role that LIPs play in this system, respond to the cycle of exclusion in which many LIPs are caught, and reaffirm the importance of the family court as a vital institution of family justice.

1. Litigants in Person and the Family Justice System

The relationship that LIPs have with the family justice system is inextricably shaped by its capacity to support them in reaching appropriate resolutions and meaningfully including them in the processes of family justice. As explored throughout the preceding chapters, this capacity is frequently limited, not only by the limited availability of lawyers to provide litigants advice and representation, but also by the assumptions, norms, and working practices on which the court process continues to rely in their absence.

Despite the fact that LIPs have always been a common feature of the justice system, the family court process remains predicated upon a full-representation model. The assumption that parties typically come to court with the benefit of both prior legal advice and comprehensive legal representation is, however, quite divorced from the everyday reality of the family court. Traditionally, different court users – judges, lawyers, and litigants – each perform distinct, prescribed roles within the process. Through the effective co-ordination of these roles, the system is able to efficiently gather all required information, apply relevant law, and determine appropriate solutions. The presence of LIPs disrupts this normal functioning, because LIPs occupy a unique and arguably disjointed role within court proceedings: one in which they must simultaneously play the roles of both litigant and lawyer. As a consequence, the traditional routines and expectations of the court process are disrupted, because other professionals are also forced to adapt their own roles in order to mitigate the delays and problems that stem from LIPs' lack of familiarity with the legal system.

This incongruence starkly underpins the various journeys that LIPs take through the family justice system, because it posits them as *unexpected* within court hearings, despite the fact that they appear in the majority of cases. It places the onus on LIPs to navigate both explicit and implicit expectations about who the family court is for and parameters that dictate how it should be used. The norms and rules that govern the justice system come in a variety of forms, each of which pose distinct and complicated challenges for LIPs. Perhaps the most obvious example of these are the procedural requirements that structure the different contributions that court users make within the system, as well as the scope, format, and order in which family problems are considered and decisions are made. Procedurally, individuals are expected to follow the steps of the court process by pre-empting the requirements of each hearing in advance, preparing information or arguments, and conveying and negotiating that content in certain formats, such as through court paperwork or verbal submissions. In theory, this process ensures that all family court decisions are reached efficiently and with sufficient clarity and consistency. In reality, its efficacy ultimately rests upon an assumption that court users are both familiar with these rules and invested in their wider significance for the family court.

For LIPs, procedural rules pose a variety of barriers, which can affect their experiences of both individual hearings as well as the process as a whole. By dictating when and how certain issues may be raised, what aspects of a family dispute are legally relevant, and who is permitted to discuss those issues within hearings, their combined effect is to limit and prescribe the ways that LIPs can talk about their family problem within individual proceedings. From completing court forms to preparing paperwork, to participating in advocacy, LIPs are continually required to extract and translate specific aspects of their lives into strictly prescribed written and oral formats. The effects of these rules vary depending on the circumstances and characteristics of individual LIPs, with those who struggle with written or oral forms of communication potentially limited in terms of the points they can convey within proceedings, and significant barriers imposed for the many LIPs who may face challenges with both.

These challenges are further compounded by the fact that LIPs are rarely familiar with the way that these individual hearings fit together to constitute a complete process. LIPs do not have an 'insider' to check that they have correctly prepared for the right type of hearing, or to explain the purposes of the different kinds of hearings that are used within the process. As an 'outsider' to the routines and patterns of the court system, hearings do not necessarily link together in a linear sense. Rather, hearings may be experienced as erratic, and there may be no clear path towards an ultimate outcome. After all, for those who do not have prior experience of this procedure, it is difficult to appreciate why information is presented and collected in these unique formats and how these hearings are designed with specific procedural objectives in mind.

Procedural requirements may be the most apparent example of how LIPs are not a natural fit within the family court, and it is for this reason that procedural reform is so frequently posited as a solution to the inaccessibility of family justice. However, the misalignment between the family justice system and LIPs also manifests within the legal norms that govern decisions in the family court. While procedural rules dictate the format and means by which family disputes are managed, the decisions made in the family court are underpinned by a nuanced legal framework, comprising statutory principles and a rich history of case law.

During court hearings, a key part of the lawyer role is to negotiate how these legal norms should be interpreted and applied to the circumstances of the given case. Due to the specialist nature of legal vocabulary and knowledge, LIPs are not privy to these legal norms. Of course, judges and legal professionals do not expect LIPs to be legal experts, and as such frequently adapt their traditional roles in order to avoid placing them in situations where they might be expected to discuss or negotiate using specialist legal concepts. When hearings turn to matters of family law, therefore, LIPs' lack of knowledge means that they are regarded more as lay clients without representation, instead of representatives in and of themselves. However, this positioning conceals the reality that many aspects of the family court process nevertheless require specialised legal skills, even if they do not involve technical legal language or knowledge. Advocacy and cross-examination, for instance, can be undertaken without the use of legal concepts or terminology, but still require LIPs to coherently present their position in a specifically 'legal' way, for instance by focusing on formulating legally relevant submissions and questions. Similarly, although legal jargon may be minimised, the task of preparing a court bundle remains a specialist activity which requires an understanding of how such paperwork informs the wider court process. Even when LIPs are shielded from explicit discussions about legal rules, they are implicitly still expected to meet significant, and often unclear, performative demands, even if legal professionals themselves do not realise that this is what the process requires.

Further, the shielding of LIPs from explicit legal norms may, in some circumstances, facilitate their segregation within proceedings. The practice of judges and lawyers holding separate conversations about relevant legal frameworks and then extending explanations to LIPs is undoubtedly indicative of professionals trying to make proceedings more accessible for LIPs. However, isolating LIPs in a bid to protect them from legal knowledge they are unlikely to understand may in fact facilitate a sense of disadvantage among LIPs, because it prevents them from actively contributing first-hand to negotiations about how the law should apply to their circumstances. While fully unrepresented hearings are invariably more chaotic and difficult for legal professionals, the experiences of LIPs indicate that these hearings were experienced as more inclusive. Rather than having to wait for professionals to finish a 'legal' conversation before it is translated, these hearings required a more inquisitorial approach from judges, characterised by a continuous translation of knowledge and process.

While it is tempting to simplify legal rules as phenomena which are simply inaccessible to LIPs, their inaccessibility in fact has a great deal more to do with the way that the court process is set up to manage and mediate these norms. Simplifying explicit legal rules as the aspects of family proceedings that LIPs should be shielded from, has the effect of concealing the 'legal' nature of many tasks that LIPs are expected to engage with. Doing so also limits consideration of other approaches, such as inquisitorial judicial management, that might deviate from the usual ways of working with legal norms, but would better empower all court users.

The hesitancy to depart from understandings of how the family court should work is unsurprising, given that the process is itself rooted in long-accepted cultural and social norms. Beyond procedural and legal rules, the family court process is governed by a complex web of social hierarchies, cultural customs, and established modes of professional behaviour. They include things like knowing how and when to speak or where to stand during proceedings, to being able to preempt how others will act and permissible options available for responding to them. These informal modes of regulation are rarely acknowledged let alone scrutinised by those working in the process, because they are based on unspoken but shared understandings about the ways that things are done. For instance, there is an inexplicit understanding that in the court process, litigants and lawyers will pay due deference to judges. This expectation manifests in the design of the court process as well as in the physical arrangements of courtrooms. Elevated seating, separate entrances, or large divisions of space in the courtroom, are all common signifiers of judicial authority and power.

Navigating these inexplicit rules is complicated for LIPs who, by virtue of their unique dual role in the process, do not have the understanding of cultural norms that comes with frequent engagement with the legal system, nor fit cleanly into professional hierarchies. However, while LIPs may not be familiar with how and why the court process works the way it does, many are keenly aware that there are certain ways that they may be advantaged and disadvantaged by these unspoken rules. Making good impressions on judges, for instance, is crucially important to some LIPs, who may attempt to do this by presenting themselves as professional, polite, or well-organised. This does not mean that LIPs are necessarily invested in these customs and hierarchies – while some may welcome signifiers of judicial authority, others may perceive them as crudely undemocratic. In other words, LIPs are well aware that someone else is setting the rules of the game, and their interpretations and responses within proceedings are often motivated by a desire to do well in spite of this.

Taking all of this together, it is possible to appreciate that an increased presence of LIPs in the family justice system is disruptive to the long-agreed procedural, legal, and cultural norms that characterise the family court process. The assumption that parties come to court with full advice and representation underpins every aspect of the process, including the relationships that court users have with one another, the ways that conversations are negotiated, and the perceived legitimacy of decisions reached in this context. LIPs disrupt the usual workings of this process by occupying a disjointed role within proceedings and by being unable to pre-empt and navigate rules in the manner expected. Their presence in hearings forces judges and legal professionals to change their approach, and in many ways renders the traditional working practices of the family court redundant. Despite the efforts of other professionals to support them, LIPs are continually positioned as an external force which departs from the norm, because the onus is on them to refute full-representation assumptions at every stage of the court process.

The relationship between LIPs and the family justice system can therefore be understood as one characterised by tension. This has significant implications for how LIPs relate to others within the process, as well as how they may come to understand and perceive the legitimacy of the system as a means of reaching resolutions to family law problems. In turn, the ways that LIPs interpret and respond to their interactions with the legal system are also mediated by the broader structures of inequality and disadvantage that frame experiences of society more generally. Some LIPs may try to occupy a neutral role within the process by attempting to ascertain and comply with these rules, to varying degrees of success. Others may attempt to forge a role for themselves by trying to evade or work around these constraints, by trying to maximise their efforts in some stages of the process in order to offset the disadvantages they face in other stages.

The effectiveness of these efforts is in part down to the circumstances and resources of individual LIPs, with some LIPs being more able to draw upon privileged skills and knowledge necessary for either navigating prescribed rules or identifying margins of flexibility within them. However, the ability to play a meaningful role within proceedings also hinges significantly on the relationships that LIPs have with other individuals in the family justice system. On one hand, productive and positive relationships with judges and opposing lawyers can help LIPs to play an active role in proceedings, such as through genuine opportunities to communicate their needs, raise concerns, and to feel that both have been meaningfully addressed. On the other hand, unconstructive relationships characterised by misunderstandings or mistrust may lead LIPs to either constructing an adversarial role for themselves or resigning themselves to playing the role of passive observer within their own hearings.

In reality, given the diverse range of circumstances in which people are self-representing, LIPs are likely to respond in a variety of different ways. Some may channel their efforts into preparing extensive written bundles in order to allay their anxieties about not being able to speak up during oral procedures like advocacy and cross-examination. Others may conceptualise opportunities to speak in court as their chance to challenge the arguments of the other side and come out as the 'winner' in the eyes of the judge. Some may even draw upon the assistance of McKenzie Friends in order to ensure that they are heard within proceedings, which can either aid or impede these efforts, depending on the motivations and capabilities of those they rely upon. In each of these scenarios, the court process is undermined, because disruption of these oral and written procedures can impair the efforts of other professionals, and the further entrenchment of adversarial attitudes is unproductive for the objectives of reaching appropriate outcomes.

The complicated and often unpredictable dynamic that exists between LIPs and the family justice system has several important consequences. Based on the findings presented in this book, I have chosen to emphasise three here that are particularly crucial for thinking about the possible future of this relationship. The first is the likelihood that LIPs may be dissatisfied with the experiences they have of the family justice system. Given the experiences explored here, it is not difficult to see how some LIPs may leave the court process feeling that they have been unable to contribute, that what they have said has been ignored, or that they had to 'fight' to be heard. This is particularly apparent within LIPs' descriptions of the legal professionals who are positioned to support them in the process. Many are concerned about being taken advantage of by opposing lawyers, or disappointed that their judges did not listen to them more carefully or help them enough. While it is not possible to know the detail of these interactions, these perceptions themselves are enough to suggest that the family court is falling short of LIPs' expectations. In the process itself, this may mean that it is more difficult for judges and lawyers to gain an accurate understanding of the case, and to build inroads through which LIPs can be empowered to participate in discussions. Dissatisfaction is also evident in the way that some LIPs perceive outcomes reached through the court process. At least among those interviewed for this book, decisions were either based on matters of luck or they were pre-determined by set patterns. In either circumstance, LIPs were dissatisfied with the decision-making process because, in their view, this process did not incorporate their contributions as relevant, necessary or valuable.

The second consequence of this dynamic is the risk of mistrust that may stem from this dissatisfaction. In many ways, the full-representation assumption of the family court process can operate to threaten and constrain the relationships that LIPs have with judges and lawyers. Within the process, lawyers are naturally positioned as LIPs' adversaries, rather than as potential sources of support or fellow collaborators to the court process. This can mean that LIPs regard them with suspicion, especially when lawyers attempt to narrow down issues within hearings or try to encourage them to negotiate. Relationships with judges are similarly fragile, and easily tainted when judges do not have sufficient time to read extensive bundles, or if LIPs suspect professional loyalty and informality between judges and lawyers. In several circumstances, this can limit opportunities for court users to openly communicate with one another, and by extension, build trust and shared understandings about the important issues at stake. Mistrust may not only inhibit the efficacy of the court process, but may also have the effect of disenfranchising individuals from the justice system. In chapter seven, I drew upon the experiences of four LIPs who had received unsatisfactory outcomes in the form of unsafe child arrangements with their abusive ex-partners. These LIPs explained to me that despite their current concerns, they would not return to the family court by choice. Mistrust, therefore, can facilitate a cycle of exclusion in which the process is no longer perceived as a safety net by those who require it.

The final consequence is the danger that LIPs are positioned as the source of the problems that currently characterise the family justice system. Without a clearly defined role in the court process, LIPs are forced to negotiate their own functions within the court process, which may either accord with or subvert the expectations of other court users. In turn, this may position them as disruptive, litigious, or unreasonable, which can have a cyclical impact on their ability to foster positive working relationships and play a meaningful role in the court process. As explored in chapter one, most LIPs in fact do not fit the profile of an angry litigant seeking a personal sense of justice or their own 'day in court'. Rather, they have most often been those caught in the gaps of legal aid provision, and now are likely to be those using the family court as a last resort. If LIPs are regarded with trepidation by others in the process, this will only perpetuate the tension and incongruence that already characterises their relationship with the family justice system, further impair the capacity of the safety net that the family court can provide, and reiterate the risk of dissatisfaction and mistrust among LIPs.

II. LASPO: The End of Family Justice?

Traditionally, the procedural, legal, and cultural barriers that define the relationship LIPs have with the family justice system have been mitigated through the provision of legal aid funded lawyers. Through legal aid, litigants have historically been able to draw upon lawyers' professional familiarity with the system through representation. Even in the absence of legal representation, advice from a lawyer at the very least gives LIPs an understanding about what to expect from the court process. Due to the work that lawyers have historically done to bridge the divide between lay clients and the legal system, the full-representation assumptions have endured even despite the reality that legal aid eligibility was significantly eroded during the lifetime of the scheme.

As such, arguments in favour of promoting access to justice are frequently bound up with arguments for preserving access to legal aid, even if this access is limited. In the family justice context, expert advice is invaluable for giving LIPs accurate understandings of their legal positions as well as realistic expectations for the possible outcomes of their cases. Advice is also a crucial means through which the family court process is demystified – for instance, even a small amount of advice may be enough to debunk misinformation that LIPs may have encountered, such as by explaining in advance how opposing lawyers may try to help them during proceedings, or how the family court expects them to try and compromise. The model has therefore continued to assume that lawyers are necessary to reconcile the different worlds of the legal system and the lay individuals that rely upon it. Yet this model has become increasingly strained within a context of neoliberal policies which simultaneously encourage self-sufficiency and stigmatise dependency on public services. In reality, the family justice system has been under significant pressure for several decades, with free legal advice and representation becoming increasingly inaccessible, and a deepening chasm between those relying on legal aid and those who could afford to instruct private legal services.

The wholesale withdrawal of legal aid for private family law problems under LASPO has marked an important turning point for this context. By exacerbating these problems to such an extent, it is no longer possible for many lawyers or advice organisations to continue papering over this chasm. Without a minimum threshold through which individuals may establish a need for legal aid, the task of resolving family disputes now frequently hinges upon the amount of advice that individuals can afford to pay for. There are, of course, a vast range of initiatives geared towards providing free information and support to help those who are ineligible for legal aid, which can be found online or through non-legal or pro bono services. Since LASPO, these have been significantly overwhelmed by the enormous increase in the number of people who are ineligible, and many are struggling to keep up with demand. It would therefore not be too dramatic to suggest that LASPO may have marked the end of family justice, by providing a final blow to a system that was already struggling under the pressure of previous budget cuts and reforms.

Nevertheless, in this book I have proposed that the LASPO reforms may instead mark the beginning of a new era for family justice. Instead of trying to sustain the same approaches and methods with fewer resources and increasing requirements, the sweeping nature of these changes may, in effect, provide a potential opportunity to reflect on the unsustainability of continuing to expect LIPs to navigate the family justice system in the way that they currently do. Such a reflection requires critical focus on why the family court process has maintained these barriers in the first place. Writing about law and the legal profession more than 40 years ago, Caplan (1977: 93) suggested that 'the easiest way to create a monopoly is to invent a language and procedure which will be unintelligible to the layman'. The continued reliance on professional expertise, combined with the assumption that this expertise is freely available to those who need to use the family court, was problematic long before the LASPO reforms. These assumptions position LIPs as exterior to the normal running of the family justice system instead of facilitating a role for them as legitimate court users. Legal representation is one way to bridge the divide between LIPs and the family justice system. Lawyers will always be needed to do this, as there will always be a certain category of litigants who would need support to engage with the legal process, and would be difficult to quantify based on characteristics or income (Trinder et al. 2014: 121). Yet, it is imperative not to lose sight of the fact that this divide is attributable to the inaccessibility of the family court process itself. In other words, barriers do not exist for LIPs because they do not have legal representation, but rather because of how the court process is designed and how it continues to function.

If we are to consider LASPO not as the end, but rather as an opportunity to reset family justice, what might we want the future system to look like? The many possible answers to this question are far from straightforward. The family justice context remains significantly constrained by neoliberal notions of personal responsibility, self-sufficiency, and cost-effectiveness. This is perhaps most evident in the long-awaited post-implementation review of LASPO (Ministry of Justice 2019a). In this review, the government explicitly acknowledged that LASPO had not necessarily met all of its statutory aims, and that the increased number of LIPs was placing a strain on the family court. However, despite publishing an action plan setting out commitments to improve the delivery of support, political commitments to family justice have been limited to further efforts to financially incentivise mediation and the short-term provision of non-legal assistance at court.[1] These commitments have fallen disappointingly short of professional and academic hopes of substantive change which might have started to address the true current or long-term consequences of LASPO. This is most likely because such change would require economic investment, for which there is limited political appetite.

The COVID-19 pandemic created a range of significant challenges for the family justice system, and concern about the economic costs of recovery will undoubtedly only reinforce existing narratives controlling expenditure within family justice. The rapid, necessitated shift to remote methods of working and use of technology has also demonstrated that the work of this system can, at least to a certain extent, be undertaken more quickly and cheaply than ever. Various legal processes in England and Wales were already facing calls to maximise their own efficiency by increasing their use of technology and moving towards more digitalised procedures.[2] In many ways, digital mechanisms promote the openness and accessibility of justice systems, but there were (and continue to be) concerns about the communities that may be excluded or left behind as this trajectory gradually took its course (Tomlinson 2019; Creudzfeldt 2021; Denvir and Darshini Selvarajah 2022). After March 2020, this trajectory was rapidly accelerated as courts, lawyers, and advice services managed to adapt to online hearings, remote working, and increased use of email and video calls as means of providing legal advice and support. Yet, much of this was achieved despite chronic underfunding, with research indicating unsustainable working practices and precarity among professionals trying to sustain access to justice during the pandemic, as well as a concerning disengagement of several digitally excluded groups who have traditionally relied upon face to face services, and were notably absent during this period (Newman et al. 2021; Denvir et al. 2021). Now that digital working practices have been established, it may be even more difficult to make arguments that are rooted in concerns for meaningful access to justice, rather than efficiency

[1] For example, the government has introduced a mediation voucher scheme, and temporarily increased funding for the Litigant in Person Support Strategy (LIPSS) during 2019–2021. See: Ministry of Justice 2021c; 2019b.

[2] See, eg: HM Courts and Tribunals Service 2018.

and cost-effectiveness. Yet, the post-COVID context means that it is even more important to do so – as the implications of the pandemic on peoples' lives begin to unfold, it is essential that the justice system is prepared to support them.

At the same time, narratives of personal responsibility continue to dominate within family law. While these ideas have always been used to argue for curtailments to legal aid, they are now increasingly posited as means of distinguishing between legitimate and illegitimate users of the family justice system. This can clearly be seen, for instance, in the ways that government administrations have frequently exceptionalised domestic abuse as a unique and isolated circumstance in which litigants should be able to expect both legal aid and adequate support within the court process. The long-awaited commitments to review court procedures and practices that have come on the heels of the *Harm Panel* report are welcome and refreshing responses for those who have spent years campaigning for change in respect of the family court's responses to cases involving allegations of abuse. Yet, it is important not to lose sight of how these problems intersect with the broader problems that characterise the family justice system. At the point LASPO was implemented, victims of domestic abuse were the only litigants identified as those who were 'most vulnerable' and thus in genuine need of state funded legal advice and representation. While this recognition is important, the implication of this distinction was to construct all other family law disputes as those in which litigation should not be necessary. The improved commitments to addressing the family court's long-standing failures in respect of domestic abuse are to be celebrated. However, we should also be cautious not to allow this success to conceptually collapse LIPs even further into simplistic distinctions between those who are 'most vulnerable' and those who are using the court process unnecessarily. As explored throughout this book, the unpredictable nature of family problems as well as the circumstances in which people may find themselves needing to rely on the family court means that we cannot make sweeping assumptions about LIPs' capabilities or support needs. They often do involve allegations of abuse, but the picture is also frequently more complicated and varied. In reality, LIPs are a diverse population of individuals with fluctuating and often chaotic circumstances who may need to rely on the family court for a broad range of complex reasons. To ignore this complexity would limit the capacity of the process to be adequately flexible and responsive to all those who may need it.

The narratives of personal responsibility have also been employed as a means of questioning whether family lawyers and the family court any longer have a legitimate role to play in family disputes at all. Of course, as noted in chapter two, family justice policies have long been characterised by political emphasis on the importance of encouraging parties to resolve their disputes in private, away from courts and lawyers, which are thought to encourage unnecessary litigiousness. These policies are indicative of a longstanding scepticism about the presence of legal norms within family disputes, which is now gaining even more traction in the post-LASPO context. In response to the problems associated with this context, the Family Solutions Group[3] (2020) proposed an 'early triage' intervention for addressing disputes over children termed 'information and assessment meetings'. The rationale behind this suggestion was that these meetings could provide an opportunity for families to receive tailored information about their options and an understanding of what is expected of them in terms of parental responsibility and future co-parenting. Importantly, their report is explicit in disavowing the notion that this meeting needs to involve legal advice, or indeed the idea that disputes involving children have any legal dimensions at all:

> … while legal information may be helpful to understand the legal context, being directed to a legal professional enhances the view that parenting disputes are legal issues. In private law children cases where there are no safety issues, the aim is to reframe disputes away from being 'legal issues' and into 'parenting disagreements' instead (2020: 193).

Scepticism about the importance of legal norms has also been expressed by other professionals working in the family justice system. For instance, evidence submitted to the Future of Legal Aid review by National Family Mediation (2020) suggests that separating couples are likely to benefit from 'expert input', but they do not necessarily require 'legal input'. This scepticism aligns well with the government's objective of keeping costs down, because it supports the diversion of funding away from expensive legal services and instead towards non-legal support.

Earlier, I argued that LASPO may provide an opportunity to rethink the full-representation assumptions of the family court. However, there is a crucial distinction between, on the one hand, suggesting that the family justice system may be made more accessible and, on the other hand, suggesting that family problems should not be conceptualised as legal problems at all. The latter is, in fact, a potentially perilous route that should be regarded with significant caution. First, legal norms do not only exist within the family court process. Rather, legal norms provide guiding principles to inform private negotiations and agreements. Family disputes are never purely 'private' disagreements in which only those involved have an invested interest in the outcomes. Rather, post-separation arrangements regarding children will always hold wider consequences for society as a whole. While there will always be scope for debate about the types of legal norms that should underpin family law decisions, the significance of the role that these norms play should not be underestimated. A framework of legal principles helps to ensure that children's welfare is promoted and that their parents both have sufficient resources to care for them, and in many cases, family law plays an important role in ensuring an equality of arms between parties as they negotiate suitable arrangements. Leaving the law out of family disputes risks perpetuating power imbalances and undermining opportunities for families to effectively negotiate by themselves.

[3] A subgroup of the Private Law Working Group, formed to give attention to improving opportunities for separating families away from the Family Court.

Fundamentally, scepticism about the role of law in family disputes also risks undermining the important role of the family court within the wider family justice system. It is unquestionable that many LIPs may be better off if they had been able to make use of alternative dispute resolution, and it is also true that litigation has the potential to exacerbate family problems, by entrenching conflict and potentially extinguishing any hope of positive future relationships between separated parents. But this does not erase the reality that the family court is, for some individuals, the most appropriate and effective route to resolution. The family court has traditionally operated as a safety net for families for whom alternative dispute resolution is inappropriate or ineffective, providing essential intervention to secure and stabilise some of the most chaotic and difficult circumstances for both parents and children. Conceptualising family disputes as disagreements instead of legal problems runs the risk of undermining the importance of ensuring that this safety net is accessible for those who require it.

There are, of course, clear concerns about the navigability of legal norms, especially in the post-LASPO context where support and advice in relation to family law is now very difficult to access for most people. Nevertheless, it is important to avoid assuming that delegalisation of family justice is an appropriate way to address these concerns. Rather, as I have demonstrated throughout this book, the problems faced by many LIPs are not related to the presence of legal norms but the way that the court process was capable of managing and translating these norms. This is a crucial distinction, and it relates specifically to the way that the family justice system itself operates. This distinction is all the more important in the post-LASPO context because of the ways that LIPs are often stigmatised for relying on formal mechanisms of family law and the reality that there is very limited political appetite for any initiatives or reforms that might make legal norms more accessible to lay individuals.

The future of family justice is therefore likely to be just as complicated as its past. Any reform proposals, regardless of scale, will need to be negotiated within a complex political context that prioritises cost-effective and privatised solutions. Such negotiations will also need to include sustained resistance to narratives that risk concealing the diverse range of users that may need to rely on family law, and perhaps even staunch defence of the legitimate and necessary role of family law and the family court in many of these disputes. Nevertheless, the process of rethinking family justice has already begun. The combined effects of the LASPO reforms and the COVID-19 pandemic have facilitated major disruptions to the otherwise accepted norms that underpin the family court process. As Rossner (2021) has argued, remote hearings are not merely diminished versions of traditional court hearings, but rather an opportunity to forge new dynamics rooted in egalitarianism, whilst retaining appropriate levels of formality. While the family court process may once have been perceived as an inviolable structure of procedures and rules, it is now forced to adapt on a daily basis – both in terms of guiding LIPs through court hearings, as well as adapting proceedings so that they may take place in virtual or hybrid formats. These events have even further impaired LIPs' ability to seek support and participate in their hearings by further isolating them from sources of advice as well as court professionals.

A re-evaluation of how the family court should respond to LIPs was already overdue even before it was faced with the unsustainable demands that came with increased self-representation after LASPO. The outbreak of the COVID-19 pandemic was, of course, another crucially compounding factor in this trajectory, but the scale and nature of its impact are inextricable from the deleterious state of family justice that existed before March 2020. Of course, a great deal of further work is needed to build a stronger understanding of how LASPO and the pandemic have intersected and impacted LIPs' experiences of family justice. However, even at this early stage, it is possible to see that the disruption caused by these events is forcing change within the family justice system. Now is therefore a prime opportunity to begin asking questions about how the full-representation assumption has historically impeded the relationship between LIPs and the legal system, and undertake a long-overdue re-evaluation of the appropriateness of this assumption in light of the present family justice landscape. In doing so, LASPO need not be the end of family justice, and instead can provide an opportunity to harness disruption and think about ways to build a more democratic system that is responsive to the needs of those who rely upon it.

III. How to Break a Cycle of Exclusion

At the core of this challenge is the need for a fundamental shift in how LIPs are conceptualised within the family justice system. As explored in chapter three, socio-legal researchers, especially those working on access to justice issues, are frequently torn between the impetus to produce short-term, impactful evidence that highlights clear routes for reform, and the importance of being more broadly critical of the systems that frame experiences of law. To forge meaningful change for LIPs and the family justice system, I argue that both of these short-term and long-term goals are important. Without broader theoretical critique of the family justice system, the potential impact of short-term empirical evidence about the challenges LIPs face will inevitably be limited. In turn, without this short-term evidence, such critique will achieve very little in terms of meaningful change.

This can be seen, for instance, in the limitations of the ways that the family justice system currently attempts to accommodate LIPs. Throughout this book, I have highlighted several ways that judges and lawyers go above and beyond their traditional roles in efforts to help LIPs engage with family court proceedings. Offering procedural leeway, attempting to initiate pre-hearing negotiations, and explaining legal concepts in lay terms are just some examples of how professionals try to extend guidance and support to LIPs within the confines of the family court process. It may be possible, with further qualitative research, to produce empirical evidence that informs methods of best practice for judges and lawyers that enable these well-intentioned efforts to be more effective and responsive to LIPs' needs.

However, this short-term and sporadic flexibility will never achieve large-scale, meaningful change within the process. Rather, these efforts simply provide work-around solutions to the deep-rooted cultural norms and social hierarchies that operate to isolate LIPs within the process. Further, the task of incorporating any of these accommodations into the current process invariably places greater burden onto already-strained workloads of those working in the family justice system.

Meaningful change therefore requires empirical efforts to be combined with broader critique of how this system works, and reflection on the kinds of assumptions that underpin its practices. In reality, LIPs have always faced exclusionary norms and have always struggled to navigate a system premised upon a historically-reiterated set of roles to which they do not belong. Moreover, LIPs are – especially after LASPO – not a homogenous group with clearly identifiable needs around which a role can be constructed for the purposes of the existing court process. As demonstrated in this book, LIPs are a diverse population of users with varying circumstances and needs. There is no simple fix through which the various requirements surrounding communication and participation can be adapted in order to be accessible to lay court users. Rather, what is needed is a process that can be responsive and flexible to the diversity of circumstances in which LIPs appear. Most importantly, this requires the family justice system to shed implicit expectations about how the court process should work, and instead start to reconsider how the process may properly start to account for the different kinds of court users that are relying on the safety net of the family justice system.

To this end, I argue that accounting for the experiences and perceptions of LIPs should be the first step on the journey towards a new future for family justice. In this book, I have drawn together a rich array of experiences, perceptions and understandings and used these to demonstrate the value of evaluating the justice system from the perspectives of its most marginalised users. Exposing and centring LIP voices is an invariably political task because it focuses critical attention on the ways that the design and practices of the court process can, in many ways, compound and exacerbate the disadvantage that LIPs face in this context. Even in the most sensitively managed hearings, the very fact that they are dependent on others working to create space for them within proceedings is indicative of their institutional exclusion.

It also sharply clarifies the chasm between how LIPs perceive the family justice system, and how they are perceived within this system. It is understandably tempting to attribute LIPs' problems to their lack of understanding, and for professionals to try to remedy this by assimilating LIPs into the system. However, this alone does nothing to rectify LIPs' exclusion within this system. The challenge of achieving appropriate outcomes in LIP hearings is markedly broader than simply helping LIPs to understand the rules of the game. Rather, there are important lessons to learn about how and why LIPs may feel more or less able to contribute and participate in hearings, and to consider how they may be empowered to dispute, correct, or question aspects of the decision-making process without being branded as disorderly, litigious disruptions to the court process. Of course, given the personal and emotional nature of family disputes, it is inevitable that individual perceptions of the system are likely to be heavily influenced by whether LIPs agree with the outcomes reached. However, this alone vastly oversimplifies how much there is to learn from LIPs' perceptions. Drawing together the different ways that LIPs view the family court process is a valuable opportunity to untangle the level of trust that LIPs feel they can place in the family justice system, and the extent to which LIPs recognise the family court as a legitimate means of obtaining resolutions to family problems.

Further, a failure to incorporate LIPs' perceptions in debates about the future of the system is dangerous for family justice. It is dangerous because it risks perpetuating the cycle of exclusion that underpins the current system. When perceived – and actual – exclusion from the motions of family justice is cyclical, this means that these negative encounters with the legal system will repeat time and time again and are no longer limited to the experiences of individual LIPs. Conceptualising barriers, problems, and disadvantage as isolated to individual injustices is short-sighted, especially given the increasing prominence of informal online support and the frequency with which LIPs go on to help others going through the process. The attitudes and understandings that LIPs have when they leave the family court process have never been more important for appreciating the ways that negative perceptions and experiences of the court process may be circulated among others engaging with the family justice system. Such attitudes may close off access to the potential mechanisms of support and flexibility that lawyers and judges are working to build into the current system. At worst, this may further reinforce existing stereotypes and tropes about LIPs as disruptive, litigious, uncooperative individuals, thus only bolstering the cycle of exclusion that underpins the journeys that LIPs take through this system.

As such, I argue that family law scholars, professionals, and policymakers need to make explicit efforts to seek out an understanding of LIPs' diverse experiences, perceptions and understandings, and centre these within debates about what comes next for family justice. While it may not be a politically appealing conclusion to draw, this book has demonstrated that it is necessary to use these accounts to further complicate our understanding of family justice before we can begin building a new future for this system. However, it is only by committing to this learning process that it will be possible to meaningfully harness the disruption that has been brought by LASPO and reiterated by the COVID-19 pandemic. In short, the sustainability of the family justice system will ultimately depend upon its capacity to learn from those that it has so far operated to systematically exclude, and to safeguard the family court as an essential safety net for families in crisis.

BIBLIOGRAPHY

AdviceNow (2020) 'How to Apply for a Child Arrangements Order Without a Lawyer' (London, AdviceNow).

All Party Parliamentary Group on Domestic Violence (2016) *Domestic Abuse, Child Contact, and the Family Courts* (Bristol, Women's Aid).

Alrouh, B et al. (2022) *What do We Know About Ethnicity in the Family Justice System in England?* (London, Nuffield Family Justice Observatory).

Ashiagbor, D (1999) 'The Intersection Between Gender and 'Race' in the Labour Market: Lessons for Anti-Discrimination Law' in A Morris and T O'Donnell (eds), *Feminist Perspectives on Employment Law* (London, Routledge).

Bach Commission (2017) *The Right to Justice: Final Report of the Bach Commission* (London, The Fabian Society).

Baiocchi, G et al. (2013) 'Actor-Network Theory and the Ethnographic Imagination: An Exercise in Translation' 36 *Qualitative Sociology* 323.

The Bar Council (2013) *A Guide to Representing Yourself in Court* (London, The Bar Council).

The Bar Council, CILEx and the Law Society (2015) *Litigants in Person: Guidelines for Lawyers* (London, The Bar Council, CILEx and the Law Society).

Barlow, A et al. (2017) *Mapping Paths to Family Justice* (London, Palgrave).

Barnett, A (2020) *Domestic Abuse and Private Law Children Cases: A Literature Review* Ministry of Justice Analytical Series.

—— (2017) 'Greater Than the Mere Sum of its Parts': Coercive Control and the Question of Proof' 29 *Child and Family Law Quarterly* 379.

—— (2016) 'Family Law Without Lawyers – A Systems Perspective' 39 *Journal of Social Welfare and Family Law* 223.

—— (2015) 'Like Gold Dust These Days': Domestic Violence Fact-finding Hearings in Child Contact Cases' 23 *Feminist Legal Studies* 47.

—— (2014) 'Contact at All Costs? Domestic Violence and Children's Welfare' 26 *Child and Family Law Quarterly* 439.

—— (2000) 'Contact and Domestic Violence: The Ideological Divide' in J Bridgeman and D Monk (eds) *Feminist Perspectives on Child Law* (London, Cavendish).

Barnett, H (1998) *Introduction to Feminist Jurisprudence* (London, Cavendish).

Bartlett, KT (1990) 'Feminist Legal Methods' 103 *Harvard Law Review* 829.

Barry, KA (2020) 'The Barriers to Effective Access to Justice Encountered by Litigants in Person in Private Family Matters Post-LASPO' 42 *Journal of Social Welfare and Family Law* 416.

—— (2019). 'McKenzie Friends and Litigants in Person: Widening Access to Justice or Foes in Disguise?' 31 *Child and Family Law Quarterly* 69.

—— (2000) 'Contact and Domestic Violence: The Ideological Divide' in J Bridgeman and D Monk (eds) *Feminist Perspectives on Child Law* (London, Cavendish).

Bendall, C (2014) 'Some are More 'Equal' than Others: Heteronormativity in the Post-White Era of Financial Remedies' 36 *Journal of Social Welfare and Family Law* 260.

Bennett, T et al. (2009) *Culture, Class, Distinction* (Abingdon, Routledge).

Bevan, C (2013) 'Self-represented Litigants: The Overlooked and Unintended Consequence of Legal Aid Reform' 35 *Journal of Social Welfare and Family Law* 43.

Birchall, J and Choudhry, S (2018) *'What About my Right Not to be Abused?' Domestic Abuse, Human Rights and the Family Courts* (Bristol, Women's Aid).

Bourdieu, P (2005). *The Social Structures of the Economy – Pierre Bourdieu* (Cambridge, Polity Press).
—— (1987) 'The Force of Law: Towards a Sociology of the Juridical Field' 38 *Hastings Law Journal* 805.
—— (1986) 'The Forms of Capital' in J Richardson (ed) *Handbook of Theory and Research for the Sociology of Education* (Westport, Greenwood).
—— (1984) *Distinction* (Cambridge, Harvard University Press).
Bourdieu, P and Wacquant, L (1992) *An Invitation to Reflexive Sociology* (Cambridge, Polity Press).
Bowcott, O (2015) 'Barristers Threaten to Walk Out Over Legal Aid Cuts' *The Guardian* Available from www.theguardian.com/law/2015/may/21/barristers-threaten-walk-out-legal-aid-cuts.
Boyd, S and Treloar, R (2014) 'Family Law Reform in (Neoliberal) Context: British Columbia's New Family Law Act' 28 *International Journal of Law, Policy and The Family* 77.
Bridgeman, J and Monk, D (2000) 'Introduction: Reflections on the Relationship Between Feminism and Child Law' in J Bridgeman and D Monk (eds) *Feminist Perspectives on Child Law* (London, Cavendish).
Brown, W (2015) *Undoing the Demos: Neoliberalism's Stealth Revolution* (New Jersey, Princeton University Press).
Burke, C et al. (2016) 'Introduction: The Development of Bourdieu's Intellectual Heritage in UK Sociology' in J Thatcher et al. (eds) *Bourdieu: The Next Generation* (Abingdon, Routledge).
Buzelin, H (2005) 'Unexpected Allies: How Latour's Network Theory Could Complement Bourdieusian Analyses in Translation Studies' 11 *The Translator* 193.
Byrom, N (2020) *What We Know About the Impact of Remote Hearings on Access to Justice: A Rapid Evidence Review* (London, Nuffield Family Justice Observatory and the Legal Education Foundation).
Byrom, N et al. (2020) *The Impact of COVID-19 Measures on the Civil Justice System* (London, Civil Justice Council).
CAFCASS and Women's Aid (2017) *Allegations of Domestic Abuse in Child Contact Cases* (London, CAFCASS).
Carlen, P (1976) *Magistrates Justice* (London, Martin Robertson and Company Ltd).
Caplen, A (2016) 'The View from the Law Society' in E Palmer et al. (eds) *Access to Justice: Beyond the Policies and Politics of Austerity* (Oxford, Hart).
Caplan, J (1977) 'Lawyers and Litigants: A Cult Reviewed' in I Illich et al. (eds) *Disabling Professions* (London, Marion Boyars).
Citizens Advice (2016) *Standing Alone: Going to the Family Court without a Lawyer* (London, Citizens Advice).
Clark, J (2021) *Evaluation of Remote Hearings During the COVID-19 Pandemic* (London, HMCTS).
Cloatre, E (2018) 'Law and ANT (and its Kin): Possibilities, Challenges and Ways Forward' 45 *Journal of Law and Society* 646.
—— (2013) *Pills for the Poorest: An Exploration of TRIPS and Access to Medication in Sub-Saharan Africa* (London, Palgrave MacMillan).
Conaghan, J (2013) *Law and Gender* (Oxford, OUP).
—— (2009) 'Intersectionality and the Feminist Project' in E Grabham et al. (eds) *Intersectionality and Beyond: Law, Power and the Politics of Location* (Abingdon, Routledge).
—— (2007) 'Intersectionality and UK Equality Initiatives' 32 *South African Journal on Human Rights* 317.
Cookson, G (2013) 'Analysing the Economic Justifications for the Reforms to Social Welfare and Family Law Legal Aid' 35 *Journal of Social Welfare and Family Law* 21.
Corbett, NE and Summerfield, A (2017) *Alleged Perpetrators of Abuse as Litigants in Person in Private Family Law: The Cross Examination of Vulnerable and Intimidated Witnesses* (London, Ministry of Justice).
Cornford, T (2016) 'The Meaning of Access to Justice' in E Palmer et al. (eds) *Access to Justice: Beyond the Policies and Politics of Austerity* (Oxford, Hart).
Coulthard, M and Johnson, A (2007) *An Introduction to Forensic Linguistics: Language in Evidence* (Abingdon, Routledge).
Cowan, D and Carr, H (2008) 'Actor-Network Theory, Implementation, and the Private Landlord' 35 *Journal of Law and Society* 149.
Coy, M et al. (2012) *Picking Up the Pieces: Domestic Violence and Child Contact* (London, Rights of Women).

Crenshaw, K (1991) 'Mapping the Margins: Intersectionality, Identity Politics, and Violence Against Women of Color' 43 *Stanford Law Review* 1241.
—— (1989) 'Demarginalizing the Intersection of Race and Sex: A Black Feminist Critique of Antidiscrimination Doctrine, Feminist Theory and Antiracist Politics' 1 *University of Chicago Legal Forum* 139.
Creudzfeldt, N (2021) 'Towards a Digital Legal Consciousness?' 12 *European Journal of Law and Technology* 1.
Creudzfeldt, N and Sechi, D (2021) 'Social Welfare [Law] Advice Provision During the Pandemic in England and Wales: A Conceptual Framework' 43 *Journal of Social Welfare and Family Law* 153.
Cusworth, L et al. (2021) *Uncovering Private Family Law: Who's Coming to Court in England?* (London, Nuffield Family Justice Observatory).
—— (2020) *Uncovering Private Family Law: Who's Coming to Court in Wales?* (London, Nuffield Family Justice Observatory).
Davies, M (2017) *Law Unlimited: Materialism, Pluralism and Legal Theory* (Abingdon, Routledge).
Davis, G et al. (1994) *Simple Quarrels* (Oxford, Clarendon Press).
Denvir, C and Darshini Selvarajah, A (2022) 'Safeguarding Access to Justice in the Age of the Online Court' 85 *Modern Law Review* 25.
Denvir, C et al. (2021) *We Are Legal Aid: Findings From the 2021 Legal Aid Census* (London, Legal Aid Practitioners Group).
De Simone, T and Hunter, R (2009) 'Causes of Inaction: Barriers to Legal Aid Services' 34 *Alternative Law Journal* 265.
Dewar, J (1998) 'The Normal Chaos of Family Law' 61 *Modern Law Review* 467.
Dewar, J et al. (2000) *Litigants in Person in the Family Court of Australia* (Sydney, Family Court of Australia).
Diduck, A (2000) 'Solicitors and Legal Subjects' in J Bridgeman and D Monk (eds) *Feminist Perspectives on Child Law* (London, Cavendish).
Diduck, A and O'Donavan, K (2006) 'Feminism and Families: Plus ça Change?' in A Diduck and K O'Donovan (eds) *Feminist Perspectives on Family Law* (London, Routledge).
Dunne, P (2016) '(Trans) Marriage Equality? Challenging Europe's Marital 'Dissolution Requirements'' 28 *Child and Family Law Quarterly* 325.
Eekelaar, J et al. (2000) *Family Lawyers: The Divorce Work of Solicitors* (Oxford, Hart).
Edwards, AD (1976) *Language in Culture and Class* (London, Heinemann).
Ewick, P and Sibley, S (1998) *The Common Place of Law* (Chicago, University of Chicago Press).
Family Solutions Group (2020) *What About Me? Reframing Support for Families Following Parental Separation* Judiciary.gov Available from: <https://www.judiciary.uk/wp-content/uploads/2020/11/FamilySolutionsGroupReport_WhatAboutMe_12November2020-2.pdf-final-2.pdf>
Fineman, MA (2017) 'Vulnerability and Inevitable Inequality' 4 *Oslo Law Review* 133.
—— (2016) 'Equality, Autonomy, and the Vulnerable Subject in Law and Politics' in MA Fineman and A Grear (eds.) *Vulnerability: Reflections on a New Ethical Foundation for Law and Politics* (Abingdon, Routledge).
—— (2011) 'The Vulnerable Subject and the Responsive State' *Emory Law Journal.*
—— (2008) 'The Vulnerable Subject: Anchoring Equality in the Human Condition' 20 *Yale Journal of Law and Feminism* 1.
—— (1996) *The Neutered Mother, The Sexual Family, and Other 20th Century Tragedies* (London, Routledge).
Fraser, G (2020) 'Reflections on Changing Family Law Practice During the COVID-19 Lockdown' 4 *Family Law* 1115.
Fraser, N (2013) *Fortunes of Feminism: From State-managed Capitalism to Neoliberal Crisis* (London, Verso).
—— (2008) 'From Redistribution to Recognition? Dilemmas of Justice in a "Post-social" Age' in K Olson (ed) *Adding Insult to Injury: Nancy Fraser Discusses her Critics* (London, Verso).
Galanter, M (1974) 'Why the 'Haves' Come Out Ahead: Speculations on the Limits of Legal Change' 9 *Law and Society Review* 95.

Genn, H (1999). *Paths to Justice: What People Do and Think About Going to Law* (Oxford, Hart).

Goodin, RE (1985) *Protecting the Vulnerable: A Reanalysis of our Social Responsibilities* (Chicago, University of Chicago Press).

Grabham, E (2016) 'Time and Technique: The Legal Lives of the 26-week Qualifying Period' 45 *Economy and society* 379.

—— (2014) 'Legal Form and Temporal Rationalities in UK Work-life Balance Law' 29 *Australian Feminist Studies* 67.

—— (2009) 'Intersectionality: Traumatic impressions' in E Grabham et al. (eds) *Intersectionality and Beyond: Law, Power and the Politics of Location* (Abingdon, Routledge).

—— (2006) 'Taxonomies of Equality: Lawyers, Maps and the Challenge of Hybridity' 15 *Social and Legal Studies* 5.

Grabham, E et al. (2009) *Intersectionality and Beyond: Law, Power and the Politics of Location* (Abingdon, Routledge).

Harris, P (2015) 'Casualties of Friendly Fire: Counterproductive Campaigning on Public Funded Legal Services' in M Maclean et al. (eds) *Delivering Family Justice in the 21st Century* (Oxford, Hart).

Hartsock, N (1990). 'Foucault on Power: A Theory for Women?' in LJ Nicholson (ed) *Feminism/Postmodernism* (London, Routledge).

Harvey, D (2005) *A Brief History of Neoliberalism* (Oxford, OUP).

Hester, M (2011) 'The Three Planet Model: Towards an Understanding of Contradictions in Approaches to Women and Children's Safety in Contexts of Domestic Violence' 41 *The British Journal of Social Work* 837.

Hester, M and Radford, R (1996) *Domestic Violence and Child Contact Arrangements in England and Denmark* (Bristol, Policy Press).

Hester, M et al. (1997) *Domestic Violence: A National Survey of Court Welfare and Voluntary Sector Mediation Practice* (Bristol, Policy Press).

Hirsch, D (2018) *Priced Out of Justice? Means Testing Legal Aid and Making Ends Meet* (London, Law Society).

Hitchings, E et al. (2013) *Assembling the Jigsaw Puzzle: Understanding Financial Settlement on Divorce* (Bristol, University of Bristol).

HM Courts and Tribunals Service (2018) *The HMCTS Reform Programme* Gov.UK Available from www.gov.uk/guidance/the-hmcts-reform-programme.

House of Commons Justice Committee (2015) *Impact of Changes to Civil Legal Aid Under Part 1 of the Legal Aid, Sentencing and Punishment of Offenders Act 2012* HC 311 2014-15.

House of Commons Public Accounts Committee (2007) *Legal Services Commission: Legal Aid and Mediation for People Involved in Family Breakdown* HC 396.

Hunter, C (2016) 'Solar Panels, Homeowners and Leases: The Lease as a Socio-legal Object' in D Cowan and D Wincott (eds) *Exploring the 'Legal' in Socio-legal Studies* (London, Palgrave MacMillan).

Hunter, R (2017) 'Paid McKenzie Friends: The Case for Regulation' 1 *Family Law Journal* 13.

—— (2013) 'The Gendered 'Socio' of Socio-Legal Studies' in D Feenan (ed) *Exploring the 'Socio' of Socio-Legal Studies* (London, Palgrave Macmillan).

—— (2008) *Rethinking Equality Projects in Law: Feminist Challenges* (Oxford, Hart).

—— (1998) 'Litigants in Person in Contested Cases in the Family Court' 12 *Australian Journal of Family Law* 171.

Hunter, R et al. (2020) *Assessing Risk of Harm to Children and Parents in Private Law Children Cases* (London, Ministry of Justice).

—— (2018) 'Introduction: Contact and Domestic Abuse' 40 *Journal of Social Welfare and Family Law* 401.

—— (2003) *Legal Aid and Self-representation in the Family Court of Australia* (Brisbane, National Legal Aid).

—— (2002) *The Changing Face of Litigation: Unrepresented Litigants in the Family Court of Australia* (Sydney, Law and Justice Foundation of New South Wales).

Hunter, R and Barnett, A (2013) *Fact-finding Hearings and the Implementation of the President's Practice Direction: Residence and Contact Orders: Domestic Violence and Harm* (London, Family Justice Council).

Hynes, S (2012) *Austerity Justice* (London, Legal Action Group).
Hynes, S and Robins, J (2009) *The Justice Gap* (London, Legal Action Group).
Illich, I (1977) *Disabling Professions* (New York, Marion Boyars).
Ingleby, R (1992) *Solicitors and Divorce* (Oxford, OUP).
Jacob, MA (2017) 'The Strikethrough: An Approach to Regulatory Writing and Professional Discipline' 37 *Legal Studies* 137.
Jones, O (2012) *Chavs* (London, Verso).
Joseph Rowntree Foundation (2022) *UK Poverty 2022* (London, Joseph Rowntree Foundation).
Judicial College (2021) *Equal Treatment Bench Book* (London, Judicial College).
Judiciary of England and Wales (2015) *Report of the Vulnerable Witnesses and Children Working Group* (London, Judiciary of England and Wales).
Kaganas, F (2017) 'Justifying the LASPO Act: Authenticity, Necessity, Suitability, Responsibility and Autonomy' 39 *Journal of Social Welfare and Family Law* 168.
Larner, W (2000) 'Neoliberalism: Policy, Ideology, Governmentality' 63 *Studies in Political Economy* 5.
Latour, B (2005) *Reassembling the Social: An Introduction to Actor-Network-Theory* (Oxford, OUP).
Law, J (2004) *After Method: Mess in Social Science Research* (London, Routledge).
Law, J and Singleton, V (2013) 'ANT and Politics: Working In and On the World' 36 *Qualitative Sociology* 485.
Law Centres Network (2020) *Law for All: The 50th Anniversary Campaign for Law Centres* (London, Law Centres Network).
Leader, K (2017) *Fifteen Stories: Litigants in Person and the Civil Justice System* (London School of Economics, PhD thesis).
Lee, R and Tkacucova, T (2018) *A Survey of Litigants in Person at Birmingham Civil Justice Centre* (Birmingham, CEPLER Working Paper Series).
Lefebvre, H (1991) *The Production of Space* (London, Wiley-Blackwell).
Lefevre, M and Damman, J (2019) *Practice Direction 12J: What is the Experience of Lawyers Working in Private Law Children Cases? Report of a Survey Conducted in the South-East of England August-October 2019* (Sussex, University of Sussex).
Legal Aid Practitioners Group (2017) *Manifesto for Legal Aid* (2nd edn, London, Legal Aid Practitioners Group).
Legal Services Commission (2007) *Legal Aid Reform: The Way Ahead* Cm 6993.
Legal Services Consumer Panel (2014) *Fee-charging McKenzie Friends* (London, Legal Services Consumer Panel).
Levi, R and Valverde, M (2008). 'Studying Law by Association: Bruno Latour Goes to the Conseil d'Etat' 33 *Law and Social Inquiry* 805.
Local Government Association (2021) *Tackling the Digital Divide* (London, House of Commons).
MacFarlane, J et al. (2013) *The National Self-Represented Litigants Project: Identifying and Meeting the Needs of Self-Represented Litigants* (Ontario, The Law Foundation of Ontario).
Mackenzie, C et al. (2014) *Vulnerability: New Essays in Ethics and Feminist Philosophy* (Oxford, OUP).
Maclean, M (2015a) 'New Ways to Seek Legal Information and Advice on Family Matters in England and Wales: From Professional Legal Services to Google and Private Ordering' in M Maclean et al. (eds) *Delivering Family Justice in the 21st Century* (Oxford, Hart).
—— (2015b) 'The Impact of Socio-legal Studies in Family Justice: From Oxford to Whitehall' 42 *Journal of Law and Society* 637.
Maclean, M and Eekelaar, J (2019) *After the Act: Access to Family Justice after LASPO* (Oxford, Hart).
—— (2016) *Lawyers and Mediators: The Brave New World of Services for Separating Families* (Oxford, Hart).
—— (2012) 'Legal Representation in Family Matters and the Reform of Legal Aid: A Research Note on Current Practice' 24 *Child and Family Law Quarterly*, 223.
—— (2009) *Family Law Advocacy: How Barristers Help the Victims of Family Failure* (Oxford, Hart).
Marsh, J (2014) 'A View from the Personal Support Unit' in *'Rise of LIPs': Three Perspectives on the Increased Number of People who Represent Themselves in Court* Inner Temple Yearbook 2013–2014.
Marshall, E et al. (2018) *Family Law and Access to Legal Aid* (London, Public Law Project).

Massey, D (2005) *For Space* (Thousand Oaks, Sage).
McFarlane, A (2021) 'Interesting Times' *Speech to the Family Law Bar Association National Conference* Manchester, 16th October.
McKeever, G et al. (2021). 'The Snakes and Ladders of Legal Participation: Litigants in Person and the Right to a Fair Trial Under Article 6' 49 *Journal of Law and Society* 71.
—— (2018) *Litigants in Person in Northern Ireland: Barriers to Legal Participation* (Ulster, Ulster University).
McKenzie, L (2016). 'Narrative, Ethnography and Class Inequality: Taking Bourdieu into a British Council Estate' in J Thatcher et al. (eds) *Bourdieu: The Next Generation* (Abingdon: Routledge).
Melville, A (2017) 'Giving Hope to Fathers: Discursive Constructions of Families and Family Law by McKenzie Friends Associated with Fathers' Rights Groups' 31 *International Journal of Law, Policy and the Family*, 147.
Ministry of Justice (2021a) *Family Court Statistics Quarterly: October – December 2021* (London, Ministry of Justice).
—— (2021b) *Legal Aid Statistics Quarterly: October – December 2021* (London, Ministry of Justice).
—— (2021c) *Family Mediation Voucher Scheme* Gov.UK. Available from: www.gov.uk/guidance/family-mediation-voucher-scheme.
—— (2020) *Assessing Risk of Harm to Children and Parents in Private Law Children Cases: Implementation Plan* (London, Ministry of Justice).
—— (2019a) *Post Implementation Review of Part 1 of the Legal Aid Sentencing and Punishment of Offenders Act 2012* (London, Ministry of Justice).
—— (2019b) *Legal Support: The Way Ahead* (London, Ministry of Justice).
—— (2011) *Reform of Legal Aid in England and Wales: The Government Response* (London, Ministry of Justice).
—— (2010) *Proposals for the Reform of Legal Aid in England and Wales* (London, Ministry of Justice).
Minnoch, C (2021) 'Will Amending the Means Test Actually Increase the Number of Clients Receiving Legal Aid?' *Legal Action Group* Available from: https://www.lag.org.uk/article/211396/-will-amending-the-means-test-actually-increase-the-number-of-clients-receiving-legal-aid
Moorhead, R (2007) 'The Passive Arbiter: Litigants in Person and the Challenge to Neutrality' 16 *Social and Legal Studies* 405.
—— (2004) 'Legal Aid and the Decline of Private Practice: Blue Murder or Toxic Job?' 11 *International Journal of the Legal Profession* 159.
Moorhead, R and Sefton, M (2005) *Litigants in Person: Unrepresented Litigants in First Instance Proceedings* (London, Department for Constitutional Affairs).
Mulcahy, L (2010) *Legal Architecture: Justice, Due Process and the Place of Law* (London, Routledge).
Mulcahy, L and Rowden, E (2020) *The Democratic Courthouse: A Modern History of Design, Due Process and Dignity* (London, Routledge).
National Audit Office (2014) *Implementing Reforms to Civil Legal Aid* (London, Ministry of Justice and Legal Aid Agency).
National Family Mediation (2020) *Evidence to the Future of Legal Aid Inquiry* Parliament.UK Available from: committees.parliament.uk/writtenevidence/12876/html/.
Newman, D et al. (2021) 'Vulnerability, Legal Need and Technology in England and Wales' 21 *International Journal of Discrimination and the Law* 230.
Oakley, A (1990) 'Interviewing Women: A Contradiction in Terms' in H Roberts (ed) *Doing Feminist Research* (London, Routledge).
Page, RM (2015) *Clear Blue Water? The Conservative Party and the Welfare State Since 1940* (Bristol, Policy Press).
Parveen, R (2018) 'Religious-only Marriages in the UK: Legal Positionings and Muslim Women's Experiences' 6 *Sociology of Islam* 316.
Pereira, I et al. (2015). *The Varying Paths to Justice: Mapping Problem Resolution Routes for Users and Non-users of the Civil, Administrative and Family Justice Systems* (London, Ministry of Justice).
Pleasance, P et al. (2006) *Causes of Action: Civil Law and Social Justice* (2nd edn, London, Legal Services Commission).

Pleasence, P and Balmer, NJ (2014) *How People Resolve 'Legal' Problems* (Cambridge, Legal Services Board).
Rackley, E (2010) 'The Art and Craft of Writing Judgments: Notes on the Feminist Judgments Project' in R Hunter et al. (eds) *Feminist Judgments: From Theory to Practice* (London, Sage).
Ramshaw, S (2013) *Justice as Improvisation* (London, Routledge).
Refuge (2020) *Refuge Response to Home Affairs Select Committee Report on Domestic Abuse During Covid-19* (London, Refuge).
Richardson, K and Speed, A (2019) 'Restrictions on Legal Aid in Family Law Cases in England and Wales: Creating a Necessary Barrier to Public Funding or Simply Increasing the Burden on the Family Courts?' 41 *Journal of Social Welfare and Family Law* 135.
Ridley, S (2014) 'A View from the Bar' in *'Rise of LIPs': Three Perspectives on the Increased Number of People who Represent Themselves in Court* Inner Temple Yearbook 2013–2014.
Riles, A (2006) *Documents: Artifacts of Modern Knowledge* (Ann Arbor, University of Michigan Press).
—— (2000) *The Network Inside Out* (Ann Arbor, University of Michigan Press).
Rock, P (1993) *The Social World of an English Crown Court* (Oxford, Clarendon Press).
Rollock, N (2007) 'Legitimizing Black Academic Failure: Deconstructing Staff Discourses on Academic Success, Appearance and Behaviour' 17 *International Studies in Sociology of Education* 275.
Rossner, M (2021) 'Remote Rituals in Virtual Courts' 48 *Journal of Law and Society* 334.
Russell, P (2019) Willingness to Innovate in Family Law Solicitor Practice in England and Wales: A Qualitative Study 41 *Journal of Social Welfare and Family Law* 153.
Ryan, M et al. (2021) *Remote Hearings in the Family Court Post Pandemic* (London, Nuffield Family Justice Observatory).
—— (2020a) *Remote Hearings in the Family Justice System: A Rapid Consultation* (London, Nuffield Family Justice Observatory).
—— (2020b) *Remote Hearings in the Family Justice System: Reflections and Experiences* (London, Nuffield Family Justice Observatory).
Sandefur, R (2015) 'Elements of Professional Expertise: Understanding Relational and Substantive Expertise Through Lawyers' Impact' 80 *American Sociological Review* 909.
—— (2010). 'The Impact of Counsel: An Analysis of Empirical Evidence' 9 *Seattle Journal for Social Justice* 51.
Savage, M (2015) *Social Class in the 21st Century* (London, Pelican Books).
Skeggs, B (1997) *Formations of Class and Gender: Becoming Respectable* (Thousand Oaks, Sage).
Smart, C (1989) *Feminism and the Power of Law* (London, Routledge).
Smart, C and Neale, B (1999) *Family Fragments?* (Cambridge, Polity Press).
Smith, L (2019) 'Representations of Family Justice in Online Communities' in M Maclean and B Dijksterhuis (eds) *Digital Family Justice: From Alternative Dispute Resolution to Online Dispute Resolution* (Oxford, Hart).
Smith, L et al. (2017) *A Study of Fee-charging McKenzie Friends and their Work in Private Family Law Cases* (London, The Bar Council).
Sommerlad, H and Sanderson, P (1998). *Gender, Choice and Commitment: Women Solicitors in England and Wales and the Struggle for Equal Status* (Abingdon, Routledge).
Thiara, RK and Humphreys, C (2017) 'Absent Presence: The Ongoing Impact of Men's Violence on the mother-child Relationship' 22 *Child and Family Social Work* 137.
Thomas, L (2016). *The Lottery of Justice: Exploring Some of the Consequences of the Legal Aid Sentencing Punishment of Offenders Act 2012* (Birmingham, CEPLER Working Paper Series).
Thompson, S (2015) *Prenuptial Agreements and the Presumption of Free Choice: Issues of Power in Theory and Practice* (Oxford, Hart).
Tkacucova, T (2020) 'The Changing Landscape of Advice Provision: Online Forums and Social Media Run by McKenzie Friends' *Child and Family Law Quarterly* 397.
—— (2016). 'Communication in Family Court: Financial Remedy Proceedings from the Perspective of Litigants in Person' 38 *Journal of Social Welfare and Family Law* 430.
—— (2010) 'Cross-examination Questioning: Lay People as Cross-examiners' in M Coulthard and A Johnson (eds) *The Routledge Handbook of Forensic Linguistics* (Abingdon, Routledge).

Trinder, L et al. (2014) *Litigants in Person in Private Family Law Cases* (London, Ministry of Justice).
Toy-Cronin, B (2015) *Keeping Up Appearances: Accessing New Zealand's Civil Courts as a Litigant in Person* (University of Otago, PhD thesis).
Tyler, TR (2003) 'Procedural Justice, Legitimacy and the Rule of Law' 30 *Crime and Justice* 283.
—— (1990) *Why People Obey the Law* (Oxford, Princeton University Press).
Tyler, T and Ho, Y (2002). *Trust in the Law: Encouraging Public Cooperation with the Police and Courts* (New York, Russell Sage Foundation).
Wallace, DO (2016) 'Reinterpreting Bourdieu, Belonging and Black Identities: Exploring 'Black' Cultural Capital Among Black Caribbean Youth in London' in J Thatcher et al. (eds) *Bourdieu: The Next Generation* (Abingdon, Routledge).
Wallbank, J (2014). 'Universal Norms, Individualisation and the Need for Recognition: The failure(s) of the Self-managed Post-separation Family' in J Wallbank and J Herring (eds) *Vulnerabilities, Care and Family Law* (London, Routledge).
—— (1995) 'Returning the Subject to the Subject of Women's Poverty: An Essay on the Importance of Subjectivity for the Feminist Research Project' 3 *Feminist Legal Studies* 207.
Webley, L (2015) 'When is a Family Lawyer a Lawyer?' in M Maclean et al. (eds) *Delivering Family Justice in the 21st Century* (Oxford, Hart).
Williams, K (2011) *Litigants in Person: A Literature Review* (London, Ministry of Justice).
Wilkinson, R and Pickett, K (2010) *The Spirit Level: Why Equality is Better for Everyone* (London, Penguin).
Women's Aid (2016). *Nineteen Child Homicides* (Bristol, Women's Aid).
—— (2014) *Virtual World, Real Fear: Women's Aid Report into Online Abuse, Harassment and Stalking* (Bristol, Women's Aid).
Wong, S and Cain, R (2019) 'The Impact of Cuts in Legal Aid Funding of Private Family Law Cases' 41 *Journal of Social Welfare and Family Law* 3.
Wright, K (2007) 'The Role of Solicitors in Divorce: A Note of Caution' 19 *Child and Family Law Quarterly* 481.
—— (2006) 'The Divorce Process: A View from the Other Side of the Desk' 18 *Child and Family Law Quarterly* 93.
Zimmerman, N and Tyler, T (2009) 'Between Access to Counsel and Access to Justice: A Psychological Perspective' 37 *Fordham Law Journal*, 473.
Zorza, R (2009) 'Self-represented Litigants and the Access to Justice Revolution in the State Courts: Cross-pollinating Perspectives Towards a Dialogue for Innovation in the Courts and the Administrative System' 29 *Journal of the National Administration of Administrative Law* 63.

INDEX

Milton Keynes UK
Ingram Content Group UK Ltd.
UKHW020228260124
436735UK00004B/154

9 781509 947355